How to Read a Shakespeare Play

How to Study Literature

The books in this series – all written by eminent scholars renowned for their teaching abilities – show students how to read, understand, write, and criticize literature. They provide the key skills which every student of literature must master, as well as offering a comprehensive introduction to the field itself.

Published

How to Do Theory	Wolfgang Iser
How to Write a Poem	John Redmond
How to Read a Shakespeare Play	David Bevington

How to Read a Shakespeare Play

David Bevington

Blackwell
Publishing

© 2006 by David Bevington

BLACKWELL PUBLISHING
350 Main Street, Malden, MA 02148-5020, USA
9600 Garsington Road, Oxford OX4 2DQ, UK
550 Swanston Street, Carlton, Victoria 3053, Australia

The right of David Bevington to be identified as the Author of this Work has been
asserted in accordance with the UK Copyright, Designs, and Patents Act 1988.

First published 2006 by Blackwell Publishing Ltd

1 2006

Library of Congress Cataloging-in-Publication Data

Bevington, David M.
    How to read a Shakespeare play / David Bevington.
        p. cm.—(How to study literature)
    Includes bibliographical references (p.) and index.
        ISBN-13: 978-1-4051-1395-3 (hardcover : alk. paper)
        ISBN-10: 1-4051-1395-2 (hardcover : alk. paper)
        ISBN-13: 978-1-4051-1396-0 (pbk. : alk. paper)
        ISBN-10: 1-4051-1396-0 (pbk. : alk. paper)   1. Shakespeare,
    William, 1564–1616—Study and teaching.   2. Shakespeare,
    William, 1564–1616—Appreciation.   I. Title.
    II. Series: How to study literature (Malden, Mass.)

    PR2987.B48 2006
    822.3'3—dc22

                                                                    2005024137

A catalogue record for this title is available from the British Library.

Set in 10.5/13pt Minion
by Graphicraft Limited, Hong Kong
Printed and bound in Singapore
by C.O.S. Printers Pte Ltd

The publisher's policy is to use permanent paper from mills that operate a sustainable
forestry policy, and which has been manufactured from pulp processed using acid-free
and elementary chlorine-free practices. Furthermore, the publisher ensures that the text
paper and cover board used have met acceptable environmental accreditation standards.

For further information on
Blackwell Publishing, visit our website:
www.blackwellpublishing.com

In loving memory of my dear colleagues,
Wayne Booth and Ned Rosenheim

Contents

Illustrations

1

How to Read a Shakespeare Play

This book makes no attempt to be comprehensive. It examines a few of Shakespeare's plays with the view of suggesting different ways in which one might go about trying to read this remarkable and in some ways difficult author. One must learn to cope with a vocabulary that is vast and sometimes unfamiliar, as we might expect in an author who wrote some four hundred years ago. Film and video presentations of his plays, and especially live theatre, can do much to reveal to us how funny and exciting and terrifying his plays can be when well acted, even if we may miss a few words. Reading a play out loud in a reading group can bring the characters and the dialogue to life; actually being in a production is even better. Whether one reads aloud with a group or alone with a copy of the play, one needs to ask questions of the sort a theatre director might ask, about setting, costumes, props, ages of the characters, their social background, their professional or working status. Because Shakespeare's plays do not usually have long descriptions of costume, setting, and the like, in the fashion of novels or short stories, we as readers of a dramatic text must engage in the participatory act of fleshing out what is often laconic or hidden in the script. We must clothe the characters and place them in the setting where they belong. Reading a play is an active and cooperative process involving ourselves and the dramatist, much as watching a play in the theatre also expects us to imagine what the actors describe for us. A Shakespearean play is not like film or television, where the director tells us where we are by using the camera to 'see' for us.

All sorts of materials are available to provide help: introductions and commentary notes in good recent editions, class discussion, talking with friends who know the play, office hours with a teacher, recordings, VCRs and DVDs, seeing performances, taking part in performances, a good bibliography (often available in modern editions), and, perhaps most of all, our own active inquiry into what the text or script is inviting us to visualize and hear. Why are the characters saying what they say, to each other, to themselves? When are they being ironic, or surprised, or angry, or pleased, or coy, or standoffish? What is each character after, in a given scene, and overall in the play? What, in the terms proposed by the great early-twentieth-century director and theorist, Konstantin Stanislavsky, is the character's superobjective? Imagine how you would say the lines yourself if you found yourself in a situation as described by Shakespeare. What are you trying to prove to some other character or characters, or find out from them? Do this with villainous or unlikable characters as well as the more likable ones. What is driving Edmund in *King Lear* to deceive his brother and father as he does? Why does he boast so to the audience about his skill in deception? Why are Goneril and Regan so intent on denying their aging father the hospitality that he expects from them? What is motivating old Egeus in *A Midsummer Night's Dream* to insist that his daughter Hermia marry Demetrius, when she is in love with Lysander? Why is Tybalt, in *Romeo and Juliet*, so offended by the presence of Romeo at the Capulets' evening party? Why is Claudius, in *Hamlet*, unable to pray for forgiveness for his crime of having killed his brother and then marrying that brother's wife? To what extent, if any, is Queen Gertrude implicated in that same brother-murder? Why is Antonio, in *The Tempest*, so impenitent about having plotted the overthrow of his older brother Prospero? Why is it that brothers are so often antagonistic toward one another in Shakespeare?

Shakespeare does not answer such questions so much as he questions our answers. We need to be constantly attuned, in Shakespeare, to ambiguity and a multiplicity of critical approaches. Is Falstaff, in *1 Henry IV*, a jolly old rogue with whom Prince Hal can relax and enjoy himself, or an incorrigible law-breaker who aims to use the future King of England as his protection against arrest, or something of both? Does *A Midsummer Night's Dream* invite us to approve or disapprove of Oberon's teaching his wife a lesson by tricking her into a humiliating relationship with Bottom the Weaver, or is this the wrong question to ask? Is Friar Laurence to blame for the tragic ending of *Romeo and Juliet*, or is it Tybalt, or Romeo for deciding to kill Tybalt, or the family feuding, or bad luck and bad timing, or 'the stars' that are sometimes thought to govern our destiny? Or all of the above? How are we to find meaning in this tragedy? Is Hamlet's delay in avenging his father's death the result of a personality defect, or a justifiably sane course of action given the problematic nature of determining how to

Hamlet, Act 1, scene 2. Ethan Hawke as Hamlet, Diane Venora as Gertrude, and Kyle MacLachlan as Claudius in Michael Almereyda's modern-dress film set in New York in the year 2000. Gertrude attempts to reconcile her son to his new step-father. (Miramax / The Kobal Collection / Larry Riley)

act in a world where choices are anything but simple? How much are we meant to sympathize, in *King Lear*, with old men who are testy, easily duped, persuaded of their own supreme self-importance, and clinging to myths about the gods' justice that are increasingly shown to be outmoded and inadequate? Why is Cordelia so unwilling, at the start of that play, to say what she knows her father wants to hear her say? Why must Cordelia die?

Perhaps most clearly in *The Tempest* we can see that a Shakespeare play is not one play, to be understood in terms of a simple moral lesson, but a series of overlapping plays, each with its own complex set of issues demanding a different approach to reading. We need to understand that the very idea of what 'Shakespeare' means is constantly changing, and that the 'Shakespeare' of fifty years ago, or even twenty years ago, has transmuted itself into a new dimension of critical understanding. Perhaps no author has a richer history of interpretation, and it is one to which, as readers and audience, we can both respond and contribute. As we read and respond and talk about his plays with each other, we become a part of a process by which 'Shakespeare' helps define ourselves and our evolving culture.

How do I read a play by Shakespeare? This is a question frequently asked. The prospect is in some ways daunting. Shakespeare wrote some four hundred years ago, in a language – call it Early Modern or Elizabethan – that has changed steadily ever since. His mammoth vocabulary is roughly twice that of any other author writing in English. He is famous for having coined new words, often by adding prefixes or suffixes to existing words, like 'deboshed', 'decoct', 'entame', 'intreasured', 'intermissive', and 'Juno-like'. He invents new comparatives, like 'rawer', and uses double comparatives like 'more braver' and 'more kinder', along with double superlatives like 'most worthiest' and 'most unkindest'. He is fond of newly formed compounds, like 'foul-faced', 'fore-foot', 'fore-past', 'kingly-poor', 'eye-offending', 'pistol-proof', 'merchant-marring', 'ill-composed', and 'point-devise'. He frequently introduces words from other languages, like 'passado', 'passant', 'punto reverso', and 'strappado'. He writes at times in Welsh dialectical pronunciation, with 'peaten' for beaten, 'Pible' for Bible, 'fehemently' for vehemently, and 'Cheshu' for Jesu. His stage Scottish dialect substitutes 'gud' for good, 'sall' for shall, and 'suerly' for surely; his stage Irish includes phrases like 'By Chrish, la, 'tish ill done!' One scene in *Henry V* is mostly in French (and is written in such a way as to be entirely intelligible in the theatre).

Shakespeare often revels in the musical sound of foreign places and proper names: Peloponnesus, Arragon, Lepidus, Lacedaemon, Lombardy, Madeira, Margarelon, Mesopotamia, Messina, Ptolemy, Phoenicia, Lydia, Parthia, Cappadocia, Paphlagonia, Pont, Comagene, Lycaonia, and legions more. He cites many classical myths and authors about Pythagoras, Leda, Hyperion, Plautus, Phaethon, Hippocrates, Philomela, Cerberus, Orpheus, Atalanta, Tarquin, and still others. His familiarity with the Bible takes him to stories of Adam and Eve, Cain and Abel, Jacob and Laban, Solomon, Job, Jezebel, Daniel, Jesus, Herod, Pilate, Saint Luke, and Saint Paul (though interestingly he never mentions Moses, David, Isaac, or John the Baptist). He refers familiarly to folk and church customs and occasions such as Lammas-tide and Lammas-eve, Pentecost, Lipsbury pinfold, and loggats. He imports Latin and other foreign terms like 'quoniam', 'quandam', 'reguerdon', and 'relume'. He forms Latinate compounds like 'peregrinate', 'prolixious', 'proportionable', 'propagation', 'quotidian', 'recountments', and 'intenible'. He is expert in terms of warfare with which we are no longer familiar, like 'petard', 'alarum bell', 'linstock', 'poniards', and 'counter-mines'. His characters brandish colorful terms of insult and profanity like 'rampallian', 'fustilarian', 'latten bilbo', 'By'r lakin', 'Zounds', 'By God's liggens', ''Sblood', 'By Cock', and ''Od's heartlings'.

He freely changes parts of speech, using adverbs for adjectives ('my most stay'), adjectives for adverbs ('I was like to die'), adjectives for nouns ('the inward of thee'), adjectives made into verbal forms (as when someone is 'lated', i.e., made late), and still other transformations. He uses many words whose meanings are no longer familiar to us: lawn (fine lace), pash (to smash), jordan (a privy), leaping-house (house of prostitution), liefest (most beloved), loaden (loaded), swoopstake (indiscriminately), escrimers (fencers), bewray (reveal), forwhy (because), gramercy (many thanks), and askant (aslant). Some words that seem familiar are in fact used in now-lost senses, like 'an' (if), 'nice' (trivial), 'marry' (by Mary, indeed), 'policy' (prudent or cunning course of action), 'politic' (crafty), 'friends' (relatives), 'sometime' (former), 'suddenly' (immediately), 'happy' (fortunate), 'sad' (serious), 'physic' (medicine, often specifically purging), 'retreat' (withdraw), and 'ribald' (base, worthless).

Given the difficulties of language, where does one begin? One helpful strategy can be to see a production, or take part in one, or look at film and video versions that are often widely available; see the Epilogue to this present book, in Chapter 8, for detailed listings. Another strategy is to read a play aloud with a group of friends. At first encounter, the best thing probably is to read through the play without stopping for discussion (though you can of course stop for an intermission). When the play is somewhat well known to the group, one can do a scene at a time and then discuss it at some length. This can be a productive method for classroom reading, too. Whether or not the instructor has any experience in the theatre, that instructor can energize group discussions by starting with an out-loud reading of the text. Parts are assigned to individuals in the group, through volunteering or by assignment. Once one has gotten into the swing of doing this, there will be plenty of volunteers. Casting need not be gender specific; women can read men's roles, and vice versa. If a scene is largely given over to a single character, you might want to divide the role in mid scene. Often it helps to do the scene, or a portion of the scene, more than once, to see if different interpretations emerge.

Discussion should, of course, flow from the out-loud reading. Each reader can offer suggestions as to why he or she spoke certain lines with a particular emphasis. More pointedly, each reader can reflect on what that reader has just said to another character or group of characters. To whom is each remark addressed? What is the subtext of each character's approach to the particular scene? That is, what is motivating the character to react as he or she does? What is the character after in this scene? In what way is this important? How old is each character, and how does age difference figure into the conversation? In what ways are gender differences important?

Getting at such questions can be helped if one asks about a whole host of background issues. Where is the scene taking place? Why are the characters here? What are we to imagine as to physical surroundings? If the characters are indoors, what is the room like? Is it a throne room with royal furnishings, or a bedroom, or a kitchen, or a tavern interior with fireplace and tables and chairs, or a brothel, or a banqueting hall, or a meeting room, or a courtroom, or a prison, or perhaps some lobby or antechamber? If outdoors, are we on a battlefield, or facing the walls of a castle, or in the piazza of some Italian town surrounded by houses, or in a garden, or in a forest, or on a seacoast, or at the mouth of a cave or a tent, or on board ship?

What are the characters wearing? One should approach this matter individually for each character being read in the present scene. Be specific about details of costume, even if the dialogue doesn't convey information on every detail. Are the ladies wearing gloves? Are they veiled? Are they in long dresses with farthingales or hooped petticoats? Are they carrying fans? Are the men wearing hats, jerkins (tight-fitting jackets), padded breeches? Do some of them wear swords by their sides? What are the 'hangers' like that attach the swords to their belts? Do their breeches have codpieces to give decorative emphasis to the genitalia? Are some of the men bearded and with moustaches? What are the shoes like for both men and women? Do they have high cork heels? How do the men and women walk?

How can we tell a king from a duke and a duchess from a lady-in-waiting? Does a king wear a crown all the time or only for certain ceremonial occasions? How does the 'coronet' in scene 1 of *King Lear* differ from a crown? What is suitable wearing apparel for a justice of the peace, a provost, a Franciscan friar, an apothecary, a doctor, a porter, a merchant, a schoolboy, a soothsayer, a goddess, a fairy, an airy spirit, a ghost? How does one outfit the speaker of a chorus?

What are the physical differences between moneyed people and their servants? Of what materials are their caps, garments, and shoes made? In other words, how does the stage mark social gradations? We tend to minimize sartorial distinctions today as emblems of social rank, but for the Elizabethans such distinctions were essential and omnipresent. When servants dress in a livery uniform, what does it look like? What would cooks wear? Innkeepers? Tavern wenches? Courtesans? Witches? Peasants? Hostlers or stablemen attending on horses? Gravediggers? Are the jesters, professional fools, and clowns outfitted with cap and bells, coxcombs, and motley or parti-colored attire?

What about distinctions in military rank? How does a corporal look different from a lieutenant? What distinguishes a herald visually? What do sailors wear, as in the opening scene of *The Tempest*, when mariners are instructed to enter, '*wet*'? Do characters who are Dutch, German, Italian, Welsh, Irish, or Scottish reveal their nationality by what they wear (as Portia suggests in *The Merchant of Venice* when she satirizes the sartorial fashions of her wooers of various nationalities)? How are we to imagine 'Moors' like Othello, Aaron the Moor in *Titus Andronicus*, and Portia's wooer, the Prince of Morocco, in *The Merchant of Venice*? How exotic is their dress, or that of Cleopatra and her attendant ladies in *Antony and Cleopatra*, or Caliban in *The Tempest*? Do the Roman senators wear togas and laurel wreaths in *Julius Caesar* or *Coriolanus*? When musicians appear, what do they wear and what sorts of musical instruments do they bring with them?

These are questions that one should also ask when one is reading alone. They point to a significant difference between novels or short stories on the one hand and plays on the other: fictional narrative can easily tell us about the characters' ages, personal appearance, dress, and physical surroundings, whereas drama does so mainly through stage directions and what we can infer from the dialogue. Shakespeare's plays, like those of his contemporaries, are generally sparse in their use of stage directions; often, the authorial manuscript or playbook that might later serve as copy for a printed edition was conceived of more as a playhouse document than as a reading text, with the result that the original stage directions are often limited to entrances and exits. Even exits are often left out, presumably because the actors themselves were assumed to know when to get offstage. Interpretive stage directions for the actors to speak '*aside*' or to some particular character, '*fall asleep*', enter '*invisible*', '*sit*', '*rise*', '*stand aside*', '*weep*', '*read a letter*', give something to another person, strike or restrain someone, hide something, enter '*disguised*', unlock or open something, etc., were supererogatory for the actors, whose business it was to know whom they should speak to or give a letter. Generally today such stage directions are added by the modern editor, putting them in square brackets so as to distinguish them from the original language.

Reading a play, then, calls on skills quite unlike those needed to read non-dramatic fiction (which requires an interpretive expertise of its own). Reading a play asks the reader to flesh out the scene as it is implied in the dialogue. Editorially added stage directions, and the occasional original stage directions, do of course help, but even they tend to be sparse in the editing of Shakespeare. And rightly so. Some modern dramatists, like Henrik Ibsen and George Bernard Shaw, write lengthy stage directions in a novelistic manner, specifying in concrete detail how the furniture of the set is to be arranged, what the characters are wearing, and sometimes the way the actors are to deliver their lines – wearily, enthusiastically, angrily, and so on. Shakespeare does better with a minimum of clutter, even if some added stage directions can be helpful. For the most part, the reader must do what an actor or director does: conceptualize the role that is embedded in the dialogue and give it voice. Group readings, audio recordings, and film can help us visualize the dialogue, but essentially the task of 'staging' the play in our minds as we read is the responsibility of the individual reader. It is exhilarating, since each reader is in effect given the responsibility and the privilege of directing the play by deciding how it is to be interpreted.

'Let us . . . On your imaginary forces work', urges the Chorus at the start of *Henry V*. 'Piece out our imperfections with your thoughts.' 'Think, when we talk of horses, that you see them / Printing their proud hoofs i'th' receiving earth. / For 'tis your thoughts that now must deck our kings.' The Chorus is talking to his spectators, who are standing (in the original Globe Theatre, in 1599) on three sides of a large thrust stage or sitting in the galleries, but he might as well be directing his admonitions at us. The advice is aimed exactly at what a dramatic text asks us to do. Theatre operates through the interrelated rhetorical devices of metonymy and synecdoche, by means of which a thing is made to represent a larger entity of which it is a part: the part is made to stand for the whole. *Henry V*'s Chorus repeatedly describes how this device can work. Since, he argues, something as insignificant as a few ciphers or zeroes can, when appended to a number like '1', turn it into a million (1,000,000), the same magnification can be applied by us to the actors of *Henry V*, the 'ciphers to this great account'. 'Into a thousand parts divide one man', he instructs us, 'And make imaginary puissance.' We as audience are asked to be co-creators of illusion. 'Suppose within the girdle of these walls / Are now confined two mighty monarchies.' Part of our assignment is to visualize what the great historical events of the early fifteenth century looked like. The Chorus is standing in front of a handsome theatrical facade that can be imagined to resemble the walls of Harfleur or some French castle, but it can hardly pictorialize the entire military campaign that has led Henry V from London to northern France and finally to the battlefield at Agincourt. Whether in the theatre or as we sit reading a book, we are asked to stage these great events in history by our powers of imagination. In the theatre, or when we listen to a sound recording, the actors will do much to help. When we sit with a book, we are on our own, and yet the process is essentially the same. We become producers of our own show.

This is an exciting and demanding challenge. It requires alert, creative participation. We, as armchair producers and directors, must decide what the actors wear, how old they are, in what accents they speak, what social class they represent, where they are located, why they are there, and, most importantly, what they are after as they interact with other characters and with us as audience. A task one can usefully put to oneself, as one reads, is to suppose oneself the director of a production, talking to one actor and then another for a given scene, and asking: why are you saying what the script asks you to say? How do you feel about the person you are talking to? What is the background of your relationship to this person, and how has that relationship set up this particular dynamic of this moment? You need not have any directing experience to figure out a way of doing this, since the questions you will keep asking are basic in this way. The possible answers are of course multiform, but the questions are essentially the same.

So, this is one way to read Shakespeare: aggressively, interactively, questioningly. As you go back to the text after a first listening or viewing or read-through, you will want to consult the commentary notes on the page with the text. (I am assuming you are using a text edited in this standard way.) The notes should help with a multitude of verbal difficulties. Again, read aggressively, in the sense of not letting something go by that you do not understand. If the notes do not take up a phrase you find difficult, or if you disagree with the interpretation offered, don't just let it pass by. Wrestle with it. Disagree as need be with the editor, who, I assure you, is capable of error. Shakespeare is wonderfully intelligent. Don't assume that something he has written just doesn't make sense. He is indeed brilliant, which means that at times he writes in ways that can be extraordinarily difficult to unpack and clarify.

If you are getting down to serious study of a particular play, perhaps with the intent of writing an essay, books and critical articles can be very helpful. Most editions of Shakespeare today have bibliographies in the back of the book with suggestions for further reading. Pick out something that looks germane to your particular interests. If you are studying the play for a class, ask the instructor or course assistant. If, when you start an essay or book you have chosen to read, you find it off the topic or disappointing, look for something else; a huge amount of critical literature is available. Recent studies are, on the whole, more likely to be up to date than books nearing the vintage of a hundred years or more, though of course there are exceptions. Some recent studies can be just as willfully bad as something ancient, so be selective, demanding, inquisitive. Argue with what you read, just as you have argued with the editor of your edition.

Any good current complete edition should have supportive and background material about the social customs, politics, and religious controversies of the Elizabethan age, along with matters of intellectual background relating to philosophy, cosmology, medicine, scientific investigation, and overseas discovery. Useful information is available about the theatres and dramatic companies of Shakespeare's day, the facts of his biography, the practices of grammar, rhetoric, and prosody to which Shakespeare apprenticed himself, and the printing practices used to produce the early printed texts of his works. The history of Shakespeare criticism, and of performance onstage and on screen, can help us grasp the extraordinary range of interpretive possibilities in the analysis of his work.

Source study can be rewarding. With few exceptions, Shakespeare did not invent the plots of his plays. He turned to the rich treasury of short stories, longer fiction, poems, plays, and historical chronicles that were pouring forth from the presses of London. Stimulated by the intellectual ferment of the Renaissance rediscovery of the ancient world, new translations of classical texts were now available. Shakespeare turned to Thomas North's vigorous translation (1579) of Plutarch's *The Lives of the Noble Grecians and Romans* when he wrote *Julius Caesar, Antony and Cleopatra*, and *Coriolanus*. He borrowed extensively from Raphael Holinshed's comprehensive *The Chronicles of England, Scotland, and Ireland*, which had been published in a second edition in 1587 just as Shakespeare was about to start writing his history plays. Other chronicles and tales were also at hand. Later, in 1606–7, he turned again to Holinshed for information about a Scottish king named Macbeth. Pretty much the whole story of *Romeo and Juliet* came to him from a long narrative poem in English by Arthur Brooke called *The Tragical History of Romeus and Juliet* (1562), itself based on older accounts of this legend. Shakespeare based *Hamlet* on recent translations of an old story of a Danish prince called Amlethus, as told originally by Saxo Grammaticus (1180–1208). *Othello* got its narrative from an Italian short story by Giraldi Cinthio, 1565; so did *Measure for Measure*. Shakespeare got much of his material for *King Lear* from a play about Lear (or Leir) written in the early 1590s; the story had been told a number of times. For the play's second plot of the Earl of Gloucester and his two sons, Shakespeare went to Philip Sidney's *Arcadia*. He based *Twelfth Night* mainly on a short story of 'Apollonius and Silla' by Barnabe Riche (1581). *A Midsummer Night's Dream* and *The Tempest* are exceptions to this general rule; their plots are essentially original with Shakespeare, though even in these instances he found ideas plentifully in his reading and theatre-going experience. By reading these sources as one gets to know the plays, one can gain revealing insight into the creative process.

The place to start, certainly, is with the plays, or, more specifically, with one particular play. Which one? *A Midsummer Night's Dream* is a fine choice; so is *Romeo and Juliet*, or *Twelfth Night*. Not by accident are these plays enduringly popular in high schools, colleges, and local drama groups, as well as with professional companies. The stories tend to be familiar to us, and they are about falling in love. These plays were great favorites from early days; the Cambridge University Library soon found that it had to replace its copy of Shakespeare's first collected edition, the so-called First Folio of 1623, because the pages were all worn out at *Romeo and Juliet*. Not infrequently, *Julius Caesar* is assigned in high school, although I think this is not a wise choice; it is a great play, but it is all about politics and ancient history, with nary a love story to be seen. I suspect that the play became a fixed part of the high school curriculum in the days when Latin was still being universally taught, so that most students, having sweated through Caesar's *Gallic Wars* ('*Omnia Gallia in partes tres divisa est*'), knew who Julius Caesar was and when he was assassinated (44 BC). *King Lear* is probably not an ideal place to start, either; it is unquestionably a towering achievement, but it is so emotionally and intellectually intense, and so relentless in its exploration of existential skeptical alternatives to traditional ideas of faith, that a careful reading of the play can be, and indeed should be, a shattering experience. Moreover, it is about aging and fear of death, and these feelings are perhaps more deeply understood when one has had some contact with old age.

Indeed, before we get started with *A Midsummer Night's Dream*, we might ponder for a bit the shape of Shakespeare's career as a writer, and the way in which he himself worked forward from romantic comedy to high tragedy. During the first decade of his productive career, from the time of his arrival in London in about 1590 (at the age of 26) until the turn of the century, Shakespeare wrote more or less a comedy a year, straight on through. The dates are not always certain, especially at first, nor is the exact ordering of these comedies, but the list includes *The Comedy of Errors, Love's*

Labor's Lost, The Two Gentlemen of Verona, The Taming of the Shrew, A Midsummer Night's Dream, The Merchant of Venice, Much Ado about Nothing, The Merry Wives of Windsor, As You Like It, and *Twelfth Night.* Ten comedies in ten or so years. *A Midsummer* is from about 1595, *Twelfth Night* around 1600–1. To be sure, Shakespeare also busied himself throughout this same period with writing plays about English history, in many of which the deaths are plentiful and gory, since the early history plays especially are about England's civil wars of the fifteenth century. Still, they are upbeat to the extent that they culminate in political and national success. The *Henry IV* plays are about the rise to greatness of King Henry V, a national hero; they are also about a young man's coming of age and facing up to the responsibilities willed to him by his father. Although Shakespeare also attempted one revenge tragedy, *Titus Andronicus,* he then set the genre aside for more or less a decade. His *Romeo and Juliet* (1594–6) is a tragedy, but it is a love tragedy that evokes the poignant experience of falling in love, and is spiritually more akin to *A Midsummer Night's Dream* and other romantic comedies than it is to the later tragedies.

Then, in the years around 1600–1, Shakespeare changes direction. He writes two 'problem' plays about intractable social difficulties, *All's Well That Ends Well* and *Measure for Measure,* ending them in marriages but in such a way that the endings raise more uncertainties than they resolve. He writes *Troilus and Cressida* in an experimental mixed-genre mode that is part history play (about the Trojan War), part tragedy (in the death of Hector especially), and part bleak satire about a love affair overwhelmed by a pointless war. Most significantly, he turns to writing one great tragedy after another: *Julius Caesar* (1599), *Hamlet* (c. 1599–1601), *Othello* (c. 1602–4), *King Lear* (c. 1605–6), *Macbeth* (c. 1606–7), *Timon of Athens* (c. 1605–8), *Antony and Cleopatra* (1606–7), and *Coriolanus* (c. 1608). Eight tragedies in perhaps eight or nine years, not all of equally high calibre (and *Timon of Athens* seems to be only partly his), but still an astonishing achievement.

And then, toward the end of this same decade of the 1600s, Shakespeare veers back to a kind of romantic comedy, suffused this time with more than a tinge of sorrow and world-weariness, in the so-called tragicomedies or romances: *Pericles* (written probably in collaboration, and not included in his First Folio), *Cymbeline, The Winter's Tale,* and *The Tempest* (c. 1611). Probably he then retired, though he seems to have come out of retirement to join with John Fletcher, his successor as chief dramatist for the King's Men, in writing *Henry VIII* and *The Two Noble Kinsmen.*

What this brief sketch may suggest is that Shakespeare worked his way forward by genres, focusing at first on romantic comedies and English history plays, and taking on the daunting assignment of writing tragedies only when he felt he was ready. This design also meant that he moved forward from delightful comedies about falling in love to the more intractable problems of marital conflict, murderous envy, politically motivated assassination, philosophical doubt, jealousy, midlife crisis, aging, and fear of the approach of death. Even when he returns to comedy in his late years, an awareness of the approaching end is strongly present. These transitions seem appropriate to the life of the author himself, as indeed to all of us in the arc of our lives from birth to death. They are also appropriate to the shape one can give to a reading program in Shakespeare: starting with romantic comedy, moving on to English history, and then scaling the heights of the great tragedies. Let's begin with *A Midsummer Night's Dream*.

2

A Midsummer Night's Dream

Read the play first, if you can, without reading the editor's introduction, or sources, or background material, or critical essays. All that can come later.

What one usually sees first is a list of persons in the play, sometimes called the '*Dramatis personae*'. Shakespeare and other Elizabethan dramatists often supplied lists of this sort, but not always, and some may have been lost before the play made its way into print. *A Midsummer Night's Dream* lacks such a list. The play was first printed in a quarto volume in 1600, that is, in a medium-sized book of about 9 by 6 inches in which the large printed sheet, with four pages of the book on each side of the sheet (hence *quarto*, in four), was folded twice before binding, thus yielding a total of eight pages for each printed sheet. In 1623, the play was included in the so-called First Folio edition, among the comedies. 'Folio' means that the printed sheet was folded only once, with two pages of the book on each side of the printed sheet, thus yielding a total of four pages per sheet or 'gathering'. Such a book would be handsomely large, about 12 by 9 inches, and would be pretty expensive. Quartos might sell for a shilling apiece; the First Folio probably cost around a pound, or twenty times the cost of a quarto. In neither quarto nor folio format does *Midsummer* have a list of characters. If added by an editor, it may be marked by square brackets to indicate that it is not original.

The list of characters can be useful as one reads, and can in fact help to sort out the major characters as we proceed. We need to know, right at the start, that Theseus is Duke of Athens, that Hippolyta, Queen of the Amazons, is betrothed to him, and that Theseus retains the services of a 'Master of the Revels' or court entertainments named Philostrate. We need to know that old Egeus is the father of Hermia, who is in love with

Lysander and is loved by him, but that another young man named Demetrius is in love with this same Hermia, while a maiden called Helena is in love (no doubt frustratedly) with Demetrius. The dramatic conflict of the play's opening can thus be savored in the list of characters: two young men are in love with one young woman, while another young woman finds her affection for one of these young men unrequited.

If we like, we can also see that the play's cast includes the King and Queen of Fairies, fairy attendants on the Queen, and a character called Puck, or Robin Goodfellow. The grouping of names in most editions will indicate that Puck is part of this fairy cluster. In still a third grouping we find the names of various tradesmen of Athens: a carpenter, a weaver, a bellows-mender, a tinker, a joiner (i.e., one who makes furniture by joining pieces of wood, unlike a carpenter, who specializes in heavier construction), and a tailor. Why they are here will appear presently; we can note for the moment that they are all artisans, i.e., not peasants or day-laborers but skilled craftsmen.

The original quarto of *Midsummer* also lacks any numbering of acts or scenes. The First Folio edition of 1623 provides breaks between the acts ('*Actus primus*', '*Actus secundus*', etc.), but without numbering the individual scenes. Whether the editors of the First Folio, Shakespeare's long-time theatre colleagues John Heminges and Henry Condell, supplied these act markings themselves or found them in the manuscript material available to them, we cannot be sure; they evidently took a second edition of the quarto and marked it up with some added stage directions and some minor changes from a theatrical manuscript in the acting company's possession. What this means in any case is that you can regard the act-scene divisions with a certain degree of skepticism. The text of the quarto especially shows us a play written to be performed in rapid and continuous action, with a new character or characters coming onstage immediately after the '*Exit*' or '*Exeunt*' of the previous scene. The scene divisions seem real enough when the stage is cleared, but the effect is momentary and at times even illusory. The act divisions, indebted to neo-Aristotelean criticism for the idea that a good play should have five acts, may or may not have held significance for Shakespeare.

Thus the text of *A Midsummer* begins simply enough with an entrance: '*Enter Theseus, Hippolyta, with others.*' We need to unpack Shakespeare's stage directions carefully, especially since they are so laconic. Who are the '*others*'? One of them surely has to be Philostrate, master of ceremonies, for Theseus soon addresses him on the subject of the entertainments planned for the wedding. '*Others*' must also include attendants. Theseus is a great man, a duke. He is attended by those who stand unobtrusively by, waiting to do as they are told. Hippolyta is Queen of the Amazons, and, though (as we shortly learn) she is in effect a captive, she too deserves to be attended by ladies-in-waiting or servingwomen. The acting company can provide extras for these walk-on parts. The attendants are garbed in accordance with their social station, which is lower than that of Theseus and Hippolyta.

The opening of the play needs to be stately and ceremonial. Theseus and Hippolyta are not the central characters of *A Midsummer*, but their story frames the action of the play. We learn from their opening dialogue that they are to be married in four days, in what will be a handsome state occasion. They are the human royalty of this play, and they speak with the graceful authority that comes to them naturally enough as the perquisite of their exalted rank. At the same time, if we read their dialogue carefully we detect a note of gendered conflict. Theseus has conquered the Queen of the Amazons and now plans to marry her, will she or no. Love and military might are paradoxically juxtaposed: as Theseus says, 'Hippolyta, I wooed thee with my sword / And won thy love doing thee injuries' (1.1.16–17). This is a strange way to win a woman's love, surely. It bespeaks a male triumph over the female in the face of armed resistance to male intrusion. The Amazons are not ordinary women. They are a legendary nation of women-warriors who supposedly were allies of the Trojans in the Trojan War, going so far as to invade Athens; it was in repelling this invasion that Theseus, according to legend, captured Hippolyta. The name 'A-mazon' means 'breastless', in recognition of their supposedly having removed their right breasts in order to be able to pull their bows to the fullest extent before shooting. Some women! And now Theseus has conquered their queen; he has put the genie of female transgressive unruliness back in its bottle, or so he hopes. He is eager for the marriage day to come in order that he may satisfy his importunate male desire to possess her. She for her part seems quite prepared to wait. 'Four days will quickly steep themselves in night', she languidly remarks (7). In some recent productions of the play, the actress playing Hippolyta displays her true feminist stripes by siding with Hermia against her paternalistic father. Even late in the play, Hippolyta seems to take pleasure in differing with Theseus's views, on poetry, on dramatic performances. Yet Hippolyta accepts that she is beaten, and marries with the regal grace that is her heritage.

These observations that we can deduce from the opening dialogue, a mere 19 lines, address a question with which one can always begin: why does Shakespeare start the play this way? Why does he make a point of Theseus's conquering of Hippolyta if the play is not to be about them? Several answers are of course possible. This choice starts the play with a rich panoply of wealth and power; the stage is comfortably filled with handsomely dressed people. Theseus is preeminently an authority figure, in charge of everything, including, it seems, the play we are about to witness. The setting is his court. All this, as we will see shortly, surrounds the play's main action as a contrasting world of social reality. The play will be mostly about dreaming, fantasy, nighttime, escape from social order, mixups, confusions, and the perils and pleasures of falling in love; the play begins with hierarchy, social order, and authority as a way of providing a contrastive point of view.

This portrayal of an authoritarian court, and its contrast with the world of young love and escape from social order, is underscored by the appearance, at line 20, of Egeus and his daughter Hermia, together with two young men, Lysander and Demetrius. Who is Egeus? The list of characters has told us only that he is the father of Hermia, who is in love with Lysander. Our task as readers requires us to find out about this man from what he says, not, as in most fiction, from what the author tells us about his appearance and social station. What are the clues here? What we learn first is that he is angry with his daughter for defying his wishes that she marry Demetrius. Egeus charges Lysander with having wooed Hermia by bewitching her and 'filching' her affection with bracelets, rings, and other gifts that are so potent in capturing a young girl's fancy. Egeus invokes the law of Athens, which is draconian: Hermia must bend herself to her father's will or face the full penalty of death. Theseus, as duke, is obliged to admit that Egeus is legally correct and that Hermia must comply with her father's wishes, though the Duke does offer Hermia another option of entering a convent for the rest of her life.

We learn a good bit from this exchange. Egeus is evidently a person of some consequence in the court of Duke Theseus. He addresses the Duke as one to whom he, Egeus, is tied in bonds of obedience. At the same time, Theseus owes an obligation to Egeus to enforce the law as the occasion demands. The Athenian court is a man's world, one in which men network with one another. They evidently regard women as their chattels, their possessions. Theseus has captured Hippolyta and will shortly marry her as his prize of war; Egeus insists that his daughter marry Demetrius. 'As she is mine', he declares, 'I may dispose of her' (42). Hermia belongs to her father, to be disposed of as he chooses; her own preference seems not to matter at all to him. Why Egeus prefers Demetrius is never stated. Perhaps some family or business connection could explain the choice, but we are not told. The seeming arbitrariness of Egeus's preference emphasizes the arbitrary nature of his authority. Theseus is an absolute ruler as Duke of Athens; Egeus is an absolute ruler in his family. Obedience is such a highly esteemed social value in the male world of Athens that it is reinforced by the death penalty.

The young men are strikingly alike. When Theseus points out to Hermia that 'Demetrius is a worthy gentleman', she has her answer: 'So is Lysander.' Lysander expands this point to press his case. 'I am, my lord, as well derived as he, / As well possessed', he insists to Egeus, stressing both his noble birth and wealth; 'My fortune every way as fairly ranked, / If not with vantage, as Demetrius'' (52–3, 99–102). What is more, he points out, Demetrius has been known to pay his attentions to another young lady named Helena. Why should Egeus be so stubborn? We are left finally with the impression that his main wish is simply to be obeyed.

Shakespeare has shaped the opening scene thus far in such a way as to stress a sharp disparity between age and youth along with the tensions between rulers and subjects, men and women. The older male figures are powerful; the younger men are not, and the women are least powerful of all. Of what age are Demetrius and Lysander? Nothing specific is said, but clearly they are a whole generation younger than Egeus, not yet married and eager to be so. Productions invariably see the two young men as physically alike. They talk much the same, for all their antipathy toward each other. Though rivals, they are as alike as peas in a pod. Why does Shakespeare do this? One possible answer is to stress still another kind of arbitrariness: as wooers, young men are more or less interchangeable. There are lots of good fish in the sea. Hermia happens to be in love with Lysander, but does it really matter with whom? Is she perhaps being as stubborn as her father? Undoubtedly the scene does invite us to sympathize with young love over parental authority, but even so we are invited to see something comic about falling in love. Egeus is no doubt wrong to accuse Lysander of practicing witchcraft on Hermia, but love is nonetheless presented as irrational, impulsive, unpredictable. Why does Hermia love Lysander instead of Demetrius? In a way, her choice is as unfathomable and unexplained as her father's preference. Love is a mystery. It is both wonderful and ridiculous.

The strange nature of love is indeed the subject of conversation in the portion of scene 1 that follows a general exeunt of Theseus, Egeus, Demetrius, Philostrate, and the various attendants that have filled the stage with visual pageantry. Shakespeare seems to like sudden contrasts of this sort, shifting from public ceremony to private and intimate talk. Left alone onstage, Hermia and Lysander are given the chance to share their unhappiness in Theseus's endorsement of Egeus's insistence that he be obeyed. As they reflect on their dilemma, the two young lovers speak of love as martyrdom. 'The course of true love never did run smooth', declares Lysander, by way of announcing a theme for them to explore. They do so as in a duet. For a time they speak in single alternating lines, so unlike the long, formal speeches of the opening public debate on obedience:

LYSANDER The course of true love never did run smooth;
      But either it was different in blood –
HERMIA Oh, cross! Too high to be enthralled to low.
LYSANDER Or else misgrafted in respect of years –
HERMIA Oh, spite! Too old to be engaged to young.
LYSANDER Or else it stood upon the choice of friends –
HERMIA Oh, hell! To choose love by another's eyes!
                                        (1.1.134–40)

The language is now very poetic in its rhythmic repetitions: 'Oh, cross!', 'Oh, spite!', 'Oh, hell!', and 'either', 'Or else', 'Or else', and 'Too high to be', 'Too old to be'. It is as though these young people, able to read each other's thoughts, sing in the same key. Hermia's laments offer a choric response to Lysander's litany of complaints, for she entirely agrees: love is besieged by obstacles put up by the unfeeling world. Love is frustrated by the demands of social rank ('blood'), differences in age ('respect of years'), and pressures from family ('friends'). Lysander goes on to catalogue more threats, such as war, death, and sickness. To these two young people, love itself is simple and direct; the complications are all external. Love is brief in its ecstasy, and it is fragile. This is why they resolve to flee into the forest of Athens, where, Lysander tells Hermia, he happens to have a wealthy and childless aunt who will look after them. (We never hear of this aunt again: is Lysander making up a story to get Hermia to elope with him?)

We have not yet met Helena. Shakespeare brings her on now. Having given Lysander and Hermia their chance to sing their duet about love's tribulations, Shakespeare arranges for Helena to join them. She is looking forlornly for her faithless Demetrius. This grouping provides the occasion for Hermia and Helena to compare notes on how to succeed in winning the hearts of young men. The comparison is all the more pointed in view of the fact that, as they all know, Hermia is beloved by two young men and Helena by none. 'Oh, teach me how you look, and with what art / You sway the motion of Demetrius' heart', Helena beseeches her friend. This produces another passage of one-line exchanges that again is pointedly rhythmic in its repetitions:

HERMIA I frown upon him, yet he loves me still.
HELENA Oh, that your frowns would teach my smiles such skill!
HERMIA I give him curses, yet he gives me love.
HELENA Oh, that my prayers could such affection move!
HERMIA The more I hate, the more he follows me.
HELENA The more I love, the more he hateth me.
HERMIA His folly, Helena, is no fault of mine.
HELENA None but your beauty. Would that fault were mine!
                                                    (1.1.192–201)

Here the repetitions ('Oh, that', 'Oh, that', 'The more I hate', 'The more I love', etc.) are strongly reinforced by the rhyming in couplets: 'still', 'skill', 'love', 'move' (which in Elizabethan pronunciation would be a true rhyme). The succeeding couplets of this passage are linked by an interesting kind of rhyme in which the last words are in fact identical: 'he follows me', 'he hateth me', 'is no fault of mine', 'Would that fault were mine'. The exchanges here form not a love duet, as previously with Lysander and Hermia, but a debate between rivals. Hermia and Helena engage in what the rhetoricians would call stichomythia, or rapid-fire exchange of single lines of verse. Their debate also makes use of other poetic techniques that were taught by Renaissance rhetoricians: anaphora, or the repetition of a word or words at the beginning of two or more successive clauses; isocolon, or the speaking of phrases of equal length; parison, or the even balancing of grammatical members of a sentence; and still others, all aimed at rhythmic recurrence of sounds. The rhetorical terms are not important; what does matter is that the verse is markedly structured and controlled, in such a way as to show how well Shakespeare has mastered the techniques of versification that were considered an essential part of a poet's training.

The names of Hermia and Helena are similar in sound, beginning in 'He' and ending in 'a', both trisyllabic, with the stress on the first syllable.

Why does Shakespeare do this? Perhaps to emphasize that the two young women, like the two young men, are in a sense interchangeable. They are not identical: we learn later that Helena is the taller of the two and able to run faster (3.2.288–342). Helena tends to be more self-pitying. Even so, they are like twins who, having been close childhood friends, have now become rivals in the competitive game of courtship. They are of an age, and share many interests. Shakespeare seems deliberately not to sketch them as characters with any great complexity. A reader can be pardoned for forgetting, from time to time, which is which. The two women are to be, along with the two interchangeable young men, the subjects of a comedy of misunderstanding and confused relationships in which, at some time prior to the play, A loved *a* and B loved *b*: that is, Lysander loved Hermia and Demetrius loved Helena. When the play starts, however, A and B are competing for the love of *a*. Then, when the magical love juice is mistakenly applied to A's eyes, A loves *b* and B loves *a*; then, when love juice is applied as a remedy to B's eyes, A and B compete for the love of *b*; and then finally, when a magical remedy is applied to A's eyes, we return to the state of affairs before the play began, with A loving *a* and B loving *b*. Each Jack has his Jill, after having gone through all the possible arithmetical permutations of A, *a*, B, and *b*. These delightful manipulations of an equation militate against any deep exploration of character and feeling. The love tribulations of these young people are funny in part because they display the innocent and volatile folly of love.

And now Shakespeare gives us something entirely different. Once Helena has ended the first long scene in brief soliloquy, resolving to tell her wayward Demetrius of Hermia's flight into the forest with Lysander so that Helena will be able to chase after Demetrius there, the stage is given over to a group of Athenian artisans, or 'mechanicals' as they are called, meaning that they earn their livelihood through manual labor. What is Shakespeare up to now? The artisans are about to start rehearsing a play with which to celebrate the upcoming marriage of Duke Theseus and his Amazonian bride-to-be. Why does Shakespeare include this business in his play, and why does he interrupt the story about the flight of the young lovers to the forest of Athens?

These are pertinent questions for us to ask, because Shakespeare never tells us directly. His strategy, in writing a script for actors, is to let those actors play their parts while we as audience try to figure out possible connections. Shakespeare loves to interweave the elements of his drama, starting first with one story and then another and then a third. (The scene

21

to come next will be about a quarrel between the King and Queen of Fairies.) Only as the play develops will we see how these stories impinge upon one another. Meantime, we are given the pleasure of variety and contrast. The entire first scene has been in verse, some of it rhymed in couplets; the second scene is in prose. The characters of scene one were all persons of social station and wealth, however much contrasted among themselves in terms of age, sex, and power; scene two is about 'hard-handed men of Athens'. The first scene is high-toned, appealing to sentiments of chivalry, parental authority, the harsh Athenian law, and love's martyrdom; the talk in the second scene is buffoonish, ludicrous, and funny. In scene one we experience admiration, dismay, pity, and sympathy; in scene two we laugh at the characters, even if we find them endearing and companionable. We shift from romantic high seriousness to genial satire. Shakespeare's romantic comedy is a mix of genres.

The play that the Athenian workmen are about to rehearse is called 'The most lamentable comedy and most cruel death of Pyramus and Thisbe'. Talk about a mix of genres! This play is evidently to be both comic and lamentable, both a comedy and a tragedy. Is Shakespeare laughing at his own dramatic art? His style, as we have seen already, is a mix of the comic and serious. The potential resemblances between *A Midsummer* and 'Pyramus and Thisbe' are quite striking in other ways as well. Both are being put on by artisans, for many of Shakespeare's fellow actors came from the artisan class: some of them belonged to one or another of London's trade guilds, and Shakespeare himself was the son of a Stratford-upon-Avon burgher who made and sold leather goods. James Burbage, the father of Shakespeare's leading man, Richard Burbage, had been a 'joiner' or expert wood-worker, whose skill as a workman had enabled him to build the first permanent theatre building in the London suburbs in 1576. Many players and playwrights employed by other acting companies as well came out of this prosperous artisanal community.

At the same time, we perceive already a world of difference between *A Midsummer* and 'Pyramus and Thisbe'. The Athenian artisans are clowns. The name of the lead actor, Bottom the Weaver, should warn us that he and his companions are to be objects of laughter. 'Bottom' does in fact signify something to wind thread on, and is thus pertinent to Bottom's occupation of weaving, but it clearly also suggests the base or lowermost part of his grossly physical being. The name of Snug the joiner similarly plays on his occupation: a joiner's joining of wood parts needs to be snug. 'Starveling' is a good name for the tailor in this assembly of tradesmen because tailors were much ridiculed for being effeminate and physically slight. Flute as bellows-mender calls to mind a musical wind instrument with affinities to the bellows. Bottom is eager to play all the roles himself, like many an egomaniacal ham actor; he gives us a taste of his 'lofty' tragical vein, and it is indeed 'a part to tear a cat in'. He is especially interested in deciding what color beard he should wear. Snug the joiner asks if he can have his lion's part written out for him, since he is 'slow of study'. When told by Peter Quince, the producer and director, that the lion's part is nothing but extemporal roaring, the aspiring thespians start to worry that the roaring will frighten the Duchess and the ladies and land the players in a lot of trouble. Bottom and his fellows are clueless when it comes to the sophistications of dramatic illusion.

A major concern of *A Midsummer*, it seems, is the very nature of theatre itself. How should the theatre represent its story through actors, action, costuming, and set? Later, as they rehearse, the amateur thespians will decide that they need to bring in a wall to separate the two lovers, Pyramus and Thisbe, in the adjoining households of their two estranged families. An actor (Snout) will impersonate Wall by fitting himself out with plaster or loam or roughcast (a mix of lime and gravel) and a crannied hole or chink through which the lovers are to whisper. Robin Starveling is to impersonate the Man in the Moon, complete with the Moon's conventional attributes of a lantern, a dog, and a thornbush, to insure that the lovers may meet by moonlight, as the story demands. Snug, as Lion, is to be preceded by a Prologue, assuring the ladies in the courtly audience that they need not fear the presence of a real lion; for better assurance still, Snug will tell them in so many words that he is not a lion, but Snug the joiner. Because these amateur players are so naive about the nature of their adopted craft, they approach their tasks as workmen might, by literalizing stage action. Their staging solutions are, like themselves, 'mechanical'. *A Midsummer* does not make that mistake; it relies instead on the audience's imagination to body forth 'The forms of things unknown' (5.1.14–15). At the same time, these honest workmen stand in awe of dramatic art; they fear its power to frighten and to transform. They are more attuned to the magic of theatre than are their more jaded spectators, perhaps. We laugh at them, but we feel a deep sympathy for their innocence.

The next scene introduces us fully to Shakespeare's theatre of imagination. An unnamed Fairy, identified for us in the theatre by fairy costume and talk of fairy lore, engages in conversation with another sprite, who also remains unnamed at first. In due course this second sprite is identified by his interlocutor as a creature of many names: he is 'a shrewd and knavish sprite / Called Robin Goodfellow', known also as 'Hobgoblin' and 'Sweet Puck'. Why so many names? From the outset, Puck (as he is customarily named in the speech headings) is the mischievous elf or goblin of folk legend, known in Ireland as the Leprechaun. He bears some affinity to the Troll of Scandinavian folklore. He loves to play pranks, such as preventing the cream in the churned milk from turning to butter. He misleads night travelers, mimics the neighing of horses, and pretends to be a three-legged stool on which an unwary old woman tries unsuccessfully to sit.

Where are we? If we were standing in Shakespeare's original theatre, with its absence of scenery onstage, we would be asked to imagine the surroundings. The same is true of us today as readers; we must set the scene. Well, clearly we are in the forest of Athens, and we are in fairyland. Most of all, we are in a theatre of imagination. We learn from the ensuing conversation that Oberon and Titania, King and Queen of Fairies, are at odds about a 'changeling' boy, one who has been stolen from an Indian king by the fairies and has been serving in attendance on Titania, but whom Oberon desires to serve as a 'knight of his train' or retinue. Puck's description of Oberon and Titania's quarrel invites us to picture strange and wonderful effects: starlit encounters in 'grove or green', elves so frightened that they creep 'into acorn cups and hide them there', and still more. When Oberon and Titania make their separate entrances a short time later, each accompanied by an impressive train of followers, the verbal enchantment continues. They themselves are handsomely and strangely outfitted as the monarchs of fairydom; their verbal descriptions are even more exotic. Titania discourses on unusual disturbances in the weather pattern that have brought on 'Contagious fogs', 'pelting rivers' overflowing their banks, rotting fields of grain, disease-slaughtered sheep fattening the birds of carrion, unexpected frosts blighting the buds of spring, the moon 'Pale in her anger', and every possible inversion of the orderly progression of the seasons (2.1.81–117). Her analysis of the cause is no less wondrous: the seasons are inverted because the King and Queen of Fairies cannot reconcile their differences. We are in a world where the ordinary logic of cause and effect has been left far behind. We begin to understand that in the world of fairydom, and synonymously in the world of Shakespeare's theatre, anything can happen.

Even sexuality is different in this strange new world. Or perhaps we should say, sexuality especially is different. Oberon, offended by Titania's outright refusal to turn over the changeling boy to him, resolves to punish her by putting her under such a spell that when she awakens she will instantly fall in love with whatever her eye lights upon, 'Be it on lion, bear, or wolf, or bull, / On meddling monkey, or on busy ape' (2.1.180–1). In other words, Oberon resolves to cuckold himself as a way of punishing his wayward queen. Her lover will be some wild animal, perhaps. When the opportunity provides itself for Puck to accomplish what Oberon has desired, he chooses to outfit a mortal (no less a mortal than Bottom the Weaver) with an ass's head and long, hairy ears. In this comical motif, we see Shakespeare playing with ancient legends about the gods. Jupiter was famous, or infamous, for his many affairs in which he took the shape of a swan (with Leda), a shower of gold (with Danaë), a bull (with Europa), and still others. These legends of transformation were known especially to Shakespeare from Ovid's aptly titled *Metamorphoses*. They were stories of passionate, adulterous love affairs between gods and mortals. They were epiphanies, telling of the intervention of the godhead in human history, always in a violent way and with profoundly dislocating consequences. The brusque encounter of the swan and Leda led to the birth of Clytemnestra and Helen and thus to that greatest of wars, the Trojan War. Human history begins in violence. It is also divine in its origins.

A notable feature of fairyland is its poetic versatility. Oberon and Titania speak in blank verse, that is, in unrhymed verse lines that alternate unstressed and stressed syllables, more or less ten in all to a line; e.g., 'I DO but BEG a LITtle CHANGEling BOY' (2.1.120). So do the young men and women who have fled from Athens. This is the so-called iambic pentameter (i.e., with five 'feet' of the iambic unstressed-stressed pattern) that Shakespeare often uses for dialogue among his heightened or serious characters. Some of the sprites choose more varied forms. The First Fairy begins with short two-stressed lines, alternately rhymed, and using an anapestic pattern (unstressed-unstressed-stressed) that creates a sense of onrushing speed:

> Over HILL, over DALE,
>   Thorough BUSH, thorough BRIAR,
> Over PARK, over PALE,
>   Thorough FLOOD, thorough FIRE,
> I do wander everywhere,
> Swifter than the moon's sphere.
>   (2.1.2–7)

'Thorough' is an archaic spelling of 'through', chosen here for its metrical value of being bisyllabic. Shakespeare makes good use of alliteration, or recurrent sounds at the beginning of words, to reinforce the stress pattern: BUSH/BRIAR, PARK/PALE, FLOOD/FIRE. Anaphora, or the repeating of words at the beginnings of lines, is notable in the recurrent 'Thorough'. Short as the lines are, we notice that they are really divided in half, so that 'Over' / 'Over' also gives the effect of anaphora. Lines 6 and 7 abandon the original anapestic pattern for slower lines in a trochaic configuration, that is, stressed-unstressed: 'I do WANder EVeryWHERE, / SWIFTer THAN the MOON's SPHERE.' The word 'moon's is no doubt meant to be bisyllabic, for the meter: 'MOON-es'. Puck and the First Fairy then go on to converse in rhymed couplets: 'The King doth keep his revels here tonight. / Take heed the Queen come not within his sight' (18–19). Later fairy scenes, especially 2.2, give us songs in stanzaic forms. Titania's fairies sing her asleep with a roundel or dance sung in a ring, complete with a refrain: 'Lulla, lulla, lullaby, lulla, lulla, lullaby.' When Oberon chants a spell, he sets aside his more formal iambic pentameter for four-stress trochaic couplets: 'What thou see'st when thou dost wake, / Do it for thy true love take' (2.2.33–4). Puck too speaks in this verse form, so much so that it begins to sound characteristically fairy-like:

> Through the forest have I gone,
> But Athenian found I none
> On whose eyes I might approve
> This flower's force in stirring love.
> (2.2.72–5)

When the Athenian artisans get their turn to recite the verse of their 'Pyramus and Thisbe', it turns out to be in a language that parodies its own bumbling attempts at high poetic style. Thisbe begins:

> Most radiant Pyramus, most lily-white of hue,
> Of color like the red rose on triumphant brier,
> Most brisky juvenal and eke most lovely Jew,
> As true as truest horse that yet would never tire.
> (3.1.88–91)

The long six-stress lines here call our amused attention to the alternating rhymes and alliterative effects that are so much like the verse forms of *A Midsummer*, and yet so unlike in terms of grace and aptitude. The awkwardly archaic and contrived diction ('juvenal', 'brisky', 'eke'), the absurdly trite similes comparing Pyramus to a lily, a rose, and a horse, the choice of 'Jew' seemingly for no other reason than that it rhymes with 'hue' – these are all demonstrations of how extraordinarily delicate are the factors distinguishing false from true in the writing of verse comedy.

Once Shakespeare has established for us the textures and plot-lines of his four main narrative strands – that of Theseus's court, of the young lovers, of the Athenian artisans, and of the fairies – he proceeds to interweave the last three of these, leaving the story of Theseus and Hippolyta as his framing device with which to begin and then end the play. In the forest, the young lovers experience a series of increasingly painful tribulations until fairy magic manages to sort everything out. Demetrius heartlessly runs away from the pursuing Helena after threatening her with rape. She, thus abandoned, happens across the sleeping Lysander, whose eyes meantime have been treated by Puck with a magic love juice that will induce him to fall madly in love with the first person he sees when he awakes. The love juice was intended for Demetrius, to restore his love for Helena, but Puck's instructions from Oberon were to apply the love juice to the eyes of a young man in Athenian garments, and Puck has innocently mistaken Lysander for Demetrius since they are so much alike. Lysander, awakened by Helena, sets off in amorous pursuit of her, leaving his faithful Hermia asleep and abandoned. Shakespeare's interesting premise seems to be that one cannot fall in love with a new person without instantly loathing the person one has loved until now; Lysander soon finds Hermia repellent. Hermia is no less offended by the attentions of Demetrius. Shakespeare has designed his plot so that everything is at cross purposes.

And so, when the four young lovers eventually come together, still in the forest, the unhappiness is universal. Demetrius, awakened under the influence of Puck's love juice, immediately switches his attentions to Helena, so that both young men now desire her while heaping scorn on Hermia. Helena, having been so long neglected by Demetrius, can only suppose that both young men are mocking her with their protestations of love, and then comes to the conclusion that Hermia too is part of their confederacy to make her feel miserable. Hermia, now despised by both men, is equally unhappy. The two women turn on each other. The two young men try to kill each other. All this occurs in the play's longest and centrally located scene, labeled as Act 3, scene 2. It comes at just the point where it should occur in a well-constructed comedy, as the climax and supreme complication before the play moves on to resolving its difficulties. We see now that the play has been building toward this climax from earlier scenes of exposition and elaboration: we have met the characters, followed their various odysseys into the forest, and now see them at their moment of greatest peril and confusion.

We can see also that Shakespeare likes to write comedy in which the complications are unusually fraught with danger. Hermia repeatedly speaks of seeking out death; see, for example, 2.2.162. The young men would indeed come to fatal blows if Puck were not on hand to mislead them with his mimicking voices in the dark, keeping them safely apart. Puck talks of the forest as a place of ghosts and 'Damnèd spirits' who, as suicides, have been buried at 'crossways and floods', presumably with stakes driven through their hearts (3.2.381–5). Shakespeare likes the *frisson* of impending disaster, perhaps because it makes the resolution of danger all the sweeter. Moreover, Shakespeare psychologizes the story of the four lovers in a way that adds personal depth and meaning to their unhappiness. Helena is absolutely perverse in her impulse to feel sorry for herself; when the two young men grovel at her feet in competition for her love, she can only suppose that they are mocking her. Perhaps her undergoing this painful misery brings self-awareness at last, for when she and the other three awaken in the morning, all appears to be well. Their tribulations seem to them only a dream, a nightmare, from which they awaken into better self-understanding. They are matured emotionally by having been exposed to a frightening picture of their own perverse instincts for self-destruction. Helena especially seems aware of how fragile and precious is the happiness she has found upon awakening: 'I have found Demetrius like a jewel, / Mine own, and not mine own' (4.1.190–1).

The story of Queen Titania's affair with Bottom the Weaver follows a similar parabolic curve of exposition, complication, and resolution, but here the story is one in which the battle of the sexes is settled in favor of the male. Titania has had the best of reasons for holding out against Oberon's insistent demand that he have the changeling boy. This boy was the child of a mortal woman who served as a votaress in Titania's order; the two were very close. Titania beautifully describes their loving relationship as one that was based on sharing the secrets of pregnancy and childbirth (2.1.121–37). These bonds are so sacred that Titania will not give up the boy, now that the mother has died. Does Oberon insist on having the boy because he feels jealous? As a male, he is excluded from the mysterious rites of womanhood that Titania and the boy's mother have shared. Is he motivated too by a characteristically male impulse to control female unruliness, to put down a rebellion where he claims to be master? The parallels here to the conquest of Queen Hippolyta by Duke Theseus are suggestive. Men get to rule the roost.

Oberon's triumph is evident most of all at the moment of Titania's awakening from the spell that Oberon has cast upon her by means of the love juice. Under the influence of that spell, she has been transformed into a creature quite unlike her usual self. No longer haughty and regal, she showers the ass-like Bottom with attentions, bidding her fairy attendants to bring him delicacies, to scratch where he itches, and to sing the two of them asleep. She winds Bottom in her arms as 'doth the woodbine the sweet honeysuckle', or as the 'female ivy . . . Enrings the barky fingers of the elm' (4.1.1–43). As she freely confesses, she dotes on Bottom. This liaison is an exaggerated emblem of the epiphanic experience with which the play is so concerned: the coming together of the immortal and mortal worlds. It exposes to laughter what is so ineffably gross about our mortal nature. And indeed, when the spell is taken from Titania's eyes, she sees at once how grotesquely and ludicrously opposite is Bottom's nature from her own. 'Oh, how mine eyes do loathe his visage now!' she exclaims. She does not, however, venture to reproach her husband for having subjected her to this sexual humiliation. Perhaps she glances at Puck when she asks, 'How came these things to pass?', for she has long known Puck and his mischievous ways, but she offers no remonstrance. Oberon has taught her a lesson of wifely obedience, and has won from her the concession of turning over to him the changeling boy. 'When I had at my pleasure taunted her', Oberon reports to Puck, 'And she in mild terms begged my patience, / I then did ask of her her changeling child, / Which straight she gave me' (4.1.56–9). The surrender is complete.

Bottom's own transformation is more pleasantly comic. Although he has been changed into an ass and then back again, and in the process has lost the company of his bewildered friends, he himself seems not to feel the slightest pain or humiliation. His friends worry that they have lost him for ever when he is 'translated' (3.1.113–14), and that their opportunity to perform before the Duke and Duchess is also a casualty of their jarring forest experience, but Bottom knows only that he has had 'a most rare vision', a dream that is 'past the wit of man to say what dream it was' (4.1.203–5). Although he does not say it in so many words, he has had an affair with the Queen of Fairies. He will get Peter Quince to immortalize the story in a ballad. A paradox appears to be at work: the young lovers, who suffered pangs of humiliation in the forest, awaken to a better understanding of their

A Midsummer Night's Dream, Act 4, scene 2. Bottom's friends celebrate his affair with Titania as an erotic triumph. David Waller as Bottom in Peter Brook's production for the Royal Shakespeare Company, 1970. (Courtesy of Shakespeare Birthplace Trust, photo by David Farrell)

own human weaknesses and need for charitable forbearance; Bottom, for whom the forest was a romp, seems to have learned nothing about himself. He appears to be entirely content with who he is, and we see no reason to deny him that happiness.

'Dream' is of course a key word in the play's title. What use do other characters make of dreaming? To Theseus, when he hears of the lovers' strange adventures, dreaming is a kind of madness. Their stories are 'More strange than true'. He is the play's chief skeptic, unwilling to credit these 'antique fables' and 'fairy toys'. At the same time, he is most able to see the connection between dreaming and theatre. 'The lunatic, the lover, and the poet / Are of imagination all compact', he declares to Hippolyta, meaning that all three deal with the fantastic and 'unreal'. The lunatic 'sees more devils than vast hell can hold', madly filling his brain with images of terror that ordinary mortals never even conceive. The lover 'Sees Helen's beauty in a brow of Egypt', infatuatedly supposing the dark-complected and gypsy-like wench whom he adores to be the nonpareil of feminine beauty. The poet is no less in the grip of a kind of madness that transforms reality into dream:

> The poet's eye, in a fine frenzy rolling,
> Doth glance from heaven to earth, from earth to heaven;
> And as imagination bodies forth
> The forms of things unknown, the poet's pen
> Turns them to shapes, and gives to airy nothing
> A local habitation and a name.
>
> (5.1.13–18)

This frenzy is the 'furor poeticus' of artistic inspiration, a frenzy of creation that writers from ancient times have claimed as the divinely sent gift bestowed mysteriously upon the prophet or seer. The poet is the instrument into whom the divine afflatus breathes superhuman knowledge and power – the power of imagination and insight. The poet's realm thus uniquely connects heaven and earth; his gift is to create images or shapes that do not exist in the mundane world. Through the poet, 'airy nothing' and 'forms of things unknown' achieve a kind of substance in art.

Why does Shakespeare choose to celebrate the genius of his own dramatic art in the utterances of one who is so openly skeptical of the whole business and who nonetheless describes it so well? In part, perhaps, because Theseus is uniquely able to be an objective witness. As the central figure of the play's framing plot, appearing at its beginning and end, he never experiences the magic of the forest. His only venture into the forest's bounds is at dawn, as the lovers awaken from their dream; Theseus goes to the forest with his entourage to hunt. His conversation with Hippolyta is all about his splendid hounds, in full cry as they pursue the game. The image is perfect: Theseus is one who owns the forest, invading and colonizing it for his own patrician purposes. Historically, in England, the word 'forest' connoted a tract of partly wooded land owned by the sovereign and used by him for the hunting of game; the Forest of Arden, near to Shakespeare's birthplace, was just such a royal preserve. The location of most of the action in *A Midsummer* is both a 'wood' and a 'forest' (as at 2.2.72, for example), and, when Theseus goes hunting, he calls upon the assistance of his 'forester' (4.1.102). The forest's strange secrets are never revealed to Theseus. He does not experience what Northrop Frye aptly describes as the imaginative journey to the 'green world' of Shakespearean comedy, where the realities of everyday living are transformed into an artistic vision.

Queen Hippolyta, even though she stays with Theseus and thus does not undergo the imaginative and sometimes harrowing journey of the young lovers, believes in the 'truth' of their transformative experience; she is attuned to the magic of their story in a way that Theseus is not. Seeing how their minds are so 'transfigured' by what they have undergone, she accepts that their story 'More witnesseth than fancy's images', that is, testifies to something essentially true. Their story, she insists, 'grows to something of great constancy', all the more wondrous because it is both strange and 'admirable' – i.e., a source of wonder (5.1.23–7). Even in the courtly figures of the framing plot, then, the 'truth' of the story told in Shakespeare's play is a subject of debate.

Are the fairies 'real'? Shakespeare seems to delight in teasing us with this question, for it is a question about the kind of dramatic art he writes. In one sense, the fairies are fictional. They are parts to be played by actors. Yet since all the characters in *A Midsummer* are similarly fictional, we have yet to sort out the question of whether the fairies are fictional in a special sense. Theseus evidently thinks they are. Shakespeare is certainly drawing on legends about Pucks or leprechauns who play mischievous pranks, about briers and thorns that snatch at passers-by as though animated by a desire to hinder, about ghosts that wander in churchyards, and all the rest. Are we to 'believe' in such legends? In Shakespeare's day, belief in fairies was widespread, but was also the subject of fervent controversy, especially among some theologians and learned writers (including, a short time later, King James I and VI) who were anxious to combat what they regarded as the dangerous superstition of demonology. In varied forms, the controversy lives on in our modern world.

Shakespeare seems to be interested less in the issue of demonology than in what the question of fairydom has to say about dramatic representation. By choosing a story that deals in the improbable and the fantastic, he challenges us to examine what we mean by 'belief' when we respond to his play. In one crucial sense, the fairies of *A Midsummer* are unquestionably 'real': they exist in our imaginations as shaped by Shakespeare's poetic art, and thus are immortal. They will be remembered when all of us are long forgotten. They are immortal in the very sense that Plato describes when he talks about ideal forms: just as each individual being embodies an idea that will be eternally recreated through the process of generation, even so the invented characters of Shakespeare's play will live on forever when the actors, the individual performance or reading, and the dramatist are no longer among the living.

The artisans' performance of 'Pyramus and Thisbe' engages delightfully with this idea. It is unquestionably a bad play, but it is a play nonetheless. To Theseus, the *raisonneur* of *A Midsummer*, plays are all alike in one crucial respect. When Hippolyta complains of 'Pyramus and Thisbe' that 'This is the silliest stuff that ever I heard', Theseus offers a defense that sounds rather like Shakespeare's defense of his own art: 'The best in this kind are but shadows, and the worse are no worse, if imagination amend them' (5.1.209–11). All plays are only shadows, that is, unsubstantial representations and approximations that will vanish once the play is over. Perhaps we can hear in this speech a modesty that is characteristic of Shakespeare, apologizing for the inadequacy of dramatic representation even as he simultaneously asks us as audience to supply what is missing with our imaginations. Plato mistrusts poetry because it tells untruths; Shakespeare embraces illusion. Theseus is resolved to hear and see 'Pyramus and Thisbe' in a generous spirit of finding and amplifying what is potentially good in it. 'Never anything can be amiss / When simpleness and duty tender it', he admonishes his courtiers. 'Our sport shall be to take what they mistake', that is, our pleasure as spectators will be to receive in the proper spirit what the actors intend, not what they actually perform (82–90).

'Pyramus and Thisbe' means well. However lamentable in its inappropriately comic touches, it tells a tragic tale that mirrors the plot of *A Midsummer*. It explores in a tragic vein the very tribulations that in *A Midsummer* are cheerfully resolved: parental opposition to romantic love, unlucky timing, a dangerous forest inhabited by wild creatures, misunderstood communication leading to disaster. Presumably the young lovers on stage, watching 'Pyramus and Thisbe', can see that, were it not for the grace of some forgiving comic spirit that has saved them from their worst selves, their plight might well have been that of the doomed lovers. Comedy and tragedy are separated by a hair-thin line of difference. 'Pyramus and Thisbe' celebrates, no less than the larger play of which it is a part, the exquisite sense of young love doing battle with a hostile and uncaring world.

Shakespeare gives to Oberon and Puck the last words of *A Midsummer*. They come on stage when the happily married couples have watched the performance of 'Pyramus and Thisbe' and have betaken themselves to bed. The play is over, so far as the mortals are concerned. They have never seen the fairies, of course; when Puck and Oberon wander freely among the lovers in the earlier acts, the two of them are 'invisible', meaning simply that they tell us they are so. 'I am invisible', declares Oberon, 'And I will overhear their conference' (2.1.186–7). One cannot imagine a more perfect demonstration of what Theseus means when he says that our imaginations must 'mend' dramatic mimesis. Oberon's simply saying that he is invisible makes it so; we accept in the theatre that he cannot be seen by the mortals, even though we perceive the fairies as clearly as we do the others, and understand that all are played by actors. This stage trick confers on us a kind of omniscience; we are godlike, knowing more than do the mortals, knowing even at times more than the fairies themselves. This is particularly true when we see Oberon and Puck mistaken in thinking that Lysander is Demetrius and thus in need of having the love juice applied to his eyes to restore his love for Helena. We are the gods of the play.

Appropriately, then, we share with Oberon, Titania, and Puck a moment after the play itself is over. If Theseus and Hippolyta preside over the framing or 'over-plot' of *A Midsummer*, then the fairies now officiate at a still higher level of abstraction in the theatre. They know all about, and indeed have controlled, the events of the human story in such a way that those human participants have been entirely unaware of the fairies' existence. Even this last process of framing proceeds by degrees. First, Oberon and Titania, with their retinues, sing and dance to bless the palace of Theseus, expressing through music and dance movement the new harmony that the King and Queen of Fairies have achieved, and, through that harmony, a promise of happiness for the mortals under their 'invisible' sway. Oberon offers assurance that the marrying couples will be fortunate in their progeny, with no danger of mole, harelip, or any such 'mark prodigious' that the fairies can certainly inflict on any mortals who are so rash as to displease the fairies. Are we, as audience, so rash as not to believe in these fairies? If so, better watch out! Oberon thus playfully warns us to accede to the magical spirit of Shakespeare's play or else stand in immediate danger of the fairies' wrath. The tone is playful because of the insistent reminders that we are watching a dramatic representation, an imitation of an action.

As the last stage of this progressive framing, Puck remains alone on stage to deliver the play's epilogue. Though it is not named as such, this is an epilogue (like Prospero's in *The Tempest* or Rosalind's in *As You Like It*) by virtue of the fact that Puck drops his stage persona and steps outside the play's fictional world. He speaks to us directly as 'Gentles', brazenly asking for our applause ('Give me your hands') and apologizing for any inadequacies in what we have just seen:

> If we shadows have offended,
> Think but this, and all is mended,
> That you have but slumbered here
> While these visions did appear.
> (5.1.418–21)

'We shadows' is gracefully ambivalent. It points to the fairies themselves, for whom the word is apt: Puck calls Oberon 'King of Shadows' at 3.2.347. It embraces all the characters in the play, who are shadows in the sense of being theatrical representations with no existence outside the bounds of the dramatic fiction. It embraces the actors, since it is on their behalf that Puck offers his apology. And why not include the dramatist as well, as a member of the acting company? No less importantly, this epilogue brings everything to a close by emphasizing that the inadequacies of dramatic representation must be 'mended' by the spectators themselves, by their imaginations. Puck insistently reiterates this idea thrice in his short speech: 'all is mended', 'we will mend', 'We will make amends'.

A Midsummer, as Puck insists, is a 'weak and idle theme, / No more yielding but a dream'. But then so is life itself. The spectators, by attending this play, have 'slumbered here / While these visions did appear'. Playgoing is like sleeping; the play itself is a dream; our experience of it is like having a dream. With Shakespeare's script at our disposal, the dream becomes our dream as we watch and read. Like any dream, it seems evanescent; when it is over, it is no longer there, and we grasp at it for interpretation as it fades into day-to-day reality. As Keats says, at the end of his 'Ode to a Nightingale', 'Fled is that music: – do I wake or sleep?' Sleep, dream, poetry, drama, life itself – no wonder that Shakespeare's play is able, like Keats's Grecian urn, to 'tease us out of thought / As doth eternity'.

3

Romeo and Juliet

Romeo and Juliet tells much the same story as does 'Pyramus and Thisbe' in *A Midsummer Night's Dream*. When the two young lovers of 'Pyramus and Thisbe' are forbidden by their parents to see each other, they secretly plan an elopement. By misfortune, Thisbe arrives sooner than Pyramus at their appointed rendezvous, where she is so affrighted by a lioness that she flees, leaving behind a mantle that she drops in her panic. The lioness, her mouth all besmeared with blood from having killed a prey, tears the mantle with her bloody teeth. Pyramus, convinced by seeing the mantle that his Thisbe has been killed too, takes his own life only moments before Thisbe returns in search of him. Desolated to find him dead from a self-inflicted sword wound, she slays herself with the same weapon.

This tale, as told in Ovid's *Metamorphoses*, Book 4 (a work to which Shakespeare was much indebted as he wrote *A Midsummer*, as we have seen), differs from *Romeo and Juliet* in many particulars. Although the parents of Pyramus and Thisbe are neighbors (in Babylon) and appear to have some strong reason for forbidding the match of their children, Ovid's poem mentions nothing about a feud between the two households. The poem offers no equivalent for the death in a street brawl of Romeo's friend Mercutio, prompting Romeo to retaliate by killing the slayer of Mercutio, Juliet's cousin Tybalt. Thisbe has no Nurse in Ovid. The lovers do not meet at a masked ball. Thisbe has no rival wooer like Count Paris. These and other details came to Shakespeare instead from a long narrative poem by Arthur Brooke called *The Tragical History of Romeus and Juliet*, published in 1562, which was itself indebted to an Italian version by Matteo Bandello in his *Novelle* of 1554. Bandello in turn drew heavily on Luigi da Porto's *Historia novellamente ritrovata di due Nobili Amanti* (c. 1530), which had told and substantially expanded a story of great antiquity going back through Masuccio of Salerno's *Il Novellino* (1476) to Xenophon of Ephesus's fifth-century *Ephesiaca*. Probably the story is even older than that. Shakespeare thus did not need Ovid's account of Pyramus and Thisbe in order to shape his plot of *Romeo and Juliet*. At the same time, the similarities are striking. Bad timing and miscommunication contribute substantially to the catastrophe in both cases, leading to a tragic climax in which the young man commits suicide under the mistaken impression that his beloved is already dead, and then is found by her when it is too late. In both accounts the bereaved young woman takes her own life with her lover's weapon.

Why did Shakespeare write both *Romeo and Juliet* and the play-within-the-play in *A Midsummer* that reads like a parody of *Romeo and Juliet*? In what order did he write these two works? They seem to have been staged originally at more or less the same time, around 1594–6. Was he parodying himself in *A Midsummer*, or did 'Pyramus and Thisbe' come first? The evidence for dating is so inexact that we cannot be sure which.

This pairing of *Romeo and Juliet* and *A Midsummer* points to another striking resemblance: the mixing together of comic and tragic or near-tragic. In *A Midsummer*, many of the characters undergo humiliations and dangers until they are rescued by a kind of comic providence embodied in the mock-heroic gods and goddesses (i.e., the fairies) who rule this play. *Romeo and Juliet* is painfully funny in the first three acts – painful not only because one laughs so much but also because the merriment ends in deaths that seem so avoidable. *Romeo and Juliet* has the odd distinction of being the funniest of Shakespeare's tragedies. Having been written some years before Shakespeare turned to the great and shattering tragedies of *Hamlet*, *Othello*, *King Lear*, and *Macbeth*, this early tragedy is spiritually more attuned to the romantic comedies of the mid 1590s than to what was to follow in 1599–1600 and afterwards.

The mix of tragic and comic is present in *Romeo and Juliet* from the start. As with *A Midsummer*, we want to observe closely how Shakespeare begins his play. He does so strikingly with a Prologue, one in which the story of the play is outlined for us from start to finish:

Two households, both alike in dignity,
In fair Verona, where we lay our scene,
From ancient grudge break to new mutiny,
Where civil blood makes civil hands unclean.

Before we meet any of the regular characters in the play, we are given plot exposition. In the north Italian city of Verona, two families have been at bitter enmity with one another for as long as anyone can remember. This information confirms what we can learn also if we examine the list of characters (not in any of the early printed editions, hence added by an editor) in which the Montagues and the Capulets are usually grouped in such a way as to emphasize the division of Verona into two armed camps, with Prince Escalus as an impartial ruling figure, and a few others like Mercutio, Count Paris, Friar Laurence, Friar John, and the Apothecary, not belonging to one household or the other. The Chorus goes on to tell us how two lovers emerge from this conflict only to be overwhelmed and destroyed by it. Their love will end in death. The only saving grace is the seeming promise that, although they must die, their deaths will somehow remove the rancor of their families' feuding. The opening Prologue, written in sonnet form, thus outlines the whole story and then interprets or moralizes it: the lovers will be sacrifices to hatred in such a way as to atone for it. The Prologue thus throws away all narrative suspense. The story will end in tragedy. Its young protagonists are 'star-crossed' and 'death-marked'. We must not hope that tragedy will be averted.

Why does Shakespeare choose to reveal his plot and do away with narrative suspense? One possible reason is that the story was so very well known, as it is today. Not many readers today, I suspect, can take up *Romeo and Juliet* without a general awareness that it will end in the lovers' death. The same was probably true in Shakespeare's time. A more interesting possible reason is that Shakespeare thereby creates quite a different kind of suspense: not that of wondering what will happen, since we know what will happen, but the suspense of hoping against hope, of knowing more than the characters in the story, so that we continually hear ourselves saying, 'No, don't do that!', 'Just wait a little longer!' To see the working out of the inevitable is potentially very suspenseful and tragic, as it is for example in Sophocles' *Oedipus the King* or in Shakespeare's *Macbeth*, where prophecy spells out what will happen with such devastating certainty that we tremble as we wait for the ax to fall. This is a very old pattern of tragic suspense, quite unlike the suspense of modern detective fiction.

The 'two households' of Verona, so central to the play in the Chorus's view, are indeed the subject of the play's opening scene. It begins not with Romeo and Juliet but with a noisy and violent encounter. Servants of the two households come across one another in the streets of Verona, eager to fight. Although Shakespeare does not say so directly, he seems intent on presenting to us the anatomy of a feud. What drives these two families to bitter enmity? Several factors emerge as we listen to the dialogue. The quarrel is an 'ancient grudge', as the Chorus has told us. The servants seem to know only that 'The quarrel is between our masters and us their men' (1.1.19–20): that is to say, the servants are ready to fight because for some reason their masters have become sworn enemies. No one in fact knows how the hostility began. Whatever that cause was, it has been forgotten, leaving in its wake an unending reciprocal process of insult and retaliation.

A macho code of honor obligates the men of the Capulet household to hate all Montagues and their servants, and vice versa. One provocation leads to another. A Capulet servant bites his thumb at the Montagues, which, as he says to his fellow servant, 'is disgrace to them if they bear it' (42–3). The biting of one's thumb is an obscenely provocative gesture, more or less equivalent today to giving someone the finger. The code of honor impels these men to prove their manhood and their loyalty to their own group by daring the enemy to respond to a demeaning insult. At the same time, these servants show their cowardice by hiding behind the law. When the Capulet servant who bites his thumb is twice asked by a Montague, 'Do you bit your thumb at us, sir?', meaning, are you offering that insult to us, the Capulet servant confers with his comrade. 'Is the law of our side if I say ay?' he asks, and when assured that the law will not take his side, he retreats to a face-saving equivocation: 'No, sir, I do not bite my thumb at you, sir, but I bite my thumb, sir' (43–51). This is typical of the hair-splitting wordplay of this whole encounter. Some of it is overly precious and hard to decipher without consulting the notes, but the gist of the conversation is clear: the hair-splitting banter is symptomatic of the small-minded, cowardly, legalistic, macho ethos that fuels the perverse spirit of feuding to which these men are so prone. They might well belong to street gangs today, as indeed they are portrayed in *West Side Story* (1961) and in Baz Luhrmann's *Romeo + Juliet* (1996).

Juliet's cousin Tybalt demonstrates that at least some of the servants' social superiors are as relentlessly hostile as the men. Not until he arrives on the scene do the Capulet servants dare openly to challenge their opposite numbers; under cover of his authority and daredevil courage, they engage in fighting. When Romeo's friend, Benvolio (whose name means 'the well-wishing one'), draws his sword in an attempt to stop the skirmishing, Tybalt has nothing but contempt for such peacemaking: 'What, art thou drawn among these heartless hinds? / Turn thee, Benvolio. Look upon thy death.' When Benvolio insists that he has drawn his weapon solely for the purpose of keeping the peace, and urges Tybalt to join in such a public-spirited move, Tybalt is implacable: 'What, drawn and talk of peace? I hate the word, / As I hate hell, all Montagues, and thee. / Have at thee, coward!' (66–71). Even Tybalt's use of 'thee' is symptomatic. Employed in addressing a friend or a child, it is an intimacy; used in addressing an enemy, it is a taunt. Tybalt is implacable. Like the servants, he never reflects upon what may have been the original enmity of the two households. The name of 'Montague' is enough to set him off.

The older heads of households, 'old Capulet' and 'old Montague' (as they are identified in the stage directions at 1.1.74 and 78), speak more reasonably once their tempers have had time to cool, but in the heat of the moment they too respond to the challenge of the street fighting like war stallions answering the call of a trumpet. 'What noise is this? Give me my long sword, ho!' shouts Capulet as he enters '*in his gown*', betokening the age that should bring him the wisdom of his many years. Montague is no less ready for a fight. 'Thou villain Capulet!' Their wives strive in vain to hold them back; the macho spirit of the hour is indomitably male. Any unwillingness to fight, like Benvolio's, is branded as cowardice.

Only when Prince Escalus arrives on the scene can any semblance of sanity be restored. He lectures his subjects sternly, redefining their fierce encounter in terms of an entirely new ethic: that of law. He calls them 'beasts' (83) for the outrage they have committed. Escalus will not tolerate an ethic of revenge; to him, the macho code of honor is no more than a pretext for savagery. He is echoing dogmas of the Elizabethan state, in fact: deeply concerned with the factionalism that had torn England apart during much of the sixteenth century, Elizabeth's government insisted on the primacy of law in settling disputes. Vendettas and dueling were outlawed. Escalus is thus a ruler in the Elizabethan mode: an absolute overlord, impartial, wise, judicious. He takes care not to side with Montagues or Capulets; instead, he calls both to account, and will confer further with both heads of households on the crucial matter of keeping the peace.

That Escalus is right so to insist is borne out by the acquiescence of both offending parties. A short time later, in scene 2, we hear Capulet telling Count Paris that he and Montague are now bound to an agreement that they fully accept: ''tis not hard, I think, / For men so old as we to keep the peace'. Paris readily concurs: 'Of honorable reckoning are you both, / And pity 'tis you lived at odds so long' (1.2.1–5). Sane persons agree that feuding is senseless. Yet Tybalt is remorseless, and he is still to be reckoned with.

The comedy of *Romeo and Juliet* begins hard on the heels of the opening violence, still in scene 1. This abrupt juxtaposition of the tragic and the comic is in fact the burden of Romeo's first conversation with his friend Benvolio. Romeo has become a recluse, hiding from his family and acquaintances. His behavior expresses itself repeatedly in the rhetorical figure of oxymoron, or inherent contradiction. He inverts day and night, wandering about all alone in the dark and then returning to his room as day approaches. 'Away from light steals home my heavy son', says old Montague, punning on the opposition of 'light' and 'heavy', with 'light' meaning both 'the light of day' and 'light in mood', and with 'heavy' meaning both 'dark', as in 'a heavy sky', and 'sad'. The punning on 'son' and 'sun' intensifies what is both sad and witty in this wordplay (1.1.131–42).

Romeo sees nothing but contradiction in everything: in his own unhappy existence, in the factionalism of Verona's two leading families, in the nature of love itself. In an extraordinary series of oxymorons, he attempts to tell Benvolio what troubles him so. He begins by commenting on the visible signs of the scuffle just ended, at which he was not present:

> Oh, me! What fray was here?
> Yet tell me not, for I have heard it all.
> Here's much to do with hate, but more with love.
> Why, then, O brawling love, O loving hate,
> O anything of nothing first create,
> O heavy lightness, serious vanity,
> Misshapen chaos of well-seeming forms,
> Feather of lead, bright smoke, cold fire, sick health,
> Still-waking sleep, that is not what it is!
> This love feel I, that feel no love in this.
> (1.1.173–82)

Oxymorons are puzzles – riddling, sententious, proverbial. They pithily strive to catch at something inherently paradoxical in human nature and in life itself. They are witty, gnomic, mind-teasing, sometimes obscure and difficult. Why should the street fighting have to do 'more with love' than with hate? One can readily understand violent conflict as a product of hate, but why of love? One possible explanation is that the image here is proleptic, that is, having more to do with the future story of the play itself. Certainly Romeo and Juliet's story is to be one of love being born in the midst of hate. As Juliet says, when she learns that the young stranger she has fallen in love with at her parents' masked ball is a Montague: 'My only

41

love sprung from my only hate!' (1.5.139). Part of what binds these two young people to each other is that they both express themselves in what sound like logically impossible contradictions.

Other paradoxes in Romeo's discourse to Benvolio are no less thought-provoking. What is 'anything' that is first created out of 'nothing'? Thus abstractly stated, the saying has a proverbial ring, calling to mind the teachings of ancient philosophers and poets like Heraclitus and Hesiod as to how life itself came into being out of Chaos and Night, that is, out of a flux in which matter itself was constantly changing. Romeo seems to hint at great oppositions in the nature of things, as between being and non-being, life and death, order and disorder. These ideas too will be developed in the play lying before us, especially by Friar Laurence, who draws a plain-spun homily from the herbs in his garden that can act either as a poison or as a curative medicine. 'Two such opposèd kings encamp them still / In man as well as herbs', he intones, 'grace and rude will; / And where the worser is predominant, / Full soon the canker death eats up that plant' (2.3.28–30). Life is a battleground between good and evil, love and hate. The comedy-tragedy of Romeo and Juliet will constantly negotiate its way between these eternal oppositions.

For all his sadness, the Romeo of the play's first scenes might easily belong in a Shakespearean romantic comedy, like Orlando or Silvius in *As You Like It* or Orsino in *Twelfth Night*. He is not in love with Juliet at all, having in fact never even heard of her. Instead he is in love with a certain Rosaline. Shakespeare astutely never brings Rosaline on stage. As a result, we learn about her from what people say about her and thereby form an image for ourselves. She is known as 'the fair Rosaline' (1.2.85); her imperious beauty is her trademark. Although Romeo grovels before her, she is un-responsive to his pleadings. 'She hath Dian's wit', Romeo tells Benvolio, meaning that she is witty in chaste denial. 'In strong proof of chastity well armed, / From Love's weak childish bow she lives unharmed' (1.1.209–11). She is invulnerable to Cupid's arrows. Nothing Romeo can do prevails with her, not even 'saint-seducing gold' – the gifts he fruitlessly bestows on her. Rosaline is thus the abstract embodiment of the scornful beauty in many a Renaissance love poem who takes pleasure in the power of denial. Mercutio refers to her as 'that same pale hardhearted wench' who torments Romeo so 'that he will sure run mad' (2.4.4–5). Romeo, for his part, seems to take a kind of masochistic pleasure in being refused by Rosaline. He has no interest in pursuing other women. He is thus like the stereo-typical young male of much Renaissance love poetry: self-pitying and self-absorbed, sleepless with anxiety, ready at all hours to wallow in grief as he converses with his long-suffering friends. Romeo and Rosaline are what we might call Petrarchan figures, after Francesco Petrarca or Petrarch, whose Italian *Canzoniere* set the standard in English poetry for sonnets and odes celebrating the worship of an unattainable and idealized beauty (Petrarch's Laura).

Juliet likewise, when we first meet her, is oblivious of Romeo's existence. Instead, she appears to be on the verge of an arranged marriage. Count Paris has already spoken with her father, as a proper young aristocrat might do, obtaining the father's consent before speaking to the young lady herself. His intents appear entirely honorable, and he is certainly a very eligible young bachelor. As Count Paris, he outranks the Capulets by a considerable margin. What can we determine of their social rank? They are sometimes identified in modern editions as Capulet and Lady Capulet, as though he were a lord and she his lady, but this is misleading: the first reliable quarto of 1599 identifies her more simply in the stage directions and speech headings as 'Capulet's Wife', 'Wife', and 'Mo.' for 'Mother', though the Folio of 1623 does also use 'Lady' as a speech heading. When the Nurse and Juliet refer to Capulet as 'my lord', they do so as a mark of obedient respect; Juliet twice refers to Capulet as 'my lord and father', but she uses the term 'lord' more often to refer to Romeo, who, as her new husband, becomes her 'lord' in that sense. All the signs indicate that the Capulets, though prosperous enough, are below the ranks of the aristocracy and eager to marry into its privileged domain. Marriages of this sort were not uncommon in Elizabethan England and in the drama of the period. They provided an opportunity for well-born sons to recoup, by acquiring a handsome dowry, the fortunes they may have spent, and for families of less exalted station to aspire to social prominence. Capulet is careful to specify that Juliet's consent be a precondition of her betrothal to Count Paris, but the father sees little reason to doubt that he can prevail upon her to say yes. Though she is not yet fourteen (1.2.9, 1.3.13–15), he puts aside any hesitation he may feel about haste. Paris is the catch of the social season. 'A man, young lady!' exclaims Juliet's Nurse. 'Lady, such a man / As all the world – why, he's a man of wax.' To which Juliet's mother readily accedes: 'Verona's summer hath not such a flower' (1.3.76–8). In his direction of the modernized film version *Romeo + Juliet* (1996), Baz Luhrmann is not far wrong when he pictures Capulet as the owner of an ostentatiously large and expensive mansion in which he and his socially ambitious wife host a glittering masked ball for all the 'right' people.

One of the pleasures of *Romeo and Juliet* is to see how Shakespeare moves his story toward the meeting of the lovers. At first we see them, in alternating scenes, in their separate worlds. Juliet's world is domestic and feminine; we see her chiefly with her mother and Nurse. Romeo keeps company with his male friends, especially Benvolio and Mercutio. We form our impression of the young lovers in good part through the different sorts of company they keep. The contrast is especially marked when we compare the Nurse and Mercutio.

We learn quite a lot about Juliet's Nurse through her garrulous talk. She is well on in years, and has only four teeth left. She has been married, but her husband is now dead; so too is their daughter Susan, who, as the Nurse says, 'is with God'. The Nurse remembers them both with simple piety. 'God be with his soul!' she says almost reflexively. ''A was a merry man' (1.3.40–1). She was taken on by Juliet's family nearly fourteen years ago as a wet nurse for Juliet, perhaps so that Juliet's mother would not have to undergo the indignity of breast feeding. Having given birth to her Susan at the same time that Juliet was born, the Nurse was lactating. She remembers with extraordinary gusto the process of weaning Juliet on Juliet's third birthday or thereabouts. Perhaps because she is illiterate, the Nurse remembers it all as spots of time: Lammas Eve in early August, the hot sun beating against the wall of a dovecote, the bitter-tasting wormwood that she applied to her nipple, the child repulsed by the unpleasant taste. Now, some eleven years later, the Nurse is still a member of the household as a caretaker and companion for Juliet, a duenna or governess.

The Nurse lingers repetitiously over a bawdy and often-told story about her husband and Juliet: how Juliet as a child fell and bruised her forehead, at which point the Nurse's husband (perhaps also a servant in the household) took up the child and comforted her with a crude witticism that she would do better, when she came of age, to fall not forward but backward – that is, into a position suited to receiving a man sexually. The recollection of Juliet's naive agreement amuses the Nurse so greatly that she says it no fewer than four times: 'It stinted and said "Ay"' (1.3.45–58). The story, embarrassing as it is to Juliet now, tells us a good deal about their relationship as one in which Juliet's youthful innocence is offset by the Nurse's earthiness. At the same time, we sense a deep mutual fondness arising from the many ways in which the Nurse is more a mother to Juliet than is Capulet's wife. Moreover, the jesting about women falling on their backs seems imminently prophetic, for Juliet is being asked to consider marriage with Count Paris. She is on the verge of womanhood at a very early age, and the Nurse, for better and for worse, is her counselor and guide.

Mercutio offers male companionship to Romeo in ways that are complementary to those of the Nurse and Juliet. Romeo, like Juliet, is young and innocent (though he certainly is not as young as she: is he perhaps eighteen?). Mercutio is more worldly wise, sardonic, skeptical, voluble, wit-cracking. His 'Queen Mab' speech is a tour de force of inventiveness, as he imagines a diminutive fairy queen purveying dreams to all sorts of people. Being no bigger than a semi-precious stone in an alderman's ring, Queen Mab rides in a chariot made out of an empty hazelnut and driven by a grey-coated gnat, with wagon spokes made of spiders' legs, a whip of cricket's bone, and other details similarly reduced in proportion. Her dreams are teasing, even mischievous: courtiers dream of ceremonious bows and hoped-for preferment, lawyers of fees, ladies of kisses (which Mab plagues with blisters because the ladies are so addicted to candy), parsons of comfortable church livings, soldiers of military heroism, wenches of sexual adventure, and the like. These images are, he freely confesses, 'the children of an idle brain, / Begot of nothing but vain fantasy' (1.4.53–98). He views love in much the same terms, as a wryly amusing mad obsession.

What he offers Romeo, then, is male companionship in a spirit of scorning the effete ways of romantic courtship. He views Romeo as a casualty in the battle of the sexes, and indeed is quite splendidly bawdy in his satirical picture of Romeo as one who must be conjured 'by Rosaline's bright eyes, / By her high forehead and her scarlet lip, / By her fine foot, straight leg, and quivering thigh, / And the demesnes that there adjacent lie' (2.1.18–21). This catalogue of Rosaline's charms is a spoof of the literary tradition known as the blazon, and is considerably more graphic about her sexual anatomy than the usual effusion in that genre. Similarly erotic is his jesting to Benvolio that one might anger Romeo 'To raise a spirit in his mistress' circle / Of some strange nature, letting it there stand / Till she had laid it and conjured it down' (25–7). Mercutio uses the language of conjuration to suggest a male rival who achieves erection and sexual penetration of Rosaline, followed by satisfaction of his craving and detumescence. Mercutio is sublimely irreverent toward the worship of Love as a goddess. He is happiest when Romeo seems to have gotten over his love melancholy. 'Why, is not this better now than groaning for love?' he asks Romeo. 'Now art thou Romeo; now art thou what thou art' (2.4.87–9). One's truest self is to be found in friendship and in manly badinage. Mercutio does not know that Romeo's newfound ebullience is in fact the result of his having found reciprocal love with Juliet.

Having tantalized us by delaying the actual meeting of the two lovers until the end of Act 1, Shakespeare gives to this moment an aura both of high romantic sensibility and of exciting danger; romantic comedy and the threat of tragedy meet at an instant. The lovers' first conversation is intensely poetic, so much so that it takes the form of a sonnet. As he approaches Juliet in the dance, Romeo takes her by the hand and offers to kiss her, as though his lips were bashful pilgrims venturing to worship at the shrine of her beauty. He says this in four lines of verse, alternately rhymed. She responds in a similar four-line unit, parrying his bold offer by suggesting, in a continuation of his metaphor, that touching hand to hand might be a sufficient display of pilgrim-like devotion. His insistence on the primacy of lips then meets her counter-proposal that lips should be used in prayer. When he suggests that prayer take the form of kissing, and that as petitioner he will despair if his request is refused, she gracefully yields. Their first kiss thus appears to come at the end of the fourteen-line sonnet stanza, with its concluding couplet bringing the music of their first duet to a cadenced resolution:

JULIET Saints do not move, though grant for prayers' sake.
ROMEO Then move not, while my prayer's effect I take.
> [*He kisses her.*]
> (1.5.94–107)

At the same time, the banqueting hall is filled with ambient commotion. Though Romeo and his masked companions have not been invited to the event, Capulet as host welcomes them and invites them to dance. He joshes the ladies by suggesting that if they refuse to dance, they will be suspected of having corns on their feet. More ominously, Tybalt surmises from a voice he hears that Romeo is present, not just as an interloper but as one of the hated clan of Montagues. Tybalt's quarrel with his uncle Capulet over this matter ends in Capulet's heated insistence that he will not have his guests insulted in his own house, but Tybalt is not appeased. The fact that Capulet has heard good things specifically of Romeo opens up a wonderful irony: how easy it seemingly would be to end the quarrel of two households in a marriage! Yet we know that this cannot be.

Romeo and Juliet, Act 1, scene 5. Leonardo DiCaprio as Romeo and Claire Danes as Juliet meet at the masked ball in the Capulet house, in Baz Luhrmann's 1996 film. (20th Century Fox / The Kobal Collection / Merrick Morton)

The oxymoronic coming together of love and hate is nowhere more beautifully expressed than in Juliet's sad realization that the young man she has just met and kissed is a Montague:

> My only love sprung from my only hate!
> Too early seen unknown, and known too late!
> Prodigious birth of love it is to me
> That I must love a loathèd enemy.
> (1.5.139–42)

'Must' is a powerful word. Young as she is, Juliet at once realizes that she has no control over her having fallen in love with Romeo or over the ominous circumstances that bear down upon that fateful event.

Romeo too is in the grip of a compelling desire, so much so that he cannot go home. He makes his way around to the garden in back of the Capulet house, evades his friends by climbing the orchard wall, and looks about. He has no plan; he simply needs to be near Juliet. He knows now that she is a Capulet. What is he to do? The ensuing scene between them, once she has appeared at her window and has been overheard speaking of her love for Romeo, is a study in contrasts. He is giddy with happiness, as though in an ecstatic dream; she is practical, concerned for his safety, asking sensible questions. How did Romeo get here? Is he aware that her kinsmen may kill him if they find him? His answer suggests that he is floating in the clouds:

> With love's light wings did I o'erperch these walls,
> For stony limits cannot hold love out,
> And what love can do, that dares love attempt;
> Therefore thy kinsmen are no stop to me.
>
> (2.2.66–70)

To her inquiry as to how he found this place, his reply is no less airy: 'By love, that first did prompt me to inquire' (80).

Juliet seems intent on setting Romeo straight as a wooer. She will have none of his fulsome Petrarchan vows. When he offers to affirm his devotion to her 'by yonder blessèd moon . . . / That tips with silver all these fruit tree tops', she interrupts him with her insistence that he 'swear not by the moon'. It is too changeable. She would prefer that he 'not swear at all' (107–29). Her language throughout this encounter is simple, almost monosyllabic, free of elegant terms. 'Dost thou love me?' she asks him. 'I know thou wilt say "Ay."' Yet she knows that 'At lovers' perjuries, / They say, Jove laughs' (90–3). Earlier, before Romeo has made known to her his presence, she speaks with the same utter simplicity. 'What's Montague?' she asks in soliloquy. 'It is nor hand, nor foot, / Nor arm, nor face, nor any other part / Belonging to a man.' 'What's in a name? That which we call a rose / By any other word would smell as sweet' (40–4). She mistrusts names, labels, appearances, preferring the thing itself.

Romeo's language meantime is highly metaphorical, burdened with the conventional images of the stereotypical male lover. He compares her eyes, unsurprisingly, to stars:

> Two of the fairest stars in all the heaven,
> Having some business, do entreat her eyes
> To twinkle in their spheres till they return.

Not content with this sugary conceit, Romeo proceeds to lengthen it into a little allegory:

What if her eyes were there, they in her head?
The brightness of her cheek would shame those stars
As daylight doth a lamp; her eyes in heaven
Would through the airy region stream so bright
That birds would sing and think it were not night.

(2.2.15–22)

Romeo seems in love with his own words. Juliet would prefer that she and Romeo think about their real problems. How can she communicate with him next day? Will he marry her, if she agrees to elope with him? We are left to wonder if the marriage would ever have taken place at all if the arrangements had been left up to Romeo.

Friar Laurence, the cleric to whom Romeo turns for counseling as he has done in the past, shares Juliet's view of the impracticality of the young man. As a surrogate father, Laurence has often chided Romeo for behaving like a typical youth 'with unstuffed brain'. He is amused to learn that Romeo is now in the grip of a new romantic passion:

Holy Saint Francis, what a change is here!
Is Rosaline, that thou didst love so dear,
So soon forsaken? Young men's love then lies
Not truly in their hearts, but in their eyes.
Jesu Maria, what a deal of brine
Hath washed thy sallow cheeks for Rosaline!
How much salt water thrown away in waste
To season love, that of it doth not taste!

(2.3.65–72)

The proverbial sententiousness of these utterances is underscored by the comically rhymed couplets. Yet despite his amusement, Laurence shares Juliet's hope that Romeo is not incorrigibly foolish and that a marriage might actually make sense.

The brief and private ceremony in which Romeo and Juliet are married by Laurence testifies to this hope. Romeo does seem like a new man. The lovers sing now in one key: he is more down to earth than he was, she more poetically elegant. The marriage ends what might so easily have been a Shakespearean romantic comedy, in which marriage traditionally provides the fifth-act resolution. The trouble is that we are only at the end of Act 2. We were promised a tragedy, and it comes down with a vengeance upon the play in Act 3.

The busy scene that follows, in which Tybalt seeks out Romeo to avenge the insult of Romeo's having dared to invade the Capulet party and dance with Juliet, stands at the center of the play. We begin and end the play in violence, and violence is now the business at hand in Act 3, scene 1. One thing leads to another with dismal inevitability. When Tybalt insists on being answered in a duel, Romeo declines, but Mercutio takes his place. Mercutio is fatally wounded by Tybalt when Romeo attempts to intervene. Romeo, appalled at the death of his friend, takes on Tybalt in a fury and kills him. Prince Escalus, having given public warning that he will tolerate no more feuding, banishes Romeo from Verona. The tragedy is set inexorably in motion.

What are we to make of Romeo's involvement in all this? A tragic hero should to some degree be responsible for his fate, or else the story is likely to seem unjust. Miscalculation does of course play a major role in the disastrous turn of events: Mercutio is hurt under Romeo's arm in the scuffle as Romeo is trying to stop the carnage. Still, Romeo has choices to make. Shakespeare presents his dilemma with sympathy but also perhaps with implied judgment.

Romeo's first response, when insulted by Tybalt, is to turn the other cheek. The insult is intentionally a grievous one. 'Romeo', says Tybalt, 'the love I bear thee can afford / No better term than this: thou art a villain.' Tybalt's use of 'thee', as earlier in 1.5, is demeaning, and 'villain' (i.e., worthless wretch, scoundrel) is a term no gentleman can accept. The code of honor to which the men of this play are generally bound demands the 'satisfaction' of a reply with a weapon. Romeo knows this, and knows that his own friends are watching to see how he will respond. He chooses his words carefully:

> Tybalt, the reason that I have to love thee
> Doth much excuse the appertaining rage
> To such a greeting. Villain am I none.
> Therefore farewell. I see thou knowest me not.
>
> (3.1.61–4)

Romeo could hardly have done better. He avoids the challenge and also denies the charge of villainy by saying, in effect, that Tybalt must have the wrong person in mind. He speaks warmly to Tybalt. We know, as audience, that Tybalt is now Romeo's close relative by marriage. Romeo realizes that he has every good reason not to fight Tybalt. He owes it to Juliet, and to her wise teaching, to practice forbearance. The trouble is that

Tybalt hears Romeo's 'thees' and 'thous' not as the affectionate address between kinsmen but as the very words Tybalt himself has used in insulting Romeo.

Mercutio interprets Romeo's behavior in the same way. 'Oh, calm, dishonorable, vile submission!' (72), he exclaims, as he steps into the role of respondent to Tybalt's challenge. Mercutio's motives are mixed, some of them admirable. He feels protective of Romeo and longs to defend him against his detractors. At the same time, he clearly feels that Romeo has disgraced his manhood. And Mercutio wants to fight Tybalt anyway. Mercutio is keenly aware of Tybalt's reputation as a swordsman in a trendy new fashion of dueling that one could learn (in London) from Italian instructors of fencing. Mercutio contemptuously dismisses this new school as fighting 'by the book of arithmetic' (101). Now he falls victim to Tybalt's sword, but only because Romeo has ineffectually come between them. Romeo really meant well, in seeking to end a fight between his dear friend Mercutio and his new cousin by marriage, but circumstances have conspired against him. 'I thought all for the best', he laments (103).

Thus far, indeed, Romeo's motives and conduct have seemed above reproach in an impossible situation. But what is he to do, now that Mercutio lies slain? Appeasement no longer appears possible to him. His actions have seemed cowardly to himself, to Tybalt, and to his friends, most of all to the dear friend whose life has paid the forfeit of Romeo's refusal to fight Tybalt when challenged. As he sizes up his dilemma, Romeo decides that he must now explicitly repudiate Juliet's teaching of charitable love: 'O sweet Juliet, / Thy beauty hath made me effeminate, / And in my temper softened valor's steel.' He no longer hesitates, when, after a brief interval, Tybalt returns:

> Alive in triumph, and Mercutio slain!
> Away to heaven, respective lenity,
> And fire-eyed fury be my conduct now!
> (3.1.112–23)

Later, of course, he is remorseful. Juliet has a hard time forgiving him. But it is too late. Romeo has knuckled under to the macho mystique that has hovered over the divided city of Verona for as long as anyone can remember.

Once the banishment has taken place, the tragedy proceeds with the same ineluctable force, depending on a mix of personal choice, bad luck in timing, and fatal misunderstanding. Capulet and his wife, who have longed to have Paris as their son-in-law in any case, now hasten along a marriage between Paris and Juliet in the hopes that the event can mitigate the gloom surrounding the death of Tybalt – who is, by the way, lovingly remembered by all his family, including Juliet, as a dear kinsman; his seeming role as villain in the play needs to be qualified by this perception that he was a gentle person among those with whom he felt at home. Juliet, horrified at the prospect of bigamy, has her reasons for being unable to tell her parents what has happened; they in turn have their good reasons for angrily concluding that Juliet is being wilfully stubborn in her refusal to go along with their plan. Capulet is really a good enough father, but he explodes in anger when Juliet can give him no reason for her reluctance, after he has arranged a marriage that seems ideally suited to make her happy. The Nurse, who does know of the secret marriage to Romeo, proves an undependable ally whose counsel to Juliet is to make the best of her new situation. Paris pursues his wooing of Juliet, innocently unaware that she might have any reason to deny him. The scene in which they confer about the marriage is heavy with ironic wordplay:

PARIS Happily met, my lady and my wife!
JULIET That may be, sir, when I may be a wife.
PARIS That 'may be' must be, love, on Thursday next.
JULIET What must be shall be.

(4.1.18–21)

Capulet's hastening along the marriage has the entirely unintended effect of complicating Friar Laurence's plan to provide Juliet with a sleeping potion and to send a notice to Romeo in Mantua that he should make a quick return. All participants in the story behave honorably, it seems, and with the best interests of others at heart, but they operate blindly without full knowledge of what has happened and what is at stake. We as audience know everything but can do nothing other than watch.

Romeo is of course impulsive. When he hears the news, which we know to be false, that Juliet lies dead in her family's burial vault, he resolves at once on the desperate act of returning to Verona and joining her in death. He brushes aside his servant Balthasar's urging him to have patience. He buys poison from an apothecary, knowing that such a transaction is punishable by death for the seller. He fights with a man at Juliet's grave whom he takes to be an intruder, with the result that he kills Paris, whose offense is nothing more than to have brought flowers to strew on Juliet's bridal bed of death. We see by this that Paris was sincerely in love with Juliet and was heartbroken by her seeming death. He has visited her tomb in the dead of night with no witnesses to behold his private act of devotion, as a result of which he lies slain, and by his rival. Yet their fight is not a duel of honor; it is a sad mistake, one that Romeo regrets.

The final disaster is that Laurence arrives moments too late at the burial vault. Romeo has proceeded with dispatch to swallow the poison, after bidding Juliet an eternal farewell. She awakens moments later and slays herself with Romeo's weapon. A long postlude dramatizes the way in which the bereaved families unravel the mystery of the young lovers' sad story, coming at last to understand why Romeo and Juliet acted as they did and how those who are still living have contributed unknowingly to the catastrophe. They all resolve to learn from this tragedy how to live at last in peaceful harmony.

What sort of tragedy is this, that depends so much on misunderstanding and bad luck? Romeo and Juliet are for the most part innocent victims, even if Romeo's decision to kill Tybalt does briefly give him a crucial role in sealing his own fate. Romeo and Juliet are not like Othello or Macbeth, whose unwise and self-defeating acts are at the center of their tragic story. The young lovers here are, in Capulet's words, 'Poor sacrifices of our enmity' (5.3.304). In social status they are rather ordinary, like the typical figures of romantic comedy, instead of being princes and rulers as are Hamlet, King Lear, Macbeth, and others. And Romeo and Juliet are not the primary authors of their tragedy. They do not *fall* in the sense that Macbeth and Othello fall. Their deaths must pay the price of their families' irrational hatred, and the hope is that their deaths will atone for that hatred to the extent of curing it, at least for a time. Rather than pursue a tragedy of personal responsibility, as in his later great works, Shakespeare here invites us to sorrow over innocent and unintended deaths.

The result is to give great emotional depth to the story of a love that is exquisitely and painfully brief. The play celebrates the ecstasy of young love as an experience that realistically cannot last forever except in art. Romeo and Juliet do not get to work out their day-to-day relationship and learn what it is to accommodate difference. What we know of them is that they were intensely and beautifully in love, and that they died while their romantic passion was at its most intense. They died, moreover, as sacrifices to the unfeeling world in which they lived. The play appeals to our deep feeling that the world does not understand young lovers. This is the idea at work also in 'Pyramus and Thisbe', and indeed in

A Midsummer Night's Dream. That play achieves a comic resolution of love's tribulations, but 'Pyramus and Thisbe' is there at the end to remind us that things might just as well have gone the other way. This is perhaps the profoundest sense in which *Romeo and Juliet* is spiritually akin to the comedies that Shakespeare was writing when he turned to a tragic version of the same story.

4

Henry IV, Part I

Reading an English history play by Shakespeare is quite a different proposition from reading a romantic comedy. For one thing, the subject is English history (what else did you expect?), chiefly from the time of the late fourteenth and fifteenth centuries. The events of these years, though very distant from our own modern era, were fairly recent for Shakespeare and his audience, having taken place roughly one hundred to two hundred years in the past. Those years were crucial ones in the formation of the English nationhood to which Shakespeare was heir. They gave birth to a strange new genre in late Elizabethan England, the English history play. Neither comedy nor tragedy, it sometimes took on the characteristics of one or the other, or both. The resulting genre was hard to classify as a literary form other than to say that it dealt with English history. As a genre, it came into prominence on the London stage in the late 1580s and 1590s, following England's great defeat of the Spanish Armada in 1588. Shakespeare, having arrived in London at about that time or shortly afterward, helped to create the genre and made it his own. He wrote nine plays on English history in the 1590s, more or less one a year, just as he concurrently wrote ten romantic comedies during the same decade. Collectively, eight of these nine history plays chronicle the events of a century or so, from the reign of Richard II (1377–99) through the reigns of Henry IV (1399–1413) and his son Henry V (1413–22) and then to the disputed tenures of Henry VI (1422–61) and Edward IV (1461–83), and so at last to the brief reign of Richard III (1483–5). At some point during the decade Shakespeare also wrote a play out of this historical sequence about King John (1199–1216), and then much later, in 1613, he wrote (collaboratively, it seems) a play about Henry VIII (who ruled from 1509 to 1547), son of the Henry VII who had defeated Richard III in 1485 and father of Queen Elizabeth, who would govern England from 1558 to 1603.

Shakespeare actually began with the second half of his epic story, dramatizing the civil wars of the fifteenth century between the Lancastrian forces of Henry VI (so called after his great-grandfather, John of Gaunt, Duke of Lancaster) and those of the Yorkist Edward IV (so called after his great-grandfather, Edmund of Langley, the Duke of York). These were the so-called Wars of the Roses, symbolized by the red rose of Lancaster and the white rose of York. Four early history plays, three of them named for *Henry VI* and the last for *Richard III*, made up a four-play cycle of history reaching down to the climactic moment when Richard III was defeated at Bosworth Field by Queen Elizabeth's grandfather, thereby initiating the dynasty of the Tudor monarchs (so called in honor of Henry VII's family name) that still occupied the throne in the person of Queen Elizabeth as Shakespeare wrote his plays. Hence, he was chronicling the birth of a nation. Having told the story of the Wars of the Roses, he then went back in time to the reigns of Richard II, Henry IV, and Henry V for what turned out to be a second four-play sequence, with *Henry IV* in two parts. In so doing, Shakespeare undertook to dramatize the momentous events preceding and leading up to the fifteenth-century Wars of the Roses: the usurpation of Richard II's throne in 1399 by Henry Bolingbroke, son of the Duke of Lancaster, who thereupon took the title of Henry IV; Henry IV's troubles with his political opponents and with his son; and that son's rise to triumph as Henry V, England's hero-king in the Battle of Agincourt against the French in 1415.

All this information may seem a little daunting at first, but it does have its own fascination as history, and it introduces us to one of Shakespeare's greatest plays, *1 Henry IV*. We need to see this play in the larger historical context of Shakespeare's dramatizing the birth of a nation. It helps to know that the man who became Henry IV did so by usurping the throne from his first cousin, Richard II, in a dispute over Richard's having seized the dukedom of Lancaster from Henry Bolingbroke without a constitutional right to do so. The exiled Henry thereupon returned to England to claim his birthright as the Duke of Lancaster, with the strong support of some English lords from the north country who had their own reasons to be impatient with Richard's cavalier and extravagant ways. The result was a coup d'etat through which Henry Bolingbroke became King Henry IV, and then, not knowing how to contain the threat of a return to power by the deposed Richard, consented to the murder of Richard II in prison. (These are the events of *Richard II.*) The play of *1 Henry IV* begins with a king who is uneasy in his conscience and grimly determined to calm the turbulent waters of his troubled kingdom.

If you would like to study the period of history about which Shakespeare wrote, two books have proved popular with many readers because they discuss that history with an eye to Shakespeare's history plays: Peter Saccio, *Shakespeare's English Kings: History, Chronicle, and Drama* (1977), and John Julius Norwich, *Shakespeare's Kings: The Great Plays and the History of England in the Middle Ages: 1337–1485* (2000).

These plays tend to have large casts. The politically important people are referred to at various times by their titles or by their personal and family names. They may hold more than one title at various times, and those titles can be passed on to another person or another generation. Thus, the king of this play, Henry IV, is also referred to as 'Bolingbroke' and 'Lancaster' (i.e., Duke of Lancaster) by his political enemies, who maintain that he has usurped the name of king. Henry IV's younger son John has now been named Duke of Lancaster, and is called 'Lancaster' or 'John of Lancaster' or 'Prince John of Lancaster'. King Henry's older son, Henry, is the Prince of Wales; he is also called Hal and Harry by his friends, notably Falstaff. Chief among the King's opponents are the Percies of the north: Henry Percy, the Earl of Northumberland, his younger brother the Earl of Worcester, and the Earl's son and heir, Harry Percy, known as Hotspur for his hair-trigger temper. The fact that Hotspur and Prince Hal bear the same nickname of 'Harry' emphasizes the rivalry between them that comes to a head in the fifth-act Battle of Shrewsbury. The rebels are supported by, among others, Owen Glendower, a charismatic Welshman; the Scottish Archibald Douglas, Earl of Douglas; and Lord Mortimer, Edmund Mortimer, also known as the Earl of March because that name arguably entitles him to claim the English crown, since the now-dead Richard II had named a Mortimer as his heir to the throne. (Shakespeare conflates two Mortimers to make clearer this connection.)

We will come to the amusing (and essentially unhistorical) antics of Falstaff shortly, but first the play asks us to grapple with the political situation. In fact, Shakespeare's recurring theatrical practice in this play is to alternate scenes of high seriousness at court with scenes of ebullient comedy in more private locations, including the tavern. We begin at court. King Henry IV is conferring with his senior advisers, notably the Earl of Westmorland, about a military crisis. The King, newly in the office that he has taken away from his cousin Richard II, faces enemies on all sides, especially the Scots in the north and Glendower's Welsh guerilla fighters in the west. What is at stake, and what do we learn about the King himself as a person and as a ruler?

The King's long opening speech (1.1.1–30) is a study in political rhetoric. He urges an end to civil war, to the 'furious close of civil butchery' in which 'acquaintance, kindred, and allies' turn on one another in hatred. He pleads for a cessation of a conflict in which 'The edge of war, like an ill-sheathèd knife', cuts its own master. He has every reason to urge this end to hostilities, since the fighting is against his new regime. He appeals, as a good politician might, to the ideals of religion, by wishing he could carry out a Crusade to the Holy Land. This is a pious hope. It also suggests what Henry would most like to do: unite the factional English people against a foreign bogeyman, the Saracens of the Middle East. King Henry fervently wishes he could enlist his subjects to 'March all one way' against the Enemy of Christ instead of slaughtering one another. Is Henry sincere in his appeal to the ideal of a Crusade? Probably so, since it perfectly combines personal piety and guilt over Richard II's death with political sagacity; it would solve all his problems. But such a Crusade is not to be. The military realities of the moment are too pressing.

Henry faces danger on two frontiers, to the north and west. These are traditionally the trouble spots for English monarchs, in the mountainous areas most remote from London and the fertile southeast. His two campaigns are under the leadership of Lord Mortimer in the west and the Percies in the north. The Percies are, after all, the nobles who most materially assisted Bolingbroke in his takeover of the English throne from Richard II; as proud northern lords, they resented Richard's intrusion on their prerogatives. Living as they do in their great northern counties, they are always ready to resist invasion from Scotland. We learn that young Harry Hotspur has done well indeed against the Scottish Earl of Douglas at Holmedon in Northumberland, and has taken some high-ranking captives. King Henry wishes enviously that his own son, the Prince of Wales, would show at least some glimmer of the manliness shown by the Earl of Northumberland's brave son, Hotspur. Yet Hotspur is proving troublesome about his captives by refusing to allow King Henry to collect the ransom that should, according to the law of arms, come to the King's treasury. Hotspur's uncle, the Earl of Worcester, is apparently in back of this truculence, for Worcester is, in Westmorland's appraisal, 'Malevolent to you [King Henry] in all aspects' (1.1.96). Moreover, Lord Mortimer has been captured by the very Welshmen whom he was supposed to be fighting. Thus, despite Hotspur's victory at Holmedon, the King faces much unsettled business.

This opening glimpse of Henry's strategic dilemma sets us up for an ensuing scene of a strikingly different texture. This next scene, entirely in prose until Prince Hal's ending soliloquy, is as colloquial and witty as the taut first scene is formal and businesslike. Shakespeare, as is his custom, does not tell us why he makes such an abrupt transition. Instead, we must look for connections. We must first figure out where we are, and who the speakers are. One of them is addressed in line one as 'Hal'; evidently he is the Prince of Wales. The other speaker is not actually given a last name until the scene is three-quarters over, though in a printed text the speech headings identify him as FALSTAFF. This Falstaff speaks familiarly to the crown prince, addressing him not only as 'Hal' but as 'lad', 'sweet wag', and 'mad wag'. He drops the name 'Hal' into his conversation quite often; evidently he enjoys a privilege of familiarity, and takes full advantage of it. The two men are on a tutoying basis, regularly using 'thee' and 'thou' for personal pronouns. Hal calls his interlocutor 'Jack', and refers to him, perhaps sardonically, as 'Sir John'. When Ned Poins enters the scene, he addresses the crown prince as 'sweet Hal' and 'sirrah' and 'my lord'; he addresses Falstaff as 'Sir John'. Poins uses 'thee' and 'thou' with Falstaff, but the more formal 'you' with the prince; Hal, for his part, addresses Poins as 'thee' and 'thou'. These details of speech reveal the power semantics at work in this scene. Hal allows a certain degree of familiarity in what his companions may call him, but clearly there are limits.

What sorts of companions are they? Falstaff seems just to have woken up. When he asks the time of day, Hal sardonically asks why a person so given to drinking late into the night and then 'sleeping upon benches after noon' (1.2.3–4) should care what time of day it is. Stage tradition often begins the scene with Falstaff snoring on a bench and being wakened by Hal. Their conversation is all about cups of sack (a white Spanish wine), bawds (whores), and leaping houses (houses of prostitution), and yet we see no other evidence that they are in a tavern; no raffish companions or women are present, as in the later tavern scenes. Hal and Falstaff might be in the Prince's apartments. It doesn't really matter. Shakespeare's original stage would provide no scenery here, no furniture other than perhaps a bench. The focus is on two men and their bantering, sparring conversation.

Hal and Falstaff seem to enjoy the give and take of verbal one-upmanship. It gives them ample opportunity to insult each other in colorful, pungent comparisons that are meant as friendly wit and yet also reveal an undercurrent of serious debate. What will Hal be like as king, and what will Falstaff's place be in that new order of affairs? 'When thou art king',

Falstaff begins, 'let not us that are squires of the night's body be called thieves of the day's beauty.' Falstaff, it seems, is a highwayman, doing his business by night; he and his cohorts are 'gentleman of the shade, minions of the moon' (1.2.23–6). What will their place be in the light of day when young Hal comes to power? Hal's answer acknowledges that he knows Falstaff to be one for whom a purse of gold is 'most resolutely snatched on Monday night and most dissolutely spent on Tuesday morning, got with swearing "Lay by" [i.e., "Hands up!"] and spent with crying "Bring in" [i.e., "Waiter, bring us something to eat and drink!"]', but Hal is evasive as to what he might do about this in the fullness of time. Falstaff persists. 'But I prithee, sweet wag, shall there be gallows standing in England when thou art king? And resolution thus fubbed as it is with the rusty curb of old father Antic the law? Do not thou, when thou art king, hang a thief' (56–64). The question seems direct enough, and yet once again Hal wittily equivocates. 'No, thou shalt', he replies, meaning (as Hal goes on to explain) either that Falstaff will be put as judge in charge of hanging thieves, with the result that hangings will be rare, or that Falstaff will himself hang for his thievery. Wordplay is for Falstaff a means of fencing for position, and for Hal a means of fending off the implications of Falstaff's begging for special consideration.

Their conversation becomes a game that is filled with suggestions of spiritual seriousness. When Falstaff comically laments that he has been led astray by Hal and that he intends to 'give over this life', Hal mocks this 'good amendment' in one who is ready to take a purse whenever occasion serves. Hal understands well enough who is the tempter and who the tempted in their relationship. Poins, too, when he joins them, caricatures Falstaff as 'Monsieur Remorse', asking him, 'How agrees the devil and thee about thy soul that thou soldest him on Good Friday last for a cup of Madeira and a cold capon's leg?' Hal jocularly insists that 'the devil shall have his bargain'; Falstaff will 'give the devil his due' (94–117). The interrelated themes of temptation, remorse, and spiritual reckoning hover insistently over these witty exchanges. The stakes are indeed high, for Hal will be king some day, and will need to come to terms with the life of dissipation into which he has allowed himself to be led.

These matters become the subject of serious reflection when Hal is briefly left alone at the end of the scene. Having agreed to join with Poins in a practical joke on Falstaff that will involve Hal in a highway robbery scheme, the Prince needs to reassure himself, and us as audience, that all will ultimately be well. In soliloquy he lets us know that he sees Falstaff clearly for what he is. The images are not flattering toward Falstaff: he is pictured as one of the 'foul and ugly mists' that smother up the sun of England's royalty. Hal assures us, and himself, that he will break through these unwholesome 'vapors' when the time is ripe. For now, he will use his cavorting with Falstaff and the others as 'playing holidays' to offset the tediousness of the work that must eventually be undertaken. Hal's present wayward behavior, like a dull metal sheet placed behind a jewel to set off its brightness, will make his 'reformation' seem all the more wondrous; by 'glitt'ring o'er [his] fault', Hal's sudden reform will 'show more goodly and attract more eyes / Than that which hath no foil to set it off'. Thus, Hal has a plan for 'Redeeming time' (1.2.189–211). Yet whether he is calmly and resolutely in charge of his strategic plan, or is simply rationalizing his desire to enjoy the irresponsibility of youth for as long as possible, is another question. The actor playing Hal has a range of options here, and so do we as readers.

The juxtapositions linking scenes 1 and 2 should begin to be clear by now. The king who faces political and military opposition in his country must also deal with a kind of rebellion in his own family. His political enemies are 'malevolent' toward him, like so many disobedient planets circling the sun of majesty; his son and heir keeps company with an engaging rogue who thumbs his nose at 'old father Antic the law'. Will the King's dynasty hold long enough to be inherited by one whose image is stained by 'riot and dishonor'? Will a guilt-ridden king who cannot now fulfill his vow to undertake a Crusade to the Holy Land be succeeded by a young man who jests about amendment of life and making bargains with the devil? 'Remorse' is thus a theme in both the serious and comic plotting of this play.

These thematic continuities and contrasts are reinforced by Shakespeare's return to the royal court in scene 3. King Henry has summoned young Hotspur to explain himself about the prisoners taken at Holmedon. Worcester is summarily dismissed as implacable, but Hotspur gets to say his piece, and it is an astonishing performance. He describes what it was like to be on the field of battle, sweaty and exhausted, and to be encountered by an envoy from King Henry demanding the prisoners. Hotspur grows more and more intemperate as he dwells on this encounter. The envoy was elegantly dressed, 'Fresh as a bridegroom', and fastidiously offended by the stench of battle. Why was Hotspur so angry then, and why does the anger return to him so vividly now? One can understand that he was annoyed to be 'pestered with a popinjay' in the midst of more serious matters at hand, but something about this puppy's dislike for gunpowder offends

Hotspur to the quick. The envoy is everything that Hotspur is not: a courtier, trim in appearance, not wishing to soil his beautiful clothes, and eloquent in 'holiday and lady terms' (1.3.29–69). Perhaps his effeteness reminds Hotspur of everything he dislikes about court life, and about King Henry as well. Hotspur is blunt, northern, rugged, humorless, compulsive, intensely proud. In every way he is the opposite of the King's son, Prince Hal. King Henry admires Hotspur, and even admires his spunk in talking back fearlessly. Henry would like to claim Hotspur as a kind of son by way of compensating for the seeming ignobility of his own offspring, but he insists on a relationship in which Hotspur understands that the King is the King.

We need to ask why Shakespeare makes so much of this encounter. One plausible explanation is that it sets up such an explicit contrast between Hotspur and Hal. Another possible reason is that it distinguishes Hotspur from his uncle and father. Hotspur is young and idealistic; in him, King Henry sees the potential for a fruitful dialogue. With the older Percies, everything seems to be going sour. Why? They have helped Henry to the throne and even now are supposed to be his allies against the Scots. What has gone wrong? In part, perhaps, they are now mistrustful of Henry because he is insisting on being a strong king to whom they owe obedience. No doubt they accept the notion that dukes and earls in a medieval culture owe duty to their overlord, the King, but these men helped Henry get rid of Richard II because, as proud lords in the far north of England, they wished to protect their autonomy. Henry's insistence on centralization of authority is not what they had anticipated or wanted. Northumberland was indeed Henry Bolingbroke's right-hand man in *Richard II*, enjoying a cordial and supportive relationship with him, but now Henry grows too great. Northumberland and Worcester fear that Henry mistrusts them. 'Our house, my sovereign liege, little deserves / The scourge of greatness to be used on it', Worcester complains to the King, adding, pointedly, 'And that same greatness too which our own hands / Have holp to make so portly' (1.3.10–13). Since the Percies were so instrumental in helping Henry to the throne, do they not deserve his special favor? Henry, for his part, is increasingly wary of the 'Danger and disobedience' that he sees in Worcester's defiant speech (16). These men are all willing to make some accommodation, but largely on their own terms. They do not want civil war; indeed, King Henry fears it, and the Percies know that they have much to lose if they break with the monarch. Shakespeare astutely diagnoses the causes of a conflict that originally seems avoidable and certainly proves costly.

A crucial factor in the breakdown of negotiations has to do with Lord Mortimer. Hotspur and the Percies want him ransomed at the King's expense. He is, after all, their kinsman by marriage, since Hotspur has married into the Mortimer family; Hotspur speaks of Edmund Mortimer as 'my brother', i.e., brother-in-law (1.3.156). Then, too, Mortimer was reported to be fighting the Welsh on Henry's behalf when he was captured. The trouble from Henry's point of view is twofold: Mortimer has a claim to the English throne that some persons regard as better than Henry's own, as we have seen, and Mortimer has now married the daughter of Glendower, the very Welsh captain whom he was supposed to be fighting. One can understand why Henry regards the Earl of March as a 'traitor', as 'revolted Mortimer'. Henry's intelligence sources have told him that this Mortimer never did encounter with Glendower. The marriage is proof of his having joined in armed resistance against King Henry. Yet the Percies, and Hotspur especially, see these allegations as proof instead that Henry has turned against them all and that they had better arm themselves before Henry comes down upon them with military might.

These considerations may help explain why Northumberland and Worcester, who helped to dethrone Richard II, now listen sympathetically to Hotspur when he talks of Richard as a 'sweet lovely rose' in whose place they have planted 'this thorn, this canker, Bolingbroke' (1.3.175–6). Northumberland and Worcester probably do not share his sentimental idealization of Richard as a beautiful man, but they need Hotspur to lead the rebellion that is even now in the making. One of the most dismaying aspects of the ensuing dialogue between Hotspur and the two older Percies is the way in which they maneuver him around to where they want him to be. They let him talk magniloquently of his dreams of glory, because they need a charismatic figure like him to inspire the undertaking. They are cautious, calculating, and power-seeking; he is impulsive, risk-taking, and enamored of danger because of the opportunity it provides to show manliness and courage. Sadly, he lacks the perspective to understand the truth of the matter, which is that his relatives are just as machiavellian as King Henry. He yearns to head an army of Truth against the Enemy; they more pragmatically want to protect their worldly interests. To Hotspur, all men are honorable or else villainous, and in his estimate the latter category includes 'this vile politician, Bolingbroke' and 'that same sword-and-buckler Prince of Wales' (228–40). He cannot see that his own relatives are politicians too.

When Shakespeare returns us to the comic subplot of Falstaff and Hal in Act 2, we again need to ask ourselves, what do we learn from this quick juxtaposing of high seriousness and comic buffoonery? In particular, why does Shakespeare start the robbery sequence with two carriers, one with a lantern in his hand? What are carriers? Who are these men, and where are we? Carriers, we gather from the dialogue, are what we would call teamsters or truckers. They speak of the early hour of the day (not yet 4 a.m.), the bad state of their horses, the turkeys in their carrying baskets needing to be fed, and the hams they are transporting to Charing Cross – that is, to a market in the London area. Most of all, they complain of the discomforts and dangers of traveling from rural Kent into London. They are in some roadside inn, where the sanitary facilities are non-existent and the fleas are abundant. Gradually we gather that they are south of London, on the London–Canterbury Road, near Gads Hill, the very spot where Falstaff and company are planning their highway caper.

The danger is almost tangible. These truckers are traveling with some gentlemen who have valuable cargo and money with them; they are all sticking together because the roads are so unsafe. Gads Hill is especially notorious for robberies. When a chamberlain joins the two truckers, he asks them a lot of nosey questions. What time is it? Would you lend me your lantern? When do you expect to arrive in London? The truckers answer evasively, as well they might, for, as they evidently suspect, this chamberlain or room attendant in the inn is part of the robbery team. His job is to find out when the traveling party will arrive at the spot appointed for the heist. A chamberlain has many ways, in an inn, of gathering intelligence of this sort, by overhearing the conversations of the inn guests. He passes his information on to another member of the team, named, appropriately enough, Gadshill. The robbery is all set to go.

Meanwhile, we, as audience, have learned a great deal too: we have caught a glimpse of what ordinary working people and innocent travelers must suffer on these unsafe roads. The robbery may be a caper to Falstaff and Hal, but to its victims it is in deadly earnest. The robbery is not to be a victimless crime. Shakespeare conveys all this to us in his telegraphic dramatic style, showing us the scene without spelling out what it is there for. He calls upon us to read or view it carefully, critically, looking intently at it for signs of what is going on.

Aided with this perspective, we are in a position to enjoy the high jinks of the robbery itself and at the same time measure its social cost. Falstaff is in fine fettle, complaining of the practical jokes being played on him by the hiding of his horse so that he has to waddle about on foot. He knows how to make his own fatness a subject of mirth; it is a way he uses to endear himself to the Prince. When the intended victims arrive, they are indeed terrified. Falstaff is exuberant: 'Strike! Down with them! Cut the villains' throats! Ah, whoreson caterpillars, bacon-fed knaves! They hate us youth' (2.2.83–5). Falstaff fancies himself as a kind of Robin Hood, taking from the rich and giving to the poor – that is, to himself and his comrades. He repeats his astonishing assertion that he and his friends are young: 'What, ye knaves, young men must live' (90). Falstaff, we know, is white-bearded and old, nearly sixty by his own later admission (2.4.420), but he does embody the irresponsible hedonism of youth, and he likes to think of himself as perpetually young. He forms an imaginary alliance of the young and disenfranchised, including himself, against those who are old and powerful, including the King, the royal court, and the law. Falstaff is a free spirit, and he invites Hal to join him in the company of those who refuse to grow up.

Hal, however, has not taken part in the actual robbery of the travelers. He and Poins, by prearrangement, have withdrawn from their companions in the dark in order to stage a second raid, in which Hal and Poins take the spoils of the robbery from the robbers. The stage direction is instructive: '*As they* [Falstaff and friends] *are sharing, the Prince and Poins set upon them. They all run away, and Falstaff, after a blow or two, runs away too, leaving the booty behind them*' (2.2.102.1–3). This is an original stage direction. It specifies that Falstaff is to behave differently from the others; they run immediately, while he attempts to resist the raid but then gives up and runs away too, evidently coming to the conclusion that he cannot hope to defeat two athletic younger opponents. Shakespeare is careful to differentiate his 'cowardice' from that of his companions.

After another revealing glimpse of Hotspur, this time with his wife, as he broods about the impending rebellion, we return to the robbery story in Act 2, scene 4. This is the longest and most complex scene in the play. It continually challenges our abilities to comprehend its dramaturgy. Why does Shakespeare start with the Prince, Poins, and a hapless waif of a 'drawer' or tavern waiter named Francis? We realize at once that we are in a tavern, for Hal entertains his friend Poins with an account of how he, Hal, has been carousing with Francis and the other barkeeps of the establishment. (The place is conventionally known as the Boar's Head Tavern, from an indirect hint in *2 Henry IV*, but is never named in the present play.) Hal tells how he calls them all by their Christian (i.e., first) names, and is, in their eyes, the 'king of courtesy'. They call him 'a Corinthian, a lad of mettle, a good boy'. He has been practicing their lingo, so that he knows how to call drinking deep 'dyeing scarlet' and how to bid anyone who pauses in his drinking to 'play it off', that is, drink up (2.4.4–16). He must have a reason for wanting to learn this colloquial slang: is it that he realizes he will be king some day and wishes to know what his lowest subjects talk about? We cannot be certain, for his talk of intimacy with the barkeeps is at once proud and self-critical. Hal vaunts his own skill in winning the hearts of these poor fellows even as he condescends to his accomplishment as sounding 'the very bass string of humility' (5–6).

The practical joke he and Poins play on poor Francis is similar in nature: it shows Hal as clever and witty, and able to see things from the point of view of an illiterate commoner, and yet the joke is also cruel and snobbish. The trick is to get Francis to answer 'Anon, anon!', meaning 'Coming, sir, coming!', when they call repeatedly to him from separate rooms. 'Anon' is almost all that Francis knows how to say; most of his very parochial existence is spent in answering demands for service in this tavern. Once they have set this Pavlovian response in motion, the Prince then asks Francis about his life, and whether he might not like to receive a gift from the Prince of a thousand pounds, enabling him to get away from the indentured service to which he is bound. 'Francis!' yells Poins in the next room, to which Francis of course calls out 'Anon, anon!', thereby in effect answering the Prince by saying, 'Soon, in a minute, not right now.' Francis talks himself out of a thousand pounds. It is all a bit heartless and mean, like most practical jokes, but Francis is so bewildered that he evidently has no idea what has happened. He is none the worse for the experience, and Prince Hal has found a merry way to waste time while waiting for Falstaff to arrive from the foiled robbery. The incident is puzzling and quite wonderful. We see in it what Hal means when he says that he has 'sounded the very bass string of humility' among his tavern mates. We know, by the concurrent scenes of political intrigue, that a rebellion is brewing in the kingdom and that the hour is late for Hal to be entertaining himself in this way.

Falstaff is at his most appealing in the ensuing tavern scene. He arrives in a petulant and self-pitying mood, grumbling pointedly about certain 'cowards' who did not take part in the robbery. This complaint gives Falstaff ample occasion to practice the art of colorful insult, at which he is so adept. 'I would give a thousand pound I could run as fast as thou canst', he arraigns the Prince. 'You are straight enough in the shoulders; you care not who sees your back. Call you that backing of your friends? A plague upon such backing!' (2.4.145–9). Falstaff complains about the drink, even though he manages to consume it in quantities. He warms to the task of narrating the robbery incident to Hal, in the process of which he manages to inflate the two opponents with whom he fought into four, then seven, then nine, until, as he triumphantly concludes, 'with a thought seven of the eleven I paid'. 'Oh, monstrous!' the Prince comments. 'Eleven buckram men grown out of two!' He is no less exasperatedly amused at Falstaff's claim to have been attacked by 'three misbegotten knaves in Kendal green' in the dark, when, as the Prince exclaims, 'How couldst thou know these men in Kendal green when it was so dark thou couldst not see thy hand?' (215–31).

Falstaff must now listen to the Prince's account of what happened. How will he extricate himself from the 'open and apparent shame' of his lying? The Prince and Poins exultantly await Falstaff's reply, and it is a good one. 'By the Lord, I knew ye as well as he that made ye', he tells them, presumably after a theatrical pause timed for comic effect. 'Why, hear you, my masters, was it for me to kill the heir apparent?' Instinct, says Falstaff, came to his assistance, prompting him to spare the life of the crown prince. The jest is superb, both for its resourceful inventiveness and for its sly dig at Hal's expense: instinct has shown Hal to be a true prince when his own behavior might have given one reason to doubt. Hal and Poins crow with laughter. Falstaff has delivered as they hoped; he has been the funny man the story needed. As Poins had said, back in the play's second scene as he proposed the caper to Prince Hal, 'The virtue of this jest will be the incomprehensible lies that this same fat rogue will tell us when we meet at supper – how thirty at least he fought with, what wards, what blows, what extremities he endured; and in the reproof [i.e. disproof] of this lives the jest' (1.2.180–4).

Has Falstaff really been tricked, however? Consider the evidence. Hal and Poins have played these games often enough with Falstaff to know what to expect; their pleasure in the joke is in knowing what Falstaff will do. He, for his part, is well practiced in playing the role of the comic butt in their games. He knows perfectly well that Hal and Poins agreed to go on the robbery expedition, and were there at the start until they suddenly disappeared. Then, after the robbery had taken place, two young men in buckram suits and disguised with masks (1.2.173–4) came down upon them in the dark and took away the booty. No special genius is needed on Falstaff's part to figure out what has happened. Why else, in the tavern scene, does he insist so that he fought with two opponents? 'I have peppered two of them', he boasts. 'Two I am sure I have paid, two rogues in buckram suits' (2.4.188–90). These are the two that, in Falstaff's monstrous lie, multiply into four, seven, nine, and eleven. Is there not a wonderful double meaning in Falstaff's 'By the Lord, I knew ye as well as he that made ye' (264–5)? To the Prince and Poins, it is a brilliant lie; to us as readers or audience it may also be the simple truth, conveyed with a knowing wink of Falstaff's eye. We cannot be sure; the ambiguity is part of what makes Falstaff so fascinating. Is he an inveterate liar, or a superb entertainer who understands that his role is to be the scapegoat of the Prince's wit? How else is he to hold on to the Prince's affection?

The same ambiguity applies to Falstaff's cowardice. Poins anticipates what will happen in the planned robbery and its aftermath: the robbers will run from their new attackers. 'Well, for two of them', Poins tells Hal, 'I know them to be as true-bred cowards as ever turned back; and for the third, if he fight longer than he sees reason, I'll forswear arms' (1.2.177–80). The third must be Falstaff; the others, presumably Bardolph and Peto, are 'true-bred cowards' whereas Falstaff will fight only so long as it seems reasonable for him to do so. And so it transpires after the first robbery, when Hal and Poins surprise the robbers: '*They all run away, and Falstaff, after a blow or two, runs away too.*' Shakespeare makes a careful distinction between natural cowardice and the 'cowardice' of calculating one's chances. This is the same 'cowardice' that Falstaff will celebrate at the battle of Shrewsbury, in Act 5, when he mocks the honor that Sir Walter Blunt has gained only through death and then decides himself to lie down and play possum rather than fight with that most renowned of Scottish warriors, the Douglas. Falstaff is a coward in some senses of the term, but, in the play's debate over honor vs. cowardice, his position is nuanced and even philosophical.

Of the games that Hal and Falstaff practice to amuse each other, improvised playacting is perhaps their favorite. We see their practiced skill in the alacrity with which they undertake to rehearse the cross-examining that Hal will have to undergo next morning when he goes to face his angry father at court. Falstaff gets to play the King first, outfitting himself with a joint stool as his throne, a leaden dagger as his scepter, and a cushion as a crown atop his own bald-headed crown. The playacting makes us intensely aware that we are in the theatre, watching a play-within-the-play, witnessing a theatrical performance onstage with its own onstage audience as we watch or read from our own perspective. Falstaff is superb at parody: he exaggerates the grave majesty of King Henry IV, making him sound sententious and formal. At the same time, Falstaff does not pass up the opportunity to subject Hal to some very uncomfortable questions. 'Shall the son of England prove a thief and take purses? A question to be asked.' How can

Henry IV, Part I, Act 2, scene 4. Kevin Kline as Falstaff outfits himself with a cushion for a crown as he playacts the role of King Henry IV interviewing his wayward son. Lincoln Center, New York, 2003, directed by Jack O'Brien. (Photo © Sara Krulwich/New York Times)

such a wastrel be son to the King of England? Is he possibly a bastard child, or a changeling? His only saving grace, it seems, is that he keeps company with a virtuous older man, one who is fifty at least, or inclining to sixty. Hal, deadpan, pretends not to know whom his 'father' is talking about, but of course Falstaff means himself. He has brilliantly turned their playacting into a defense of himself as a worthy companion to the young Prince. 'Him keep with, the rest banish', says Falstaff as he sums up his case on behalf of Falstaff (2.4.369–427).

When they change roles, Hal as his own father has the opportunity to address two worrisome topics: his own deplorable behavior as an 'ungracious boy', and the role of Falstaff as 'that villainous abominable misleader of youth'. The insults come thick and fast: Falstaff is a 'trunk of humors', a 'bolting-hutch of beastliness', a 'swollen parcel of dropsies', an 'old white-bearded Satan', and much more. These are endearingly funny to the onstage audience and to us, in the vein of the amicable abuse that Falstaff and Hal both practice, but an undercurrent of seriousness increasingly manifests itself. What is Falstaff useful for except 'to taste sack and drink it'? What does he accomplish in his life but 'villainy'? Falstaff's pretending not to recognize whom the Prince is talking about makes the joke all the funnier, but one senses that a moment of reckoning is at hand. After all, Hal is about to go face his real father and try to account for his unworthy behavior.

Falstaff, sensing the change of tempo and mood, realizes that it is time for him, still in the presumed role of Prince Hal, to mount his defense of Falstaff in earnest. The speech he gives is movingly eloquent and urgent. Is it wicked to enjoy sack and sugar? 'If to be old and merry be a sin, then many an old host that I know is damned.' Falstaff's language becomes biblical, homiletic, insistent in its reflections on sin and virtue, damnation and salvation. Is Falstaff really a Satan, tempting the play's young protagonist toward sin and death as Satan had done to Adam and Eve in the Garden of Eden? Is Falstaff really to be banished? Falstaff swings into his peroration:

No, my good lord, banish Peto, banish Bardolph, banish Poins; but for sweet Jack Falstaff, kind Jack Falstaff, true Jack Falstaff, valiant Jack Falstaff, and therefore more valiant being as he is old Jack Falstaff, banish not him thy Harry's company, banish not him thy Harry's company – banish plump Jack, and banish all the world.

(2.4.460–75)

Valiant! Well, perhaps it does take a kind of courage to live as Falstaff lives, though there is nothing especially valiant about his proposing that Peto and all the rest be banished except himself. Falstaff is fighting for his life. He is the one who introduces the idea of banishment; no one has uttered the word until he does. Yet it is truly the subject under consideration. Will Hal banish Falstaff when he comes to the throne? His answer is, finally, 'I do, I will.' Whether he says this seriously, or facetiously, or quizzically, is for the actor and the reader to decide. One possibility, and a movingly persuasive one in the theatre, is that Hal and his companions have grown hushed during Falstaff's summation of his defense. Hal's time of reckoning is near at hand. He ponders quietly his options, and announces calmly but firmly, to the others and to himself, that he will do what Falstaff has pleaded with him not to do. He will accept the burdens and the penalties of growing up, and will put behind him the merry companion of his wayward youth.

Hal's encounter with his father takes place the next morning, after Hal has had to deal with the embarrassment of lying to the sheriff in order to shield Falstaff from arrest for the robbery, and after we have had a glimpse of Hotspur's combative relationship with his new ally in the rebellion, Glendower of Wales. The tongue-lashing that Hal receives from his father is even worse than he had feared. The King is gravely angry. His distress at Hal's misconduct is sharply increased by the King's own guilt over the assassination of Richard II: King Henry fears that Hal is nothing other than a scourge sent by a vengeful God to settle scores with King Henry for being a regicide. Throughout much of the scene (3.2), the King will hardly allow the Prince to say even a word in his own defense. When Hal interrupts his father's tirade to promise that he will reform, the King goes relentlessly on with yet another catalogue of Hal's failures. Hal has been too familiar with common pranksters and criminals. He has not taken part in Council deliberations about the military crisis at hand. 'Not an eye / But is aweary of thy common sight', says the King, 'Save mine, which hath desired to see thee more' (87–9). Hal has allowed Hotspur, this 'Mars in swaddling clothes', to gain a glowing reputation for chivalry while Hal has played the truant at home. Most worrisomely, Hal has given his father reason to fear that the son will join the rebels because he wishes to see his father dead. Hal of course denies all this, and handsomely promises to settle his account with Hotspur. The King seems to accept his apology at last, and commissions Hal with major responsibility in the fighting that is about to begin, but we are allowed to wonder how well the breach between father and son has healed.

Indeed, in the ensuing scene of preparation for Hal's departure to the north toward Shrewsbury, we learn that he has commissioned Falstaff to lead a company of foot-soldiers (3.3.187). Why has Shakespeare inserted this business? Evidently, the process of reform is not as smooth and easy as Hal had predicted when, in 1.2, he promised a 'reformation, glitt'ring o'er my fault'. Hal cannot quickly do away with his affection for Falstaff. Nor can we; the scene in which Mistress Quickly complains to Falstaff of his mooching off her and refusing to pay her back shows him as an outrageous rascal, and yet he speaks so wittily that he ceaselessly engages our attention.

As a military officer, he is no less captivating and irresponsible. His soliloquy on the road in Warwickshire, as he marches toward Shrewsbury with Bardolph and his soldiers, is a tour de force of boastful accomplishment. He has drafted young men who were so anxious not to be taken that they have bribed their way out of service. The pitiful specimens with whom Falstaff is left are such scarecrows that observers wonder if he has 'unloaded all the gibbets and pressed the dead bodies'. Falstaff takes great pleasure in telling us all this. When Prince Hal, encountering Falstaff on the way, declares that he has never seen 'such pitiful rascals', Falstaff is cheerfully impenitent. 'Tut, tut, good enough to toss; food for powder, food for powder', he says to Hal. 'They'll fill a pit as well as better. Tush, man, mortal men, mortal men' (4.2.12–66). The contradictions in this Falstaff are stupendous. He is breaking the law by profiteering from the impending war, as indeed some military officers were accused of having done in the years when Shakespeare wrote this play; it was a current scandal. Falstaff is utterly unscrupulous about the lives of his soldiers. At the same time, his wry perspective on war is bracing in its ironic vision. War is, too often, a matter of filling some trench with the bodies of men who lose their lives for a cause they do not understand and that may indeed seem senseless to us. We have already seen how this present war is the result of a quarrel among powerful men that seems unnecessary and yet accelerates into brutal conflict. No one captures the futility of war more insightfully than the rascally captain who is also ready to use the war to his own advantage.

Perhaps Falstaff's most clear-sighted and humorous comment on war is his catechism about honor when the battle is about to begin. Advised by Prince Hal that he owes God a death, since we must all die some time or other, Falstaff sees no reason to hurry the process along. 'I would be loath to pay [God] before his day', he reflects in soliloquy after Hal and the others have left the stage.

Well, 'tis no matter; honor pricks me on. Yea, but how if honor prick me off when I come on? How then? Can honor set to a leg? No. Or an arm? No. Or take away the grief of a wound? No. Honor hath no skill in surgery, then? No. What is honor? A word. What is in that word 'honor'? What is that 'honor'? Air. A trim reckoning! Who hath it? He that died o' Wednesday. Doth he feel it? No. Doth he hear it? No. 'Tis insensible, then? Yea, to the dead. But will it not live with the living? No. Why? Detraction will not suffer it. Therefore I'll none of it. Honor is a mere scutcheon. And so ends my catechism.

(5.1.129–40)

A catechism is a set of questions and responses normally used for the religious instruction of a person preparing to be received or confirmed into the Christian faith. That religious aura hangs mockingly about Falstaff's skeptical investigation of honor. To him, it is unsubstantial, evanescent, illusory. Soldiers die for honor, but it deserts them; they will be forgotten or slandered, and the dream of honor will be gone forever. Falstaff regards honor as a mere scutcheon, that is, a kind of heraldic emblem adorning a tomb to which the world will ultimately pay little or no attention. Falstaff prefers life. One has so many more options if one is still alive. When he sees Sir Walter Blunt dead on the field of battle, having given his life to protect that of the King, Falstaff has a simple, wry observation: 'There's honor for you' (5.3.32–3).

These reflections on honor hit home especially in this play because they invite comparison with the life and untimely death of Hotspur. That young man is the soul of honor throughout: loyal to his family, willing to die for their cause, fearless in the face of danger, contemptuous of those like Prince Hal and his father whom Hotspur considers not honorable. The stance is admirable in ways, as is Hotspur himself. At the same time, it is an inflexible code that makes no allowance for the ironies to which Falstaff is so keenly attuned. Hotspur is a victim of his own code of honor, for it obliges him to regard his own family as no less honorable than he. When, in the taut negotiations preceding the battle, the Earl of Worcester and Sir Richard Vernon as envoys are offered terms of pardon if the rebels will lay down their arms, these two men do not report the offer back to Hotspur. Vernon would prefer to do so, but Worcester talks him out of it by arguing that the King can never be trusted to forgive their rebellion in any substantive way; they will remain his enemies still, mistrusted and given little freedom to pursue their own ambitions. Vernon reluctantly agrees, and so Worcester reports only that 'There is no seeming mercy in the King'

(5.2.34). The battle goes forward. It is premised on a lie; Hotspur dies as a consequence of having been lied to by his uncle. To be sure, Worcester may well have been right to appraise the King's intentions as he did, but he did not square with his nephew. There's honor for you, Falstaff might say.

The play abounds in paradoxes, some of them in the form of a chiasmus, or inverted parallelism. Hotspur, the embodiment of honor, dies as the casualty of a lie; Prince Hal, whose father has accused him of 'riot and dishonor', gains the honor of saving his father's life in the battle and then of defeating Hotspur in single combat. Shakespeare invents this confrontation; it does not occur in the chronicle sources. To Hal, it is as though Hotspur has unwittingly been Hal's 'factor' or agent, engrossing up glorious deeds in order that Hal might then take them away from his rival (3.2.147–8). The greater Hotspur's reputation for bravery, the greater is Hal's gain when he defeats Hotspur. Finally, it seems, Hal has completed the story that he has scripted from the start and that he has promised his father to fulfill: he has broken through the 'foul and ugly mists' of his unsavory reputation, 'Redeeming time when men think least I will' (1.2.196–211). In the closing of the 'glorious day' at the battle of Shrewsbury, he has been bold to tell his father that he is truly his son (3.2.133–4). He has asserted his legitimacy as heir to the throne by defeating his namesake, Harry, 'A very valiant rebel of the name' (5.4.62). Harry the Prince of Wales has claimed and won the honorable reputation of Harry Percy. For Hal, the play would now appear to be over. A triumphant victory is surely the appropriate ending for a history play about the rise and redemption of Prince Hal.

The trouble is that Falstaff is not dead, nor is his claim on Hal's loyalty. Although Hal thinks that both Hotspur and Falstaff lie dead on the battlefield, in a kind of emblematic pairing that would seem to bring a conclusion to all his difficulties, Falstaff is only pretending to be dead. Having fought with the fearsome Scots general known as the Douglas, Falstaff has decided to fall down '*as if he were dead*' (5.4.76.1–2). This original stage direction interprets the moment as a reprise of Falstaff's tactics at the Gad's Hill robbery, where, '*after a blow or two*', Falstaff decided that (to use a phrase he has made famous) 'The better part of valor is discretion' (119–20). This phrase, often reversed to read 'Discretion is the better part of valor', is a proverbial way of saying that without discretion, valor can get one into a lot of trouble. This has been Falstaff's credo all along, and it is surely a comment on Hotspur as a man of infinite valor and non-existent discretion. Now Hotspur lies dead, like Sir Walter Blunt, while Falstaff rises to live on.

The resurrection of Falstaff gives the actor, and the reader, a wonderful choice. The earlier stage direction specifies that the actor is to fall down '*as if he were dead*'. Does he 'act' dead, or do we know that he is playing possum? Stage deaths require that the actor fall and look dead; we understand that the actor is not really dead, and will get up as soon as the scene is over. If Falstaff lies perfectly still, are we not fooled into believing, with Prince Hal, that we have reached the end of the story as far as Falstaff is concerned? Even when we read '*as if he were dead*', we cannot be sure, since '*as if*' is the stuff of theatrical mimesis. In the eighteenth and nineteenth centuries, actors sometimes winked and mugged at the audience to ensure everyone that Falstaff was up to his old tricks, but a more sophisticated approach might well be to leave the audience in doubt. Such an interpretation is in keeping with the view of Falstaff as massively clever at knowing how to please by being the butt of the joke, as earlier in the robbery incident.

At all events, Falstaff '*riseth up*', and proceeds to give Hotspur's corpse a stab in the thigh, and then claim Hotspur as his prize in the fighting. Hal, returning at this point with his brother Prince John, is of course outraged at Falstaff's effrontery, but perhaps amused too, and is willing to let the old rascal take the credit. In this, Hal shows his generosity and gentlemanly graciousness, but perhaps also a certain recklessness about the question of reputation. Falstaff lives on into the ensuing play, *2 Henry IV*, to haunt the Prince as a continual reminder of his wilder days. Everyone expects Hal to sanction lawlessness when he becomes king. Reputations once gained, for better or for worse, prove to be incredibly tenacious. Meanwhile, Falstaff has shown that he is not so easily gotten rid of, by Hal or by Shakespeare. He looms larger than life, larger even than the plays in which he appears. His resurrection is a token of his eternal existence in the theatre.

5

Hamlet

Many worthwhile productions of *Hamlet* are available on film and in video, so that if you want to start by immersing yourself in one or more well-acted versions, hearing the voices and fleshing out the characters with professional actors, you can easily do so. You can compare productions to get some sense of the remarkable range of possible interpretations. Choices might include:

- Laurence Olivier's 1948 black-and-white film with Olivier as Hamlet, Jean Simmons as Ophelia, Eileen Herlie as Gertrude, and Felix Aylmer as Polonius.
- Grigori Kozintsev's 1964 Russian film with English subtitles and musical score by Dmitri Shostakovich, starring Innokenti Smoktunovsky as Hamlet, Elsa Radzina as Gertrude, and Anastasia Vertinskaya as Ophelia.
- The 1980 BBC version with Derek Jacobi as Hamlet, Claire Bloom as Gertrude, Patrick Stewart as Claudius, and Eric Porter as Polonius.
- Franco Zeffirelli's 1990 film with Mel Gibson as Hamlet, Alan Bates as Claudius, Glenn Close as Gertrude, Helena Bonham Carter as Ophelia, and Ian Holm as Polonius.
- Kenneth Branagh's 1996 four-hour virtually uncut *Hamlet* with Branagh in the title role, Derek Jacobi as Claudius, Julie Christie as Gertrude, Kate Winslet as Ophelia, and Richard Briers as Polonius.
- Michael Almereyda's film of 2000 set in modern-day Manhattan with Ethan Hawke as Hamlet, Diane Venora as Gertrude, Kyle MacLachlan as Claudius, Sam Shepard as the Ghost of Hamlet's father, Bill Murray as Polonius, Liev Schreiber as Laertes, and Julia Stiles as Ophelia.

- Harder to locate but really excellent as a well-crafted reading of the play is a 1990 televised production with Kevin Kline as Hamlet, Dana Ivey as Gertrude, Diane Venora as Ophelia, Brian Murray as Claudius, and Michael Cumpsty as Laertes.

No Shakespeare play is better served by the visual media. Then, too, your chances of seeing a live stage production are better with *Hamlet* than with most Shakespeare plays.

And you may have read the play before; it is often taught. No matter. The best thing is to start afresh, at the beginning, with as few preconceptions as possible. Ask probing questions. Why, at every point, is the dramatist doing what he is doing? Who are the characters, and what are they saying to one another? Be especially wary of clichéd interpretations, as for example that Hamlet's 'tragic flaw' lies in his morbid delaying of what his father's ghost urges him to do. Be skeptical. Does a tragedy have to have a 'tragic flaw'? Is Hamlet's delay unreasonable? What is his problem?

If we read the beginning of the play without preconceptions, we can see how Shakespeare begins by puzzling and scaring his audience. Two sentinels encounter one another at a station where a night watch is being kept. The sentinels are so nervous about something that the man coming on watch, Bernardo, challenges his mate with 'Who's there?' This is a question that the man on watch should be asking instead; that is the point of Francisco's retort, 'Nay, answer *me*.' We learn that the time is midnight: ''Tis now struck twelve.' In some productions, a doleful sounding of the hour, with twelve slow strokes on the bell, precedes the guards' taut conversation. Midnight is the time for the changing of the guard, and for Francisco to get to bed. ''Tis bitter cold', he says, 'And I am sick at heart.' About what? The watch has been quiet so far, but some trouble is anticipated. Bernardo expects reinforcements, in fact, and they soon arrive in the persons of Marcellus and Horatio. The guardsmen are all 'liegemen to the Dane', that is, sworn to serve the Danish king. Evidently we are in Denmark (1.1.1–18).

Horatio is not a regular member of the guard. He has been brought along because he is a gentleman and a scholar, well informed in matters of state affairs and theology. He is also plainly dubious about the guards' report of 'this dreaded sight twice seen of us'. 'What, has this thing appeared again tonight?' he asks. Shakespeare's choice of deliberately vague words adds to our sense of apprehension. What is 'this thing', 'this dreaded sight', twice seen by the guard? Perhaps Horatio will have an explanation, or at least confirm what the guards themselves can scarcely believe. Bernardo starts to tell what he and Marcellus saw on the previous evening, when suddenly a Ghost appears.

As readers, we need to picture this Ghost as clearly as we can. The watchmen and Horatio emphatically agree that it looks 'like the King', and is outfitted in armor like that in which 'the King' fought against the Polacks. What king? What battle with the Polacks? This Ghost has appeared twice now, at midnight, going past the watchmen 'With martial stalk'. Horatio speaks to it in vain; 'it stalks away'. Horatio, now thoroughly convinced by the 'sensible and true avouch' of his own eyes that he has seen a Ghost, concludes, as do the others, that 'This bodes some strange eruption to our state'. In the ensuing discussion, we learn from Horatio that this Ghost was the 'image' of Denmark's 'last king', that is, the king who reigned prior to the present incumbent. That previous king was named Hamlet, and he was renowned for his valor in defending Denmark against old Fortinbras of Norway (54–108). When the Ghost makes a second harrowing appearance to the guardsmen and proves invulnerable to their weapons, Horatio decides that they had better report what they have seen to 'young Hamlet', who will surely be able to speak to this apparition. From Horatio's report to young Hamlet we learn further details about the Ghost: that he was armed 'cap-à-pie', i.e., from head to foot, that he wore the beaver or visor of his helmet up, and that his face looked pale and his beard 'grizzled' or 'sable silvered' like that of the old Hamlet (1.2.200–47).

Hamlet reads in many ways like a detective story. Not only are we as readers constantly on the lookout for clues to a mystery, but so is young Hamlet himself. Is this Ghost truly that of his father? Or may it be a demon sent to tempt him to make some fatal error? Why has the Ghost returned? Hamlet can scarcely wait to join the guardsmen on their guard platform on the following night. When he does so, the Ghost appears as before. Hamlet's first response is to pray: 'Angels and ministers of grace defend us!' He cannot be sure if the Ghost is a 'spirit of health or goblin damned', and whether his intents are 'wicked or charitable', but Hamlet knows that he must speak to this apparition so strikingly resembling his own father, dressed in 'complete steel'. Hamlet's companions are no less worried that the Ghost's intents may be damnable. 'What if it tempt you toward the flood, my lord', asks Horatio, 'Or to the dreadful summit of the cliff / That beetles o'er his base into the sea' (1.4.39–74), and there tempt young Hamlet to suicide? All of these clues suggest that the Ghost is real, since he is seen by several characters.

When the Ghost of Hamlet senior and his son are alone on the battlements of the castle, moreover, the Ghost is very convincing. His story, of being murdered by his own younger brother for the love of Hamlet senior's wife and for his Danish crown, confirms everything that young Hamlet has surmised. 'Oh, my prophetic soul! My uncle!' he exclaims. The details of the murder, by means of a cunning poison poured into the ear of the sleeping older Hamlet, offer further corroboration. Father and son agree that Claudius is both an 'incestuous' and an 'adulterate beast' who has made the royal bed of Denmark 'A couch for luxury [i.e., lechery] and damnèd incest' (1.5.42–3, 83–4). Young Hamlet unhesitatingly knows what he must do. 'Haste me to know't, that I, with wings as swift / As meditation or the thoughts of love, / May sweep to my revenge' (30–2), he exclaims. After the Ghost departs, bidding young Hamlet to 'Remember me', the son insists to himself that he will wipe away 'all trivial fond records' from the 'table' or tablet of his memory so that the Ghost's commandment 'all alone shall live / Within the book and volume of my brain' (92–104). Hamlet accepts the role of the revenger in what is starting to look like a revenge tragedy, with Hamlet's uncle as the villain.

Yet Claudius, the uncle, is far from being a conventional stage villain. We meet him in scene 2, before we learn of the secret murder. What is he like as king? His opening speech makes clear that he has been king for only a month or so. The memory of the previous king is still 'green'. Despite the brevity of that time, Claudius has married his brother's widow, his own sister-in-law. Clearly he has some explaining to do; the wedding was not only hasty but, according to the teaching of some church authorities in Shakespeare's day, incestuous. Claudius's speech, composed especially for this first public occasion since the death of the old king, is an exquisitely balanced statement of justification. Denmark is still in mourning. Why the marriage? Claudius's answer is judicious and calmly reasonable. Because Denmark has been threatened by an invasion from Norway, the great need has been for reassurance and continuity of rule. Claudius has consulted with his chief counselors, and they have readily consented to the marriage, to the 'election' of Claudius to the throne, and to Claudius's taking firm charge of foreign and domestic affairs. (Denmark is an 'elective' monarchy in the sense that the choice of the monarch is made by a small and elite group of well-born 'electors'.) Mourning is understandably necessary, but that necessity must be weighed against the need for moving forward. The new king expresses this idea through a series of carefully crafted paradoxical antitheses: in taking as his wife his 'sometime sister, now our queen', he has done so 'as 'twere with a defeated joy – / With an auspicious and a dropping eye, / With mirth in funeral and with dirge in marriage, / In equal scale weighing delight and dole' (1.2.1–14). Ever the masterful rhetorician, Claudius knows the art of constructing phrases that are carefully balanced in their sound and grammatical construction. He and his courtiers are seemingly dressed for the occasion in ways that acknowledge the passing of one regime while also welcoming the next. The King is dead; long live the King! Only Hamlet is dressed in black.

When we examine Claudius as an astute and perhaps machiavellian practitioner of the art of governing, we cannot help admiring his skill. The opening speech justifying the marriage and proclaiming the new regime is a masterpiece of tactful persuasion. This king governs with absolute authority but also with the advice and consent of his chief ministers. He has the politician's gift of remembering and using people's names: when he addresses Laertes about this young man's request to be allowed to return to France after having taken part in the royal wedding festivities, the King repeats Laertes's name no fewer than four times in a speech of nine lines, and then once again as he gives his royal consent (1.2.42–50, 62). Like an astute manipulator of power, he keeps the dispensing of royal favors under his direct control, collecting political IOUs that he can call in when he needs them; he makes sure that Polonius realizes what the new king is doing for him in licensing the departure of Polonius's son Laertes. Most strikingly, Claudius shows that he truly understands the art of international relationships and that he can play hardball when necessary.

As Claudius astutely assesses the situation, Denmark is under threat of invasion from Norway because the old King of Norway, 'impotent and bed-rid', is in too weak a condition to stop his nephew, young Fortinbras, from assembling a band of desperadoes in order to force Denmark to return the territory that the old King Hamlet won from old Fortinbras in a chivalric wager. Young Fortinbras no doubt assumes that Denmark is vulnerable in a time of regime change, especially a change precipitated by the sudden and shocking death of the old king. Claudius sees at once what he must do. He dispatches two ambassadors to point out to old Norway that his nephew is assembling an army of invasion and to urge that Norway call off the attempt (1.2.17–40). Claudius wisely allows old Norway the face-saving excuse that he may not have realized what his nephew has been up to. We learn a bit later that old Norway, realizing that his bluff has been called by the Danish king, jumps at the offer and forbids young Fortinbras to attack Denmark ever again. Through his ambassadors,

Claudius also takes care to sweeten the rebuke to Norway by offering young Fortinbras free passage over Danish soil if he will only go south and attack some other country instead, namely, Poland (2.2.60–80). Fortinbras is quite content with the offer, and acts accordingly. He has accomplished what he has wanted. Eventually, though no one realizes this at present, Fortinbras will inherit the Danish throne as well, without ever firing a shot against Denmark. Practically everyone is happy. Claudius is a genius at diplomacy, and his loyal supporters like Polonius love him for it. Only Hamlet is disaffected.

As he often does, Shakespeare moves back and forth in the early part of *Hamlet* from scenes of private conversation to scenes of public ceremony. The stratagem allows him to juxtapose contrasting worlds that comment implicitly on one another. Hamlet, at the guard station in the cold of night with a few loyal soldiers and his friend Horatio, disapproves of the lavish extravagance of Claudius's court, with its glittering array of courtiers, its banquets, its plentiful supply of drink, and the noise of the kettledrum as the King 'drains his drafts of Rhenish down'. To Hamlet, this habitual fondness for drink is 'a custom / More honored in the breach than the observance' – that is, is a custom better left unobserved (1.4.8–16). Hamlet vastly prefers the intimacy of friendship and of honest conversation.

In another private scene, Shakespeare shows us what it is like to be a senior counselor living at court with his close-knit family. Laertes's farewell to his sister Ophelia and his father Polonius shows a real tenderness of affection combined with a wariness about the competitive world that surrounds them. Laertes's most urgent wish, as he leaves for France, is to warn his sister that Hamlet's interest in her as a woman will certainly lead to her downfall if she opens her 'chaste treasure' to his 'unmastered importunity'. A young woman who loses her virginity will instantly become unmarriageable; her value on the marriage market will be nil. Hamlet no doubt professes to love her, but she must fear that young men's vows are not to be trusted, and that as crown prince Hamlet cannot be expected to marry a commoner like herself. 'His greatness weighed', Laertes cautions, 'his will is not his own. / For he himself is subject to his birth. / He may not, as unvalued persons do, / Carve for himself, for on his choice depends / The safety and health of this whole state' (1.3.17–21). Ophelia does not disagree; she merely asks, in a tactful way, that Laertes himself observe the kind of propriety he is preaching to her. When it comes Polonius's turn to talk, he lectures his son on being warily prudent about the friendships he makes, the way he chooses to dress, and the way he handles money. To Ophelia, once the two of them are alone, Polonius's advice is precisely that of Laertes. The son is like the father, and both take seriously their male obligation to protect Ophelia. The father especially insists that she obey his commands about returning Hamlet's love letters to him. Father knows best. Ophelia is submissive. Clearly she has fallen in love with Hamlet, and attempts to defend his addresses to her as honorable, but she agrees to see Hamlet no more without her father's permission. In these ways, Polonius's family is symptomatic of what Hamlet deplores so vehemently in the court life of Denmark. It is 'an unweeded garden' to him, a 'prison' (1.2.135, 2.2.244–8), and Polonius is its ignoble creation.

Whether Polonius is a doddering old fool, as in many productions, or a canny politician and spy, as in Richard Briers's portrayal of him in Kenneth Branagh's 1996 film, he certainly keeps his eye on everything. He instructs a retainer, Reynaldo, in the art of spying on Laertes in Paris. Reynaldo is to suggest tactfully to Laertes's friends that he gambles, drinks, fights duels, etc., in order to see if the friends will confirm the truth of such allegations and supply new information. 'See you now', Polonius boasts, 'Your bait of falsehood takes this carp of truth.' This is Polonius's usual way of gaining intelligence: 'Thus do we of wisdom and of reach, / With windlasses and with assays of bias, / By indirections find directions out' (2.1.63–7). Polonius is proud of his sagacity and 'reach', that is, his widely extended capacity for keeping himself informed. He delights in circuitous ways of gathering information. He has a network of spies. He arranges for the King and himself to overhear, from a concealed location, Hamlet talking with Ophelia to see if the Prince is indeed mad for love, as Polonius believes. Later he secretly listens in on Hamlet's interview with his mother in her chambers, and ends up dead on the floor as a result.

Polonius also thinks of himself as having a theatrical talent. He once played the part of Julius Caesar, he tells Hamlet, and was killed by Brutus in the Capitol. Hamlet cannot resist a mordant pun: 'It was brute part of him [Brutus] to kill so capital a calf there' (3.2.98–104). Polonius dispenses freely his critical judgments about theatre. He introduces the players who visit the Danish court at Elsinore as 'The best actors in the world, either for tragedy, comedy, history, pastoral, pastoral-comical, historical-pastoral, tragical-historical, tragical-comical-historical-pastoral, scene individable, or poem unlimited. Seneca cannot be too heavy, nor Plautus too light' (2.2.396–401). He comments sourly on the First Player's recitation with the objection that 'This is too long', eliciting from Hamlet another satirical jab: 'It shall to the barber's with your beard.' Polonius's tastes, in Hamlet's view, are impossibly vulgar: 'He's for a jig or a tale of bawdry, or he sleeps' (498–501). Even Polonius's favorable judgments sound flatulent. When Hamlet admiringly repeats the First Player's 'the moblèd queen', Polonius chimes in: 'That's good. "Moblèd queen" is good' (502–4). These exchanges do more than point up for us Hamlet's dismay at a senior courtier who snoops into people's lives and fends off Hamlet's advances to Ophelia. They suggest how important good acting is to Hamlet, and how Polonius is the very model for Hamlet of how not to go about carrying out the Ghost's dread command. Hamlet must not only accomplish that goal; he must act it well. The story of his life must make a good play.

This pointed comparison of Hamlet with Polonius suggests a way in which we are to read character in this play. Hamlet is constantly comparing himself with other characters. They in turn judge him by their own lights, and see him in terms of their own obsessions. They are all seriously misled, first by concluding that Hamlet really is mad (when we know that part of the explanation at least is that he has consciously decided to 'put an antic disposition on' (1.5.181) to throw his enemy, Claudius, off the scent), and then by assessing Hamlet's seemingly mad behavior from their own limited perspective.

Polonius diagnoses Hamlet as suffering from love madness as a result of Ophelia's having returned his love letters to him, as her father has commanded her to do. Polonius explains to the King and Queen what he thinks happened next:

> And he, repellèd – a short tale to make –
> Fell into a sadness, then into a fast,
> Thence to a watch, thence into a weakness,
> Thence to a lightness, and by this declension
> Into the madness wherein now he raves,
> And all we mourn for.
>
> (2.2.145–51)

Polonius arrives at this view presumably because he is appraising Hamlet from the perspective of Polonius's own experience. 'Truly in my youth I suffered much extremity for love, very near this', he confides in an aside (189–91). Being myopically self-absorbed, he judges others through his own eyes. His language is foolishly rambling and sententious. Most damagingly, he is fatuous in his self-assurance that he has found the truth: 'If circum- stances lead me, I will find / Where truth is hid, though it were hid indeed /

Within the center' (157–9). We are drawn to Hamlet in part because he knows that truth is infinitely more complex, and that he as an individual cannot be reduced to oversimplified and schematic diagnoses. Small wonder that Hamlet loathes Polonius.

Ophelia understandably thinks, as does her father, that Hamlet has lost his wits through the maddening frustration of unrequited affection. 'Oh, what a noble mind is here o'erthrown!' she laments in her distraught fashion after Hamlet has bid her to 'Get thee to a nunnery'. For Ophelia, the heart of the matter is in her own culpability as the denying maiden:

> And I, of ladies most deject and wretched,
> That sucked the honey of his music vows,
> Now see that noble and most sovereign reason
> Like sweet bells jangled out of tune and harsh,
> That unmatched form and feature of blown youth
> Blasted with ecstasy.
>
> (3.1.153–63)

Ophelia thus dramatizes her own distress and can conceive of Hamlet's behavior only in terms of her own suffering. Like her father, she has no doubt that Hamlet is indeed mad.

Queen Gertrude has another answer to Hamlet's presumed madness, Like Ophelia, she blames herself in her capacity as woman. 'I doubt [i.e. fear] it is no other but the main', she confides to her new husband, 'His father's death and our o'erhasty marriage' (2.2.56–7). This analysis is a good deal closer to the mark, no doubt, but it too, we perceive, is driven by Gertrude's unhappy feelings about herself. It is a mother's response: she has given her son reason to feel that she has deserted both him and the memory of her dead husband, and now he has cracked under the strain.

Claudius says little, but he too looks at Hamlet's aberrant behavior from a solipsistic point of view. Is Hamlet somehow aware that Claudius has murdered his own brother and Hamlet's father? If so, what is Claudius to do about it? Alone among the characters of the play attempting to understand what is going on inside Hamlet's psyche, Claudius is convinced that Hamlet is neither lovesick nor insane: 'Love? His affections do not that way tend; / Nor what he spake, though it lacked form a little, / Was not like madness' (3.1.165–7). Best to keep an eye on Hamlet, partly through Polonius's spying, until the King can determine what Hamlet actually knows. The King has another stratagem as well: perhaps two of Hamlet's boyhood friends can worm out of him what is troubling him.

Rosencrantz and Guildenstern thus come into the story as spies for Claudius. They do so innocently enough, in a sense: the King summons them, briefs them on Hamlet's strange 'transformation' in which 'nor th'exterior nor the inward man / Resembles that it was', professes to have no idea what it should be 'More than his father's death' that has divided Hamlet from himself, and appeals to their youthful acquaintance of yore with Hamlet to glean from him what it is that 'afflicts him thus'. Perhaps a diagnosis can lead to a 'remedy', a cure (2.2.5–18). The Queen too appeals to their spirit of helpfulness; Hamlet has often talked of these two friends with notable enthusiasm. And indeed, when Hamlet first encounters them, he greets them with genuine warmth. He hasn't seen them in quite some time; he is thirty, as we learn later, and they were acquaintances of his youth before he went off to study at Wittenberg. When their talk turns to bawdy wordplay on the idea of dwelling 'In the secret parts of Fortune' (2.2.235), we catch a glimpse of the adolescent banter they must have known as young males. Yet Hamlet quickly senses that Rosencrantz and Guildenstern have been 'sent for' to spy on him. Their motives are honest enough, perhaps: to help Hamlet with his apparent emotional difficulties, and at the same time ingratiate themselves with the King, who has many benefits at his disposal. Even so, from Hamlet's point of view they are the wrong side of the great battle he must wage with Claudius. By not knowing what Claudius has done, Rosencrantz and Guildenstern are easily deceived by him and thus unwittingly drawn into his camp.

Rosencrantz and Guildenstern have their own diagnosis of Hamlet's odd behavior, and, as with Polonius, Ophelia, and Gertrude, it is driven by their own perspectives and desires. Being themselves young and eager for advancement, they imagine that Hamlet is frustrated in his ambition to be king. When Rosencrantz asks Hamlet if perhaps it is his 'ambition' that makes Denmark seem a prison to him by being 'too narrow' for his mind (2.2.253–4), the subject provokes a discussion about what it is to be ambitious. Later, when Rosencrantz begs Hamlet to name the cause of his erratic and dangerous behavior toward the King, Hamlet gives the answer that Rosencrantz and Guildenstern evidently expect: 'Sir, I lack advancement.' Rosencrantz misses the irony of this entirely: 'How can that be, when you have the voice of the King himself for your succession in Denmark?' (3.2.336–41). Claudius has indeed settled the succession on Hamlet as 'the most immediate to our throne' (1.2.109), but of course this reply of

Rosencrantz's can hardly satisfy a prince who is secretly aware that Claudius has murdered his own brother and has thereby denied Hamlet his legitimate hopes of direct succession from his father. More to the point, Hamlet complains later to Horatio of the villain who has 'killed my king and whored my mother, / Popped in between th'election and my hopes', and 'Thrown out his angle for my proper life' (5.2.64–6). Claudius's having preempted the throne properly belonging to Hamlet is thus one of Hamlet's most serious accusations against his uncle. Are Rosencrantz and Guildenstern right, then, to diagnose his behavior as the result of frustrated ambition?

Whether Hamlet does in fact cherish the ambition to rule Denmark is an open question. On the one hand, Denmark has become, in his view, so corrupt that 'things rank and gross in nature / Possess it merely' (1.2.136–7), prompting him to seek the comforting refuge of intellectual study and debate. When he speaks to Ophelia of his being 'very proud, revengeful, ambitious' (3.1.125–6), the self-accusation seems general and even homiletic rather than political: Hamlet confesses that he is a sinner, like the rest of us. Since Denmark is an elective monarchy, choosing its rulers by the decision of a small oligarchy, Hamlet cannot assume that he would have been chosen automatically to succeed his father. His riposte to Rosencrantz, 'Sir, I lack advancement', may well be a taunt sardonically calculated to see if Rosencrantz will rise to the bait of taking him literally, as Rosencrantz does. Still, Hamlet does have good reason to consider the throne as his birthright through his noble father, and he certainly regards the present incumbent as unworthy. In a better world he might indeed have proved 'most royal', as Fortinbras says of him at the play's very end (5.2.400). Earlier, Ophelia speaks movingly of Hamlet as embodying 'The courtier's, soldier's, scholar's, eye, tongue, sword', with the potential to be 'Th'expectancy and rose of the fair state' (3.1.154–5). *Hamlet* is in this sense a tragedy of wasted greatness. Whether or not Hamlet thirsts for royal power, he is certainly scornful of Rosencrantz's simplistic reading of his supposed ambition, just as he is scornful of Polonius's fatuous certainty that he understands the cause of Hamlet's distress. Human beings are too complex for facile analysis. Hamlet is proud of his own uniqueness, and touchy about those who complacently think they can unlock his secrets.

Is Hamlet mad, at least some of the time? This is another open question, and one that tests the sagacity of the characters in the play just as it tests our own reading ability. He is himself acutely aware that persons around him believe that he is mad, and he plays with the notion, throwing his interrogators off guard. 'I am but mad north-north-west', he confides to Guildenstern, as if he were letting his friend in on some big secret. 'When the wind is southerly I know a hawk from a handsaw' (2.2.378–9). We should probably not expect this to make much sense, other than to suggest that Hamlet can tell true from false; the statement is meant to puzzle, and it does. With Polonius, too, Hamlet takes delight in teasing the old spy with what might sound like clues. When asked by Polonius if Hamlet recognizes him, Hamlet replies, 'Excellent well. You are a fishmonger.' 'Have you a daughter?' he next inquires. 'Let her not walk i'th' sun. Conception is a blessing, but as your daughter may conceive, friend, look to't.' Polonius sees glimpses of meaning in this, amidst the wreckage of a disordered mind. 'Still harping on my daughter', he comments in an aside. 'Yet he knew me not at first; 'a said I was a fishmonger. 'A is far gone' (173–89). The symptoms are classically those of mental illness: failure to recognize others, morbid preoccupation, thoughts of death and suicide, etc. But of course these symptoms may well be an act, the very 'antic disposition' that Hamlet assures Horatio and the guardsmen that he will put on to mislead and confuse his enemy in the business of revenge. Shakespeare inherited this idea from his sources, from Saxo Grammaticus's *Historia Danica* (1180–1208), and from the grandfather of all English revenge tragedies, Thomas Kyd's *The Spanish Tragedy* (c. 1587). The motif was very probably an essential part of a lost play of *Hamlet* (before 1589) which Shakespeare may have known.

Hamlet knows how to act madness. The presentation of madness had become, by 1601, a stage convention. We see it in its most purely theatrical form when Ophelia does indeed go mad. She sings snatches of songs about young women deserted by young men who have promised marriage in order to obtain their maidenheads, about persons who are 'dead and gone', about tombstones strewn with flowers. She does not know with whom she is speaking (4.5.21–75, 158–203). Her hearers are dismayed and heart-broken at her affliction. No one doubts the depth of her mental distress, and it is confirmed by her sad death by drowning (4.7.167–84). Hamlet contemplates suicide, but he reasons intelligently and ethically with it as a choice, and concludes that he cannot, indeed must not, do that. The comparison with Ophelia suggests that Hamlet's madness is a pretext, even if he is also genuinely and understandably unhappy. Never does Hamlet's 'madness' seem out of his control; it fits his purposes both of keeping Claudius uncertain and of expressing Hamlet's irritation at those who keep prying into his secrets.

Hamlet's chief stratagem for keeping Claudius off balance, and also as a means of determining if Claudius is really guilty of the offenses the Ghost has accused him of, is to stage a play before Claudius depicting a crime like that he committed. Will Claudius react to this play in such a way as to betray his guilt? Despite his certainty of Claudius's culpability when he first hears the detailed account of the murder, Hamlet may have good reasons to be cautious before proceeding with revenge. 'The spirit that I have seen / May be the devil', he reflects. 'The devil hath power / T'assume a pleasing shape; yea, and perhaps, / Out of my weakness and my melancholy, / As he is very potent with such spirits, / Abuses me to damn me' (2.2.599–604). Hamlet is on sound psychological and theological grounds. Melancholy was a much discussed state of mind in the early seventeenth century, even to the point of being fashionable. Learned treatises discussed the vulnerability of the melancholic temperament to diabolical insinuation. In an age of faith, few doubted that the devil was a cunning enemy lying in wait for susceptible victims. Hamlet is a serious Christian, who rejects suicide chiefly on the grounds that 'the Everlasting' has 'fixed / His canon 'gainst self-slaughter' (1.2.131–2). He has heard his father's Ghost speak of the purgatorial terrors of an eternal 'prison house' awaiting those who die without receiving the last rites of the Church (1.5.14–21, 78–80). Some students of the play, to be sure, analyze Hamlet as incapable of proceeding against Claudius for deeply psychological reasons; Sigmund Freud's theory, reiterated by his disciple Ernest Jones in *Hamlet and Oedipus* (1949), is that Hamlet yearns with unconscious oedipal desire to possess his own mother and therefore finds it impossible to punish Claudius for having done exactly that. Yet we need to be careful before concluding that Hamlet's delay is pathological. Perhaps Hamlet is right to question what he has learned before he proceeds to revenge.

Staging a play before Claudius and Gertrude appeals to Hamlet because he is such an inveterate enthusiast for the theatre. When itinerant players arrive at Elsinore Castle, he recognizes them at once, greeting the First Player as 'old friend' and amusedly observing to the young male actor cast in the role of 'my young lady and mistress' that his voice appears to have changed since last they met. Hamlet remembers so well a dramatic speech about the deaths of King Priam and Queen Hecuba of Troy that he is able to recite some fourteen lines of it before turning the rest over to the First Player. He offers to write 'some dozen or sixteen lines' for the actors to insert into their performance that night of *The Murder of Gonzago*, which the First Player willingly agrees to take on (2.2.421–547). *The Murder of Gonzago* is one of the repertory pieces with which they travel. Earlier in the scene, Hamlet has interrogated Rosencrantz and Guildenstern with intense interest about the 'tragedians of the city', asking why they tour the provinces when they could perform more profitably in town before large audiences, and has been told that they do so because companies of boy actors have so captivated city playgoers with their impudent satires that the adult companies have been forced to go on the road. (The fact that this passage, 2.2.337–62, appears only in the Folio text and refers to a theatrical controversy in London at about the time *Hamlet* was written is further evidence of the play's fascination with theatre.)

As the players ready themselves for their performance that night, Hamlet has much to say to them about how they are to act. He will not have them saw the air with their hands or 'tear a passion to tatters' in such a way as to 'split the ears of the groundlings, who for the most part are capable of nothing but inexplicable dumb shows and noise'. Instead, the players are to 'Suit the action to the word, the word to the action.' A play must 'hold as 'twere the mirror up to nature, to show virtue her feature, scorn her own image, and the very age and body of the time his form and pressure' (3.2.1–35). Hamlet is talking at least in part about the play for that evening, of which he is now co-author: it must show to Claudius and Gertrude such a vivid and true image of the reality it represents – Claudius's murder of his brother and incestuous marriage with that brother's wife – that the guilty witnesses will recognize, and tremble at, a just representation of themselves. Such a mimesis needs to make clear the vast difference between virtue and its scornful opposite. It must address itself seriously to discerning viewers; the 'unskillful' may also come to the theatre, ready to laugh at something that is overdone, but only the opinion of the 'judicious' should be of concern to those who believe in theatre at its best. Hamlet's view is intellectually patrician; it also represents the humanist's hope that good drama can improve and correct human behavior by its warnings and examples.

How well does *The Murder of Gonzago* carry out the purposes that Hamlet has outlined for it? One clue is perhaps to be found in Gertrude's response to what she watches. The play is at least as much concerned with asking whether a wife can be faithful to the memory of her husband as it is with the actual murder – so much so that we may wonder if Hamlet's 'dozen or sixteen lines' are not aimed at the Queen. The Player King enacts the role of an old and wise monarch who, sensing that he may not live much longer, consoles his wife with the assurance that she ought to feel free to remarry and go on with her life. The Player Queen will have none of this.

> Oh, confound the rest!
> Such love must needs be treason in my breast.
> In second husband let me be accurst!
> None wed the second but who killed the first.
>
> (3.2.175–8)

Hamlet's choric 'Wormwood, wormwood' strengthens our suspicion that these lines were written by him for his mother to hear. And he won't let the matter drop. When the Player Queen goes on to utter a series of solemn vows that she will never, never remarry, ending her protestations with 'Both here and hence pursue me lasting strife / If, once a widow, ever I be wife!', Hamlet is unable to keep silent. 'If she should break it now!' he exclaims. After the Player Queen exits a few lines later, Hamlet is at his mother again. 'Madam', he asks, 'how like you this play?' Her response is justly famous: 'The lady doth protest too much, methinks' (214–28). Gertrude is acutely uncomfortable at this dramatic representation. Though she answers without openly incriminating herself, she feels the force of the portraiture. One should not make vows one does not intend to keep, and one should keep the vows that one makes.

Claudius's response to *The Murder of Gonzago* is more visceral. He sits still for as long as the situation seems bearable, managing somehow to stomach a dumb show at the start of the dramatic presentation in which some fatal substance is poured into the ear of a sleeping regal figure. The theatrical convention seems to be, as in Kyd's *The Spanish Tragedy*, that onstage viewers cannot fully interpret the meaning of a dumb show until the drama itself is performed. At any rate, when the murder actually takes place during *The Murder of Gonzago* in such a way as to verify the Ghost's story, and when Hamlet proclaims to the assembled company that the poisoner is motivated by a criminal desire to win both the King's estate and his wife, Claudius abruptly departs. He is now fully aware that Hamlet knows about the murder. He and Hamlet have been playing cat and mouse, eyeing each other warily, looking for signs as to what the other knows. Now all is out in the open between them, even if no one else is aware of what is going on.

Why does Hamlet put Claudius on notice this way by identifying himself as the would-be revenger? Perhaps he does so because he wants to fight fair; that is part of his desire to act the part of the revenger with style and grace. When, a short time later, he comes across the King at prayer, he declines the opportunity to put his sword through a villain who is defenselessly on his knees and unaware that he is in danger. Hamlet's explanation in soliloquy for this decision to hold back is that he doesn't want to send Claudius's soul to heaven; that would be poor revenge, especially when Hamlet senior has had to suffer the pangs of purgatory because the suddenness of the murder left no time for him to receive the Church's last rites. Better to kill Claudius when he is drunk or having sex or sinning in some other act 'That has no relish of salvation in't' (3.3.92). This seems vengeful enough, but it conceals what may be a stronger motive: Hamlet's distaste for cowardly villainy. Claudius killed a defenseless, sleeping man; Hamlet would prefer to kill his adversary in such a way that his name will be remembered for valor and decency. If he were to kill Claudius now, the play of *Hamlet* would be over, and we would not be reading it. The story would be one of villainy and counter-villainy in a straight revenge plot. Hamlet has a more exalted narrative in mind, and we admire him for it.

The irony is, of course, that Claudius was getting nowhere with his attempt at prayer. Claudius, like Hamlet, is a Christian – not a good Christian, mind you, but one in whom the teachings of the Church are deeply ingrained. He knows perfectly well what he would have to do in order to pray successfully. He knows that his offense is 'rank', and also that divine mercy is offered to the most heinous of sinners. Can that mean him? Yes, truly, the Scriptures say that mercy can be given to those who are truly penitent, and so Claudius looks up, hoping for one brief moment that his 'fault is past'. The insuperable difficulty is that he knows he cannot will himself to give up penitently the things for which he committed the crime: 'My crown, mine own ambition, and my queen'. 'May one be pardoned and retain th'offence?' The question answers itself. Justice may be hoodwinked in this corrupted world, but not in the world to come (3.3.36–72).

This stunning passage does at least two things. It assures us once again that Claudius is indeed guilty, as he confessed more briefly in an aside at 3.1.50–5. Hamlet has pursued the question of truth here, and he has been proven right. Second, we are shown a frightening picture of what it is to be a reprobate and damned soul even while one is still alive. Claudius has a choice to make now, and it is one that, as he fully understands, will determine the fate of his eternal soul. He sees the fearful consequences of failure, he wants desperately to repent, yet he cannot. He cannot will himself to take the steps that might make salvation possible, because he is a worldling. Shakespeare and his audience would have been familiar with what John Calvin preached on this topic: that there are reprobate people whom God has predeterminately set down for eternal destruction. This does not mean that God is the author of that evil; the choice belongs to those people, and yet God foresees that they will choose wrongly. This is a paradox, but then so are most of the central tenets of religious faith.

Hamlet's encounter with his mother in her chambers is a crucial turning point of the play. One way to read a tragedy in structural terms is to ask at what point does something happen that cannot be reversed and from which all the remainder of the tragedy follows as a logical consequence. In *Romeo and Juliet* that moment is the killing of Mercutio and then Tybalt. In *Hamlet* it is the killing of Polonius. He is not the villain that Hamlet is after, of course, but once he is dead there can be no turning back. One could argue, of course, that the murder of Hamlet senior is an event that sets all the rest in motion, but that is before the play starts and is more in the nature of a 'given' upon which the tragedy is built.

Consider what happens in Act 3, scene 4 and afterward. Polonius hides behind an arras or hanging tapestry in Gertrude's chambers to overhear the conversation of mother and son. When Gertrude cries out in alarm, fearful that her son intends to harm her, Polonius calls out also from his place of concealment. Hamlet, thinking him to be the King, stabs him through the arras, and Polonius lies slain. As a consequence, the King is more determined than ever to send Hamlet to England immediately in the custody of Rosencrantz and Guildenstern. Hamlet manages to evade the sentence of death prescribed for him in the papers they are carrying by secretly substituting their names in his stead, and makes his way back to Denmark. Laertes too returns to Denmark, determined to avenge his father's death. The shock of that death has caused Ophelia to lose her wits and then drown in what is ruled as a suicide. Laertes and Hamlet grapple at Ophelia's gravesite. A fencing match is arranged between them, in preparation for which Laertes secretly envenoms the point of his sword, having conspired with the King to do so. A poisoned cup of wine, intended as an alternative way of dispatching Hamlet, kills the Queen instead. And so on to the final catastrophe. Every event follows ineluctably from the slaying of Polonius. The tight architectonic pattern is part of what we admire in this brilliantly constructed play. Nothing seems out of place.

Hamlet of course did not intend to kill Polonius. Hamlet shows little sign of grief or remorse for one whom he has long regarded as a 'wretched, rash, intruding fool' (3.4.32); Polonius has in a sense brought this on himself. At the same time, Hamlet sees that he must pay for what he has done. In some mysterious way, he believes, the heavens have some purpose in what has happened. 'Heaven hath pleased it so', he tells his mother, 'To punish me with this, and this with me, / That I must be their scourge and minister' (3.4.180–2). Although what he did was a mistake that has cost a man his life and for which the heavens will punish the killer in some way, Hamlet senses that out of this mixup will come some larger purpose that heaven intends. He will be heaven's 'scourge' in the sense of being an agent of punishment who is himself flawed; he will be a 'minister' in the larger sense of being an instrument of divine will. One interesting way of reading the rest of *Hamlet* is to follow the path of development by which that larger purpose is, in Hamlet's own view, accomplished.

What are Hamlet's intentions with regard to the Queen during this interview? His father's Ghost, in 1.5, has urged him to take revenge on Claudius for what that man has done, but the Ghost is no less insistent that Hamlet is not to seek revenge on Gertrude. 'Leave her to heaven,' the Ghost urges, 'And to those thorns that in her bosom lodge, / To prick and sting her' (1.5.87–9). The Ghost thus sharply distinguishes Claudius from Gertrude; Claudius's crimes are unforgivable and must be punished, even with eternal damnation, whereas one can hope that Gertrude is recoverable. Is this Hamlet's intent, to steer his mother to a course promising hope of spiritual healing? Gertrude herself is so far from reassurance on that point that she cringes in terror, remonstrates with her son for effrontery, and acts at first in total denial. The Ghost, too, is so alarmed by Hamlet's hectoring of his mother that he intervenes, reminding Hamlet that he is neglecting his 'almost blunted purpose' of revenge on Claudius. The Ghost chides his son for driving his mother to 'amazement' or distraction (3.4.115–16). It is as though the Ghost fears that Hamlet has forgotten the specific command to 'Leave her to heaven'. Gertrude worries that Hamlet is gone mad again, especially now that he appears to be talking to the empty air.

Yet if we look closely at what Hamlet says to his mother, once the Ghost has departed, we can see that he is deeply concerned about her spiritual condition. If the Ghost wants thorns to lodge in her bosom, 'To prick and sting her', Hamlet can be the agent or minister for just such a sting of conscience. A short time before his coming to her chambers, he has assured himself (and us) that he intends to be 'cruel, not unnatural'; he will 'speak daggers to her, but use none' (3.2.394–5). Now that they are together, and that she is indeed beginning to show signs of remorse for the 'black and grainèd spots' that darken her soul and will not surrender their 'tinct' or dark stain, Hamlet launches into a veritable sermon. 'Confess yourself to heaven', he urges her. 'Repent what's past, avoid what is to come.' He moves on to some very practical advice. 'Go not to my uncle's bed,' he insists. 'Assume a virtue, if you have it not.' The way to recover from having surrendered to sinful behavior is to take one step at a time, mechanically at first until virtuous conduct becomes more familiar and easy. Habit works both ways; it can quickly seduce us into moral slovenliness, but it can be enlisted in the more slow and painful process of recovery. 'To the use of actions fair and good / He [Custom] likewise gives a frock or livery.' 'Refrain tonight, / And that shall lend a kind of easiness / To the next abstinence; the next more easy.' The last thing Hamlet asks of his mother is to believe that he is sane, and refrain from telling Claudius that Hamlet is mad only 'in craft' (3.4.90–203).

These admonitions ask us to consider what is the exact nature of Gertrude's 'black and grainèd spots', and also whether she then makes the attempt to recover herself that Hamlet urges. The signs are encouraging that she does. After Hamlet has left her, dragging away the corpse of the dead Polonius, Gertrude reports to her husband that Hamlet, 'Mad as the sea and wind when both contend', has slain Polonius (4.1.7–8). That is, she lies to her husband as Hamlet has asked her to do, supporting his fiction that he is mad. We see her less with Claudius in the rest of the play, as he plots with Laertes to kill Hamlet unfairly in a fencing match. The result is that, in the final scene, she knows nothing of the poisoned wine. When Hamlet does well in the fencing with Laertes, his mother showers him with attentions and then proposes to drink a 'carouse' to his good fortune. Seeing her take the poisoned cup, the distraught King bids her, 'Gertrude, do not drink', but she does: 'I will, my lord, I pray you pardon me' (5.2.291–4). Whether she surmises that the wine is poisoned and drinks it in an expiatory suicide, or, more likely, drinks the wine because she wants to make a public gesture of support and love for her son, the fact is that she directly disobeys an order from her husband. In a culture like that of Elizabethan England, wives were bound to obey their husbands. Gertrude has declared her allegiance; she has come back to Hamlet, as he asked. The two of them die in a spirit of mutual forgiveness. Probably Gertrude knew nothing of her husband's plans to kill Hamlet senior, but she has been painfully aware that she deserted her son in her new marriage. Now, at last, she joins him in death.

Hamlet's mood changes after he is banished to England and manages to make his return. Up until now he has shown himself to be under terrific emotional pressure to carry out his father's command of revenge. He has lacerated himself for being a 'dull and muddy-mettled rascal' who can say or do nothing in behalf of a father-king 'Upon whose property and most dear life / A damned defeat was made.' 'Am I a coward?' he asks himself, concluding that he must be 'pigeon-livered' to do nothing but prate when he is 'Prompted to my revenge by heaven and hell' (2.2.567–85). As late as Act 4, scene 4, just as he is about to be shipped to England, he pauses to wonder if it is 'Bestial oblivion, or some craven scruple / Of thinking too precisely on th'event' that has kept him from acting (4.4.41–2).

Yet even as he asks these hard questions of himself, Hamlet sees the problem. Immediate action does not always prove to be the best choice. Hamlet is both fascinated and puzzled by the example of Fortinbras, his Norwegian counterpart, whom Claudius has given permission to cross Denmark in order that he may attack Poland. Meeting one of Fortinbras's officers, Hamlet is curious to know what Fortinbras hopes to gain by that foray into another country. Is the land worth seizing? Well, no, it turns out; no one in his right mind would choose to farm it. Does that mean that the Polish army won't bother to defend it? No, comes the answer, 'it is already garrisoned'. Hamlet is astonished, as we are meant to be. 'Two thousand souls and twenty thousand ducats / Will not debate the question of this straw', he comments. Fortinbras and his army will undertake to expose 'what is mortal and unsure / To all that fortune, death, and danger dare, / Even for an eggshell'. War of this sort is, to Hamlet, an emblem of the sheer absurdity of some bold actions. War may seem splendid to the generals, but the stark consequence of such vainglory is 'The imminent death of twenty thousand men / That for a fantasy and trick of fame / Go to their graves like beds' (4.4.26–63). Hamlet cannot help admiring Fortinbras, even to the point of vowing to act swiftly as Fortinbras has done, but he also sees the massive irony.

If we explore this paradox further, we perceive that the play is filled with examples of misconceived action. Hamlet sees that his killing of Polonius is a prime example; he should have moved more carefully, it seems. Laertes determines on swift action when he hears that Hamlet has killed Polonius and that Ophelia has gone insane as a result, and so Laertes resolves to kill Hamlet by whatever means necessary. The result is that Laertes consents to a plot of secret poison that goes against his finer nature. He is of course right that Hamlet is the slayer of Polonius. Should he not then act at once on that perception, without waiting for further thoughts to complicate the picture? The trouble, of course, is that Laertes does not know the identity of the real villain. Claudius is in back of all that is wrong in Denmark. Laertes unknowingly conspires with Claudius to commit a secret murder. Too late, as he and Hamlet both lie dying, Laertes understands the mistake he has made, and begs Hamlet's pardon; and Hamlet, having made a mistake too, begs pardon of Laertes. They die together in reconciliation, having come to the realization that inadequately considered action can play into the hands of evil men. Laertes and Hamlet are alike in having sought to avenge the wrongful death of a father; Fortinbras is still another. All three are object lessons in the philosophical problem of when and how to act.

On his return from England, Hamlet seems calm. His conversation about death with Horatio and the gravediggers in Ophelia's graveyard is witty, ironic, almost serene, as though Hamlet is preparing himself for death. He sees with brilliant clarity the vanity of human wishes that ultimately reduces all lawyers, courtiers, and even the Emperor Alexander to becoming a handful of dust in the grave, since we all must die (5.1.183–216). Yet this wry perception does not mean that life is simply purposeless and existential. To Horatio, Hamlet expresses his profound conviction that 'There's a divinity that shapes our ends, / Rough-hew them how we will'. As before, when he killed Polonius, Hamlet feels sure that divine wisdom is somehow in charge of all that happens; now he sees that pattern with more confidence and faith in an unseen goodness. Even rashness has its place in the scheme of things. 'Let us know', he assures Horatio, 'Our indiscretion sometime serves us well / When our deep plots do pall'. His particular example, as he looks back over his own recent history, is the way in which he suddenly realized, on the sea voyage to England with Rosencrantz and Guildenstern, that he could search their luggage at night and exchange their names for his in the death warrant being carried to the King of England. Hamlet had no trouble acting decisively on that occasion, and has no qualms now about the resulting deaths of his onetime friends. 'Why, man, they did make love to this employment', he insists to Horatio (5.2.6–57).

Hamlet is confident that somehow all will come out for the best, and that his story will have the shape that such a story ought to have. When Horatio responds to Hamlet's confession that all is ill 'here about my heart' by urging that he not accept Laertes's challenge to a fencing match, Hamlet is calmly determined to go ahead:

Not a whit, we defy augury. There is special providence in the fall of a sparrow. If it be now, 'tis not to come; if it be not to come, it will be now;

Hamlet, Act 5, scene 1. Laurence Olivier as Hamlet in Ophelia's graveyard, in Olivier's 1948 film. (British Film Institute/London Features International)

if it be not now, yet it will come. The readiness is all. Since no man of aught he leaves knows, what is't to leave betimes? Let be.

(5.2.217–22)

Hamlet seems to recall the biblical injunctions: 'Are not five sparrows sold for two farthings, and not one of them is forgotten before God?' (Luke 12:6), and 'Consider the lilies of the field, how they grow; they toil not, neither do they spin. / And yet I say unto you, That even Solomon in all his glory was not arrayed like one of these' (Matthew 6:28–9). The idea that 'What must be, shall be' is a commonplace of folk wisdom. Hamlet embraces the idea now, as he waits to see what will happen in his fencing match with Horatio.

That is all very well, but it leaves us in a great puzzle as to how we are to understand the Ghost's earlier command that Hamlet revenge his murder. Was he to accomplish that revenge by letting providence decide how he was to proceed? His one most energetic intervention led to the killing of Polonius, and that was a mistake. At the same time, 'rashness' too has its proper place in the scheme of things. How is Hamlet to know what to do? His problem reminds us of another piece of folk wisdom: 'Lord, give me the strength to change things that ought to be changed, and the patience to bear what cannot be changed, and the wisdom to know the difference.'

One possible key to this paradox in *Hamlet* is to consider that the play tells two stories. One is a pagan Norse story of bloody revenge, taken from Shakespeare's chief source in Saxo Grammaticus, in which the Hamlet figure acts without remorse in accord with the dictates of the revenge code. That code has its own ethic: an eye for an eye, a brother for a brother, a father for a father. The ethic is, however, at odds with the more 'civilized' and Christian code in which Hamlet and his father have lived. In his vengeful mood Hamlet speaks of wanting to send Claudius's soul direct to hell, but more often he is a person of refined sensibility who shuns suicide and preaches repentance to his mother. The Ghost's command to revenge came out of the pagan story, and is motivated in the play by a very understandable feeling on the part of Hamlet and his father that what Claudius has done deserves death. Yet is the hero of the play to carry out the sentence in cold blood? When he sees Claudius undefended and at prayer, he draws back. Hamlet needs a way to kill Claudius with grace and style and moral justification.

The play finally provides him just that. Having resolved to put himself at the service of an overseeing providence to which he now implicitly trusts his whole life and mission, Hamlet enters into a fencing match with Laertes on honorable terms. He does well in the match, scoring points and bidding fair to win the wager. Only when he is wounded by what was supposed to have been Laertes's blunted weapon does Hamlet realize that his life is in danger. He attacks furiously, in self-defense, and kills Laertes. Then, learning from Laertes that his weapon's point was poisoned and that 'The King, the King's to blame', Hamlet turns immediately and thrusts the poisoned weapon into Claudius. 'The point envenomed too? Then, venom, to thy work' (5.2.323–4). The response is instantaneous and visceral. It involves no premeditation, even though Hamlet has spent the entire play trying to figure out how to kill Claudius. It is ethically justifiable as an act of self-defense (since Claudius has just attempted to kill Hamlet), so that Hamlet dies as a noble and heroic victim rather than as a killer. This is a remarkable achievement on Shakespeare's part, when we consider that Hamlet has killed, or contributed to the deaths of, just about every major figure in the play: Polonius, Rosencrantz, Guildenstern, Ophelia (indirectly),

Laertes, and Claudius. Perhaps we should even add Gertrude, since she drank the poisoned wine in his honor. Hamlet achieves his revenge without having had to plot it. Having longed for his own death, he also dies bravely and without committing suicide. These are the ways in which, as Hamlet sees it, a special providence has indeed shaped his ends.

Yet Horatio reads Hamlet's story in very different terms. The account that he will give Fortinbras and the other survivors is

> Of carnal, bloody, and unnatural acts,
> Of accidental judgments, casual slaughters,
> Of deaths put on by cunning and forced cause,
> And, in this upshot, purposes mistook
> Fall'n on th'inventors' heads.
>
> (5.2.383–7)

Horatio's view of history, unlike Hamlet's, is skeptical and secular. No benign guiding force oversees the events of Horatio's narrative; it is instead a story of violence, accident, and wanton suffering. To the extent that he does see a pattern, it is one of ironic turn and counterturn, in which villainy undoes itself through its own attempts at cleverness. As Laertes confesses, he is 'a woodcock to mine own springe' or trap, 'justly killed with mine own treachery' (309–10). Claudius prepares a poisoned cup as a backup method of dispatching Hamlet if the poisoned sword fails, and thereby manages to poison the woman for whom in part he committed his terrible crime. Hamlet has seen a similar grim irony at work in the fates of Rosencrantz and Guildenstern: he has contrived to delve beneath their mines and blow them up, demonstrating that it is 'sport to have the engineer / Hoist with his own petard' (3.4.213–16). Both Hamlet and Horatio see a suitable justice, then, in the way that villainy undoes itself, but Horatio is the chronicler of this process while Hamlet is the seer. With a fitting indeterminacy, Shakespeare ends his endlessly problematic play about Hamlet by showing us how it can be interpreted in such profoundly different ways. No play offers a better challenge to us as we attempt to learn how to read Shakespeare.

6

King Lear

As with *Hamlet*, a good way to read *King Lear* is to begin at the beginning, and without preconceptions. Some excellent films are available to get one started. The list includes:

- Peter Brook's starkly existential interpretation of the play in 1970–1 with Paul Scofield in the title role, Ian Hogg as Edmund, Irene Worth as Goneril, Anne-Lise Gabold as Cordelia, Jack MacGowran as the Fool, Cyril Cusack as Albany, and Robert Lloyd as Edgar.
- Grigori Kozintsev's 1970 film in Russian, with music by Dmitri Shostakovich and with Yuri Yarvet as Lear, Valentina Shendrikova as Cordelia, Elsa Radzina as Goneril, Galina Volchek as Regan, Oleg Dal as the Fool, Leonard Merzin as Edgar, and Regimastas Adomaitis as Edmund.
- Michael Elliott's 1983 film with Laurence Olivier as the aging king, Anna Calder-Marshall as Cordelia, Dorothy Tutin as Goneril, Diana Rigg as Regan, Colin Blakely as Kent, John Hurt as the Fool, Leo McKern as Gloucester, David Threlfal as Edgar, and Robert Lindsay as Edmund.
- Akira Kurosawa's *Ran* (1985), which adapts the story to the warlord culture of sixteenth-century Japan. Although it retains none of Shakespeare's incomparable language, it is a remarkably moving interpretation of the play. With Tatsuya Nakadai as the Lear figure, Hidetora Ichimonji, and Mieko Harada as the vengeful Lady Kaede.

The play is often staged. Most importantly, we have the text of the play itself, available in many current editions.

These editions vary among themselves to an unusual degree, owing to the fact that Shakespeare's Folio text of 1623 departs significantly from the earlier quarto text of 1607. The changes seem to give us different stage versions, with cuts that may have been made to shorten the time of performance along with some additions and revisions that appear to be authorial. Censorship may have played a role. These are important matters, and can affect one's interpretation of the play. Even so, my own recommendation is that the careful study of textual difficulties is better left for later on, after one has become acquainted with *King Lear*. A single text that is based on the Folio version along with restored readings from the quarto (since they may have been cut for reasons of length of performance, and are undoubtedly by Shakespeare) seems to me the best basis for starting, and a number of current editions provide just such a reading text.

Fortunately, in any case, the opening scenes do not vary much from quarto to Folio, and here is where we want to begin. A number of questions insistently present themselves. First, why does Shakespeare begin his long first scene with a brief conversation in which the Earl of Gloucester introduces his illegitimate son Edmund to the Earl of Kent? The story of Gloucester's family is to be the subplot of the play and is not mentioned again in the course of scene 1. Evidently, Gloucester's relationship to Edmund is to be important to *King Lear* as a whole, or Shakespeare would not have begun this way. We surmise that we will learn more about the story of an illegitimate son whom the Earl of Gloucester begot in a moment of extramarital pleasure. We gather that Gloucester is rather complacent about his bastardizing; he is wealthy and powerful, and, like many an aristocrat, believes that his money can pay for his pleasure. He can afford a comfortable income for Edmund, though that young man will not be able to inherit the earldom. Gloucester's purpose in introducing Edmund to Kent is presumably that of making useful contacts for Edmund. The young man is being initiated into the aristocratic life of the court; he will be a courtier. Kent accepts the role of sponsor that he is asked to assume. All seems well enough arranged. At the same time, a good actor in the role of Edmund can let us know, by means of shifting glances and a sardonic politeness, that he is restless with his father's complacency and with the arbitrary turnings of fate that have consigned him to be excluded from the line of inheritance. We will hear more of Edmund in scene 2.

In the meantime, more questions press upon us. Indeed, any reading of *King Lear* encounters a host of painful and ultimately unanswerable questions – more so, perhaps, than in any other Shakespeare play. Why does

Cordelia refuse, in the play's opening scene, to tell her father what she must know he wants to hear her say, that she loves him more than words can express? Why does he banish her for this refusal and turn the divided kingdom over to Cordelia's two older and treacherous sisters, Goneril and Regan? Why, at the play's end, must Cordelia die? That is, why does the playwright choose to dramatize this devastating triumph of injustice when his sources, and indeed an important stage version of the story that came after Shakespeare, choose to follow the traditional account in which Lear is restored to his favorite daughter? In the play's second plot of the Earl of Gloucester and his two sons, Edgar and Edmund, what are we to make of the bastard Edmund's easy success in deceiving his gullible father into believing that the older and legitimate son, Edgar, is plotting against the father's life, with the consequence that Edmund displants his older brother as heir to the earldom, then displants his father as Earl of Gloucester, and is well on his way to becoming Duke of Cornwall and even King of England until, at the last moment, he is exposed as the villain that he really is? Why is injustice able to prevail unchecked to an extent seldom seen in any literary work? And why, when he stands publicly accused of adultery and attempted murder, does Edmund agree to fight with an anonymous challenger who then proves to be Edmund's nemesis? *Hamlet* too is full of questions, but those in *Lear* seem especially devastating since they question the existence of justice not only on earth but in the cosmos, in the very scheme of things. Why does Shakespeare pursue this apocalyptic vision of human unhappiness to such extremes, and what as readers or viewers are we to make of the play's titanic pessimism?

One question which the opening scene does not explore, curiously, is whether Lear's decision to divide his kingdom among his three daughters and their husbands (including Cordelia's, once she has married) is a foolish decision. To many readers it seems unwise. Certainly it embodies an age-old anxiety among the British that their kingdom is really three disconnected territories, with Albany or Scotland to the north (where Goneril is married to the Duke of Albany), Wales and Celtic Britain to the west and southwest (where Regan is the consort of the Duke of Cornwall), and the heartland of England in the south and east, including London and the prosperous southern counties of Kent and Middlesex, where Lear plans to spend his happiest days with his favorite daughter, Cordelia, as wife of either the Duke of Burgundy or the King of France. It is to Cordelia that Lear offers 'A third more opulent than your sisters'' (1.1.86). The plan seems divisive, and yet no courtier speaks against it. The play's opening private conversation between the earls of Gloucester and Kent is full of expect-ant gossip as to which of his sons-in-law Lear favors most in 'the division of the kingdom' (4), but without a hint of disapproval of the plan itself – not even from Kent, who shortly will show himself to be the fearlessly loyal counselor willing to risk the King's disfavor by candidly protesting against the banishment of Cordelia. Clearly the division has already been deter-mined, and is accepted by the court as a *fait accompli*, awaiting only the ceremony of official ratification. Arguably, then, the division is a politically sagacious move on the King's part to hold his powerful sons-in-law at arm's length by a balancing of power in which the favorite child, Cordelia, is to play a central role at Britain's geographical center. Perhaps the courtiers present see some useful purpose in Lear's plan to marry his favorite daughter to a husband who is powerful enough as a continental ruler to fend off the contending claims of Albany to the north and Cornwall to the west. We cannot be sure. Lear seems to be in control. The division of the kingdom is his plan for coping with a succession in which he has no sons of his own to whom he can transfer power. His hope is 'that future strife / May be prevented now' (44–5).

If Cordelia is to be a key player in this delicate negotiation, she fails spectacularly to follow the script that Lear has written for her. The older sisters know what is expected of them, and they perform brilliantly. Lear wants a pledge from each of his daughters that his gift of territory and wealth will be amply reciprocated: they are to honor and venerate him, to look after him in his old age, and (as he says a short time later) to allow him to 'retain / The name and all th'addition to a king' (135–6). Goneril and Regan promise that and more. Goneril swears that she loves their father 'Dearer than eyesight, space, and liberty', while Regan professes that she is 'alone felicitate / In your dear Highness' love' (56, 75–6). They are doing what Lear asks, taking part in a public ceremony of ratifying an agreement by acceding to its terms. Their language is that of excessive and even out-rageous flattery, but such is the language of the court to which Lear has become accustomed and on which he thrives.

Such flattery is his due, as Lear views the matter. Why cannot Cordelia consent to take part in a public ritual of acknowledgment? Cordelia states that she does indeed love and honor her father, and willingly owes him obedience. These are fit duties, for, as she says, 'You have begot me, bred me, loved me' (96). Why then does she draw back from saying more? Why is she willing to break her father's heart by what he perceives to be base ingratitude? The answer must remain uncertain, but one important clue has to do with her impending marriage. Whoever that husband is to be, she insists that 'Haply, when I shall wed, / That lord whose hand must take my plight shall carry / Half my love with him, half my care and duty' (100–2). Cordelia is not the sort of independent-minded woman who questions the hierarchy of a male-centered world. Quite the contrary. Her point is rather that when she marries she will transfer some of the loyalty she owes her father to her new husband. She explicitly contrasts herself in this with her sisters, who have professed love for their father over all other considerations. 'Sure I shall never marry like my sisters, / To love my father all', she pointedly insists (103–4).

Goneril and Regan are of course lying when they make such fulsome protestations; if we don't know this now, we surely will do so by the scene's end when the two of them conspire to make sure that Lear's 'last surrender of his will' (308) will not work to their disadvantage. Cordelia refuses to lie this way, even in what might appear to be the 'harmless' platitudes of courtly flattery. She wants her father to understand the realities of aging and of having marriageable daughters: those daughters will transfer their affections in good part to their new partners. Desdemona, in *Othello*, makes a similar point to her father Brabantio when she marries Othello. She will leave her father's house to devote her loyalties to a new lord and master, just as Brabantio's wife did when he married her. This is the cycle of the generation; it is as 'natural' as life itself. But Lear is not prepared to understand that idea. To him it smacks of desertion and rejection. To him it is 'unnatural' in that it seems to abrogate the duty a child owes its parent. Cordelia does not intend, of course, to reject Lear; she will care for him and cherish him, as indeed she does in the course of the play even after Lear has rejected her. Sadly, Lear cannot hear any profession of love in Cordelia's quietly stubborn refusal to say more. He wants all. Perhaps it is because he wants all that he cannot have it. Lear feels he is entitled to all, as king, as father. The play may suggest that such a feeling of entitlement is the surest way to lose what one so desires. Nowhere is this more true than in the case of an aging father who feels that he is entitled to total and unquestioning love and obedience from his children.

Many other issues remain to be considered in the play's opening scene, but let us for the moment move on to the second plot, in scene 2. In no other tragedy does Shakespeare employ such an elaborate double-plotted structure as he does in *King Lear*. It is a device he employs much more commonly in his comedies. Why does he do so here? Shakespeare's dramaturgic strategy is to say nothing in his own person as dramatist, but instead to let the juxtaposition of scenes speak for itself; we are implicitly asked to do the critical work, as audience, of making sense of the connection. After a long opening scene in which an aging king banishes his favorite daughter and relinquishes his power to his two scheming daughters, we now encounter a scene in which an aging nobleman is persuaded by his duplicitous illegitimate younger son to disinherit his well-meaning and loyal older son and heir, Edgar. The genders are reversed in these parallel actions of scenes 1 and 2, and so are the relative ages of older and younger children – Lear's youngest child is the virtuous one, whereas Gloucester's elder son holds that position in the subplot – but the issues of loyalty and deception are much the same. Accordingly, we wonder now what it is about the Earl of Gloucester that makes him so vulnerable to the flattering insinuations of his ruthless younger son, and so unable to see through the deceptions that are made so plain to us as audience or as readers. In what ways is Gloucester like Lear?

One concept that emerges from a comparison of scenes 1 and 2 is the matter of defining what is 'natural'. The King of France, in scene 1, supposes at first that Cordelia's offense against Lear must be 'of such unnatural degree' as to make it monstrous, since nothing else would explain the severity of Lear's sentence in banishing her. Lear's explanation for his decision, however, is considerably less serious as an indictment: Cordelia should have found a way 't'have pleased me [her father] better'. 'Is it but this?' France replies. 'A tardiness in nature / Which often leaves the history unspoke / That it intends to do?' (1.1.221–41). 'Natural' for Lear means, among other things, the duty that a child owes its parent; his colloquy with France rests on the assumption that duty, obedience, and hierarchy are inherent qualities in a just and divinely ordered universe. France, for his part, thinks it 'natural' for Cordelia to have been reluctant to promise more than she intends to act. The word is in debate.

Edmund, in scene 2, proposes a radically different meaning for 'nature' and 'natural'. 'Thou, Nature, art my goddess', be begins, in a disarmingly frank soliloquy addressed to us as audience with no one else on stage. To Edmund, old-fashioned ideas of the 'natural' as demanding obedience and loyalty to parents are symptomatic of 'the plague of custom' and 'The curiosity of nations' (3–4) – that is, social custom devised by those in authority as means of enforcing the power of the entrenched social structure. The custom of primogeniture, for instance, specifying that property is to descend to the eldest male heir, strikes Edmund as arbitrary and unfair. It may seem so to us, too, from our modern perspective. In Edmund's case, the exclusion is intensified by his having been illegitimately born and hence further barred from inheritance by law and custom. Does Edmund's resentment of being treated as inferior, owing to circumstances over which he had no control, awaken our sympathy? Is there not something refreshingly skeptical and even modern in his readiness to challenge time-honored and stale custom?

Edmund is certainly more quick-witted than his father. As a young man standing outside the prescribed social order, he is an astute critic of tired old ways. The Earl of Gloucester exemplifies the old school, and in a way that does it little credit. He is what we would call superstitious. He is firmly convinced that 'These late eclipses in the sun and moon' portend trouble. Nature 'finds itself scourged by the sequent effects'. Mutinies and disorders abound, in such a way that the 'bond [is] cracked twixt son and father' (1.2.106–12). Having been credulously misled into believing that his older son Edgar is plotting against his life, Gloucester comes at once to the conclusion that the rebellion has its origin in some vast cosmic disorder, just as King Lear has fallen 'from bias of nature' in banishing his daughter Cordelia. Gloucester sees what is 'unnatural' in that rejection, and yet falls into precisely the same trap himself. Edmund is contemptuous of such mindless traditionalism. 'This is the excellent foppery of the world', he comments sardonically in soliloquy, after his father has left the stage. How fatuous we humans are, he insists, to

> make guilty of our disasters the sun, the moon, and stars, as if we were villains on necessity, fools by heavenly compulsion, knaves, thieves, and treachers by spherical predominance, drunkards, liars, and adulterers by an enforced obedience of planetary influence, and all that we are evil in, by a divine thrusting on. An admirable evasion of whoremaster man, to lay his goatish disposition on the charge of a star!
>
> (1.2.123–31)

Edmund's credo is that he is the author of his own destiny. He would be who he is 'had the maidenliest star in the firmament twinkled on my bastardizing' (134–6).

Today, we are drawn to sympathize with this credo of the self-made individual. At the same time, Edmund is self-proclaimedly a villain. He reasons cleverly that by freeing his mind of superstitious cant, he can gain a tactical advantage over those who subscribe to conventional moral views of obedience, loyalty, and just dealing. Edmund proceeds to demonstrate just how effectively his proposition can be made to work. He lies to his father about his half-brother and succeeds in turning Gloucester against Edgar by playing on the old man's fears that a son and heir might be eager to push his father out of the way. Because Edgar is trusting and decent, Edmund is also successful in persuading Edgar that Edmund has his brother's best interests at heart in bidding that older brother to flee the wrath of their incensed father. Edmund's skill in manipulating the credulous members of his family astonishes us; Edmund is a brilliant tactician, and his credo of self-fashioning is so modern that we see the intellectual force of his skepticism. Yet cannot one be a skeptic about corrupt older customs and still decide to behave decently and honorably? Need a skeptic be a villain? Shakespeare thus poses a question that hangs over the remainder of the play.

For an agonizingly long time, in both the Lear plot and the Gloucester plot, we are forced to confront the evidence that villainy can indeed go a very long way by taking advantage of those who are constrained by traditional moral obligations. Goneril and Regan agree that their best way to deal with a crotchety old father, long accustomed to having his way, is to scant their hospitality and thereby bring him to heel. Goneril orders her steward, Oswald, to make Lear uncomfortable when he pays his first visit to her and her husband, the Duke of Albany, in Scotland. 'Put on what weary negligence you please, / You and your fellows', she instructs him. 'I'd have it come to question.' She knows that Regan will do the same, since Regan's 'mind and mine, I know, in that are one, / Not to be overruled' (1.3.13–17). Lear is indeed a lot to handle; accompanied by his hundred knights and many servants, he has crowded the facilities of Goneril and Albany's castle to the extent that conflicts between the two households now living on top of each other have become inevitable. Peter Brook's film version of *King Lear* (1970–1) graphically illustrates what the continual melee would have been like. Goneril has a point; as she says of her father, 'he hath ever but slenderly known himself' (1.1.296–7). At the same time, her calculated cruelty strikes us as inhumane, especially when she goads him into leaving Scotland for the household of her sister, where, Goneril knows, Regan's reception of their father will be just as unwelcoming as Goneril's has been. Even Goneril's husband, the mild-mannered Albany, worries that she is being too abrupt and severe.

Regan's reception of Lear is indeed as callous as we have feared, knowing as we do that the two sisters have intended to act in concert. Furthermore, Regan enjoys the support of her husband, the Duke of

Cornwall, in a way that Goneril does not. Regan and Cornwall have hit upon a plan that will baffle Lear's plea for their hospitality even before the visit can commence. Forewarned by letter of Lear's coming, they determine not to be at home in their own ducal palace, but instead descend on the household of the Earl of Gloucester and await Lear's arrival there. Because Gloucester owes feudal obedience to the Duke and Duchess of Cornwall as his overlords, he cannot refuse them hospitality, and indeed such a visit would normally be considered a deep honor to the recipient. In this present instance, however, the visit is uncannily like Lear's own unwished-for arrival in Scotland a short time earlier; that is, Gloucester finds himself overwhelmed with visitors whose servants crowd his house and whose superior position in the feudal hierarchy overrides his own. The painful upshot is that Gloucester finds himself unable to intervene when Regan demands that Lear return to Goneril's residence in Scotland for the stipulated month's visit and then come to her, having meantime divested himself of half his 'train' or retinue (2.4.202–5). Again, Regan has a plausible argument on her side: 'How in one house / Should many people under two commands / Hold amity?', she asks (242–3). This is what Goneril meant earlier when she demanded of Lear 'A little to disquantity your train' (1.4.246). When Lear refuses to obey Regan, as he has refused to obey Goneril, choosing instead in his rage and distraction to rush out into a gathering storm, Gloucester is powerless to stop what is happening. Regan has declared that she will allow Lear to come back out of the storm into Gloucester's house, 'But not one follower' (2.4.294–5). Gloucester is thus denied the right to offer hospitality in his own house to the person he still honors as his king.

As Lear encounters his fearful ordeal in Goneril's and then in Regan's household, a companion on whom he increasingly depends is his Fool. The utterances of the Fool are gnomic and often hard to decipher in detail, partly perhaps because a new comic actor named Robert Armin had joined Shakespeare's acting company in about 1598 with his special 'line' of foolish wisdom as his stock-in-trade; perhaps also because the tragedy of Lear raises such complex issues of wisdom and folly. Despite the sometimes riddling nature of the Fool's witticisms, what he has to say to Lear (and us) is, on the whole, clear if also paradoxical. As a professional fool, his business is to see what is ridiculous in the supposedly sane behavior of his nominal superiors; his being a fool gives him a kind of license to say what ordinary counselors and advisers to a king would not dare to utter. From first to last, the Fool dares to suggest that King Lear is the truly foolish one – even more so than the Fool himself. Lear is foolish in many ways: to have relinquished authority to his daughters and then expect them to continue in their obedience to him (1.4.99–101), to hope that Regan will be more kind than Goneril when any fool can see that the two sisters are as alike as two crab apples (1.5.14–16), to suppose that old age will be reverenced by the young, and so on.

These plain truths spoken by the Fool take the paradoxical form of conundrums. Lear has banished his two cruel daughters, the Fool quips, and has done the third 'a blessing against his will' (1.4.97–102) – i.e., he has alienated Goneril and Regan by giving them such power that they will soon be rid of him, whereas Lear has given Cordelia the paradoxical blessing of separating her from the ruinous effects of good fortune. The Fool thus inverts the seeming truth of the matter, which is that Lear has banished Cordelia and bestowed his blessings on her sisters. The Fool next compares Lear to a hapless rider ignominiously forced to carry his own mount instead of riding on it himself in the usual course of events (159). Similarly, says the Fool, Lear has made his daughters his mothers by putting the rod of correction in their hands while taking down his own breeches to receive a whipping (169–71). He is like a hedge sparrow feeding a newly hatched chick that a cuckoo bird has planted in its nest; the sparrow is unaware until too late that the fledgling cuckoo will grow up and kill the foster-parent (213–14). Lear is a fool for having grown old before he learned to be wise (1.5.43–4). He is a fool not to let go of a wheel that is plummeting downhill, instead of hitching his wagon to 'the great one that goes upward' (2.4.70–3). He is a fool not to come out of the rain when it begins to storm (76–9).

Even though Lear scarcely hears these quaint admonishments of the Fool, we hear them as audience. We perceive, moreover, that they are offered in a profoundly paradoxical sense. Of course Lear is a fool for all the reasons that the Fool has cited. Yet we realize that the Fool has no intention of following his own advice. He will not abandon Lear when the King's fortunes are heading lower and lower, as a supposedly wise person would do. 'But I will tarry', he sings; 'the fool will stay, / And let the wise man fly' (2.4.80–1). That is because to run away is to be a fool in the deepest sense of the word. Wisdom and folly change places in the Fool's gnomic wisdom. To be wise as the world defines that term is to be in danger of becoming insolent, selfish, and indifferent to the sufferings of others. Only the foolish – i.e., those who are 'foolish' enough to practice charity and kindness even at great risk to themselves – will be rewarded with the higher wisdom of understanding what things truly matter in life. They will do so, however, at the huge cost of being frequently victimized, pushed aside, humiliated, and forgotten.

These paradoxes are often found at the heart of the world's great religions, including Christianity. To Erasmus, in his *The Praise of Folly* (1509), Christ is a kind of fool in the same paradoxical sense that the Fool in *Lear* employs. To give all that one has to the poor – not just some, but all – is to embark on a radical course of charity according to which the material things of this world are to be seen as temptations that human beings must eschew if they are to find spiritual enlightenment. This idea is 'radical' not in the sense of fomenting social revolution, but in the sense of getting back to the root meaning (Latin: *radix*, root) of Christian teaching. *King Lear* is set in pre-Christian Britain, before the time of Christ, but the ideals of charitable forgiveness and renunciation of worldly prosperity are everywhere apparent in Shakespeare's text. The Fool's paradoxes are very close to those of the King of France, who, in praising Cordelia, speaks of her as one who is 'most rich being poor, / Most choice, forsaken, and most loved, despised' (1.1.254–5). These are the oxymorons of the Sermon on the Mount in the New Testament: 'Blessed are the poor in spirit: for theirs is the kingdom of heaven', 'Blessed are the meek: for they shall inherit the earth', 'Blessed are the merciful: for they shall obtain mercy', 'Blessed are they which are persecuted for righteousness' sake: for theirs is the kingdom of heaven', and so on (Matthew 5:1–12). Cordelia embodies these paradoxes perhaps more than any other character in *King Lear*. And Cordelia is, in this spiritualized sense, a fool. That is, she practices charity and forgiveness at the expense of the worldly self-interest that is conventionally associated with wisdom.

The Earl of Kent is another such charitable fool. So distressed is he at Lear's banishment of Cordelia in scene 1 that he endangers his own welfare by speaking up when ordered by the King to remain silent, and so he too is sent into banishment. One might suppose that such a wronged nobleman would resent the king who has treated him so unjustly, but this fool further endangers his own life by coming back in disguise to serve the king who has sentenced him to death if he ever sets foot in the kingdom (1.1.179–81). Kent so loves his master that he is willing to take this risk. Once in service as 'Caius', Kent further endangers his own safety by tripping up Goneril's steward, Oswald, when that officious servant (Kent's counterpart in Goneril's household) has slighted Lear in obedience to Goneril's directive. When he is sent with letters on Lear's behalf to Cornwall and Regan, Kent again tangles with Oswald and manages to get himself thrown in the stocks for rioting and insubordination. Indeed, Kent has picked a quarrel with Oswald, whom he contemptuously regards as a servile time-pleaser, and is guilty of battery in assaulting Oswald without visible provocation; Cornwall is determined to teach such a troublemaker a lesson he won't soon forget. The fact that 'Caius' or Kent has been sent on an official ambassadorial mission by King Lear does not deter Cornwall; instead, he seems to welcome the opportunity to deliver a deliberate insult to the King in the person of his emissary. The upshot is that Kent must sleep out the night in the stocks, where Lear finds him. The stage picture of an earl suffering the humiliating indignity of being stocked (a punishment usually reserved for 'basest and contemned'st wretches / For pilferings and most common trespasses', 2.2.145–7) is an apt emblem of the appalling inversions of fortune to which this play testifies. Kent's ending up at the bottom of Fortune's wheel (176) will be followed in short order by Lear's suffering in the storm and by Gloucester's being arrested for assisting Lear in his agony.

Edgar too becomes identified as a fool in this devastating inversion of wisdom and folly. Once heir to the earldom of Gloucester, Edgar finds himself obliged to disguise himself as Poor Tom, a kind of 'Bedlam beggar' (2.3.14) or madman with his hair all in elf-knots and only a blanket to shield his body from the raging elements. Like the Fool, Edgar becomes a companion to the forlorn Lear in his madness, as they seek the shelter of an outbuilding on Gloucester's estate. Edgar is like the Fool too in that he speaks gnomically, almost crazily. His mad tale is of fiends and devils with scary names like Flibbertigibbet, Modo, Mahu, Obidicut, and Hobbididance (3.4.114–42, 4.1.58–60). These are devils from Elizabethan folklore whose names Shakespeare found in Samuel Harsnett's *Declaration of Egregious Popish Impostures* (1603). Edgar's seemingly mad ravings also dwell on licentiousness of every kind. He talks of himself as one who has been

A servingman, proud in heart and mind, that curled my hair, wore gloves in my cap, served the lust of my mistress' heart, and did the act of darkness with her; swore as many oaths as I spake words, and broke them in the sweet face of heaven. One that slept in the contriving of lust and waked to do it. Wine loved I deeply, dice dearly, and in women out-paramoured the Turk. False of heart, light of ear, bloody of hand; hog in sloth, fox in stealth, wolf in greediness, dog in madness, lion in prey. Let not the creaking of shoes nor the rustling of silks betray thy poor heart to woman. Keep thy foot out of brothels, thy hand out of plackets, thy pen from lenders' books, and defy the foul fiend.

(3.4.84–97)

None of this is true of Edgar, of course, but it is more than seeming madness. In its thematic preoccupation with depraved sexuality, oath-breaking, betrayal, and obsessive pursuit of worldly gain, Edgar's vivid imagining of a life of sinful excess touches on everything that the Fool's paradoxes portray as the essence of what is so insane about worldliness. Edgar is thus another 'fool' whose ravings expose to our view the inversions of sanity and wisdom for which *King Lear* is justly famous.

We will want to return to Edgar in his 'sane' persona as the character who, perhaps more than any other, wrestles philosophically and wisely with the existential nightmare posed by the terrifying cruelties perpetrated in the play, but first the play demands that we confront the frightening reality of those cruelties and the sufferings they inflict on the two old men, Lear and Gloucester. Lear's odyssey proceeds relentlessly downward into misery and madness. His first response to his daughters' hardness of heart is incredulity and anger. 'Ingratitude, thou marble-hearted fiend!' he shouts at Goneril as he prepares to leave her castle rather than submit to her insistence that he reduce the size of his entourage (1.4.257). He begs the goddess Nature to dry up in Goneril 'the organs of increase', so that her 'derogate body' will never be able to give birth to a child unless it be one that will be 'a thwart disnatured torment to her', just as, in Lear's view, Goneril has been to her father (275–82). He calls upon the gods to avenge the wrongs he has suffered; the gods will surely do so, since they are so much like him. 'O heavens, / If you do love old men, if your sweet sway / Allow obedience, if you yourselves are old, / Make it your cause; send down, and take my part' (2.4.190–3). Lear, like Gloucester, presupposes a cosmos in which the gods embody order and hierarchy just as human society is also hierarchically ordered. Surely then the gods will reward persons like himself and punish villains like Goneril and Regan. 'You see me here, you gods, a poor old man, / As full of grief as age, wretched in both' (274–5). He threatens the revenges that he feels sure the gods will exact on those who are wicked and disobedient. Yet are the gods listening, or do they even exist? That troubling thought edges Lear toward madness, since to imagine a universe without such gods is to imagine a world in which injustice can triumph and innocence can suffer endlessly.

A stage in Lear's sad decline toward madness is his bargaining with his daughters, and with the gods themselves, supposing that they exist. This is a stage remarkably like that we find in Elisabeth Kubler-Ross's clinical analysis of the stages through which patients invariably go when they learn that they are dying. They are first incredulous and in denial; then they are angrily resentful at what seems intolerably unjust; and then they bargain. Give me another year of life, or save the life of my child, and I will do anything. Lear's version of this is, first, to bargain with his daughters over a hundred knights that are to follow him, then fifty (2.4.205–39), then twenty-five (250), and so on. His position is so pitiably weak that he finds himself agreeing at one point to return to Goneril's household since she offers him (he thinks) fifty knights, which 'yet doth double five-and-twenty, / And thou art twice her [Regan's] love' (260–2). Yet even that reduced offer does not stand. 'What need you five-and-twenty, ten, or five'? asks Goneril, to which Regan chorically rejoins, 'What need one?' (263–5). Later, at the end of the play, Lear will bargain with the gods. Let me keep Cordelia, he seems to say, and you can keep my wealth, my kingdom, even my freedom (see 5.3.8–26). Lear and Cordelia are captured and under threat of execution, but they are together, and for Lear that is more than enough. Yet in the harsh world of this play, the gods, if they exist, do not listen, do not bargain. Lear loses Cordelia after having lost everything else.

An unexpected consolation accompanies Lear's loss of sanity during the terrible storm: he suddenly realizes, for the first time, that other human beings suffer too. 'How dost, my boy?' he says to the Fool, as they consider Kent's invitation to take shelter against the storm in a hovel. 'Art cold? / I am cold myself. – Where is this straw, my fellow? / The art of our necessities is strange, / And can make vile things precious. . . . Poor fool and knave, I have one part in my heart / That's sorry yet for thee' (3.2.68–73). Lear learns compassion in a way that he could learn only by suffering what others suffer too. His misery brings this precious sort of wisdom. It does so, paradoxically, at the very moment that Lear slips into madness. 'My wits begin to turn', he acknowledges (67).

Lear is what we would call clinically mad in the specific sense that he no longer knows to whom he is speaking. Inside Gloucester's house, he was furiously out of control, but he knew he was ranting at Goneril and Regan, and he felt the terrible injustice of their persecutions. Now, in the hovel, he acquires a new interest in fellowship among those who are miserable. He questions mad Tom (Edgar) to know his story, and pities the beggar's 'uncovered body' now exposed to 'this extremity of the skies' (3.4.101). He is eager to converse with 'this philosopher', 'this same learnèd Theban', about such topics as 'the cause of thunder' (152–5). When he thinks he is arraigning Goneril for having 'kicked the poor King her father', he is in fact talking to 'a joint stool', as the Fool points out

(3.6.46–51). Yet, paradoxically, he now speaks with a wisdom he has never known before. His compassionate view of the fallen state of the world is deeply humane in its concern for the poor, and is all the more touching in that the mad Lear now can acknowledge his own dereliction of duty in having allowed injustice to prevail as he has done:

> Poor naked wretches, wheresoe'er you are,
> That bide the pelting of this pitiless storm,
> How shall your houseless heads and unfed sides,
> Your looped and windowless raggedness, defend you
> From seasons such as these? Oh, I have ta'en
> Too little care of this! Take physic, pomp;
> Expose thyself to feel what wretches feel,
> That thou mayst shake the superflux to them
> And show the heavens more just.
>
> (3.4.28–36)

This vision is, like Lear himself, mad: it is apocalyptic, utopian, imagining a world in which inequalities of worldly prosperity are to be erased by a radical redistribution of wealth, taking it from those who have too much (and thus become insolent and hard-hearted in their indifference to the lot of the poor) and giving it to those who have too little. The image is violent and even scatological: 'superflux' suggests 'bodily discharge', as though Lear's social justice is to be achieved by the administration of a gut-wrenching purgative (a 'physic') to the rich. The wealth which corrupts their spiritually disease-ridden bodies will spew forth in order to nourish the poor. This is a utopian vision in which all would benefit, and it seems so simple, yet it is mad in the sense that we know it is never going to happen. The rich will not allow it.

Gloucester arrives at a similar kind of wisdom through his gruesome suffering. Once a French army has landed to rescue Lear from his oppressors, the charitable aid that Gloucester provides to Lear by offering him shelter and protection is technically a treasonous act. Edmund takes advantage of this situation by turning his father over to the Duke of Cornwall as one who is guilty of 'treason' (3.5.13), all the while pretending that he is in agonies of self-recrimination for having to betray his own father. Gloucester is summarily tried as a traitor (3.7.8, 23, 33, 38, 45) and is found guilty by Cornwall, who uses the 'form of justice' of a trial to justify what Cornwall is prompted to by his 'wrath'; as he insolently boasts, his 'power / Shall do a court'sy to our wrath, which men / May blame but not control' (25–8). The trial is thus a travesty of true justice, even though it proceeds through the regular forms of judicial proceeding (while concurrently in his wretched hovel King Lear is madly arraigning Goneril and Regan, showing how a truer justice is to be found in the mad company of the King, poor Tom, and the Fool).

Gloucester's paradoxical discovery of truth proceeds through the inversion of seeing and blindness, in a way that is clearly parallel to Lear's inversions of wisdom and folly, sanity and insanity. Gloucester's cruel fate is to have both of his eyes ground out by Cornwall's booted feet as the old man sits pinioned in a chair. His response, as this terrible thing is about to happen, is to insist that he will 'see / The wingèd Vengeance overtake such children'. Cornwall sees the opportunity for a grisly joke: 'See't shalt thou never', he rejoins, as he proceeds to gouge out one of Gloucester's eyes. When a servant intervenes and is slain for his presumption, gasping out to Gloucester, 'My lord, you have one eye left / To see some mischief on him', Cornwall again has a cruel rejoinder: 'Lest it see more, prevent it. Out, vile jelly!' he exclaims as he puts out Gloucester's other eye. Yet Gloucester may have meant 'see' in a non-physical sense. Certainly when he has been totally blinded, he begins to 'see' for the first time. Crying out on Edmund to revenge this 'horrid act', Gloucester is informed by Regan that Edmund has in fact 'made the overture of thy treasons to us'; he has turned his father over to be blinded in this way. Gloucester's response is quite wonderful and perhaps unexpected: 'Oh, my follies! Then Edgar was abused. / Kind gods, forgive me that, and prosper him!' (3.7.68–95). In other words, he does not cry out in fury against Edmund, as a person in his predicament might do; instead, he is entirely caught up in the terrible realization of what he has unjustly done to Edgar. Gloucester 'sees' the truth at the moment of his blinding, and accepts his own complicity in a miscarriage of justice, just as Lear has gained the wisdom of compassion and repentance just when he began to lose his wits.

The parallel is further pursued in the next scene, when the blind old Gloucester is delivered by servants into the custody of 'poor mad Tom', i.e., Edgar, still in disguise. Brokenhearted at what he has done to Edgar, and of course unaware that he is now talking to that very son whom he has so wronged, Gloucester can think of nothing but how he might make restitution. He gives his purse to the seeming beggar, not realizing that he is in a sense restoring the birthright and inheritance to the very son he thinks he has disinherited. The occasion prompts a reflection that closely parallels what Lear had said in the storm:

> Here, take this purse, thou whom the heavens' plagues
> Have humbled to all strokes. That I am wretched
> Makes thee the happier. Heavens, deal so still!
> Let the superfluous and lust-dieted man,
> That slaves your ordinance, that will not see
> Because he does not feel, feel your pow'r quickly!
> So distribution should undo excess
> And each man have enough.
>
> (4.1.63–70)

Like Lear, old Gloucester begs the gods to take wealth violently away from the rich, who have grown callously insolent in their powerful positions, and bestow it on the poor. Like mad Lear, Gloucester imagines a utopia that will benefit all parties, subjecting the rich and powerful to the kind of chastisement from which Gloucester has gained the wisdom he never could find otherwise, and redistributing 'excess' in such a way that all persons will have 'enough' and not too much. Gloucester's utopia is like Lear's in that it sounds like a perfect answer to the world's vast inequalities, and yet it is one that will never be achieved.

Edgar emerges in this same scene as the play's most thoughtful inquirer into what to make of the appalling cruelty that appears to be thriving on all sides. Like his brother Edmund, Edgar speaks often in soliloquy and in asides to us. Like Edmund, Edgar is a refreshingly iconoclastic speaker who resists the shopworn clichés of their father and of King Lear when they insist that the gods ought to intervene on the side of age and hierarchy. Edgar is too much a realist to expect that; he seeks a philosophical explanation that takes into account the existential fact of self-interested and competitive rivalry as a primal condition of human existence. Like his brother, he accepts that the conditions of life are not controlled by the gods in accord with some predetermined divine plan that will eventually bring justice to the good and punishment to the wicked. At the same time, Edgar appears to reject out of hand his brother's credo that such an existential universe necessarily invites any self-aware individual to be ruthless in seeking an advantage over others in the competition for survival. Edgar is more like Cordelia and Kent: he appears to regard decency and caring for others as worthy endeavors in their own right, not because some god may punish wayward behavior but because it is simply better to be generous and forgiving. Edgar chooses to care for his broken and blinded old father, despite Gloucester's having put a price on Edgar's head, because the old father desperately needs help. Edgar feels deeply the obligation of a son to a father, and he wants to help his father learn to forgive what he has done to Edgar, just as Cordelia needs to help her father find a way to forgive himself for what he has done to her.

Edgar encounters his blind father at just the moment when Edgar has begun to hope that things will take a turn for the better. 'To be worst, / The lowest and most dejected thing of fortune, / Stands still in esperance, lives not in fear', he soliloquizes at the start of Act 4. He is at the very bottom of fortune's ever-turning wheel, and so he supposes that eventually his fortunes must turn upward; they cannot go lower. 'The lamentable change is from the best; / The worst returns to laughter' (4.1.1–6). Those who enjoy good fortune have reason to fear that things may get worse; persons like himself who have nothing to lose have nothing to fear. Edgar shows himself to be a stoic in his philosophic outlook, having learned through hard necessity not to expect anything at Fortune's hands.

Yet he realizes, as he now encounters his blind and ruined father, that he has forgotten something: he has been thinking only of himself, of his own misery. He now discovers with a shock that things can indeed get worse through the sufferings of others. 'O gods!' he exclaims in soliloquy. 'Who is't can say, "I am at the worst"? / I am worse than e'er I was.' Being the philosopher that he is, Edgar goes on to enlarge this perception into a devastatingly candid observation on human life generally: 'And worse I may be yet. The worst is not / So long as we can say, "This is the worst"' (4.1.25–8). As long as we are alive and can still draw breath, the one thing we can count on is that things may get worse. Any attempt to comprehend meaning in human existence is doomed to disappointment if it fails to acknowledge the irrefutable truth of this profoundly non-idealized view. As a stoic and skeptical realist, Edgar struggles to come to terms with life as it exists.

Gloucester needs Edgar's ministrations not simply because he is blind and helpless, but because he is also in suicidal despair. 'As flies to wanton boys are we to th' gods', the old man bitterly concludes. 'They kill us for their sport' (4.1.36–7). Unable to give up his belief in the gods, Gloucester can only conclude that they are malicious. What is Edgar to do? He chooses the strikingly innovative expedient of allowing his father to stage a 'suicide' that involves no actual physical danger. Edgar playacts the business of leading his father to the edge of a Dover cliff, as his father has bidden him (4.1.72–6), where Edgar describes to the blind Gloucester the dizzying heights that seem to open below them. The father bids his companion to let go his hand, and falls forward. He lands, unhurt, on the stage where he has been standing. Only now do we, as audience, realize

that Edgar has misled Gloucester, and us as well: his description of the high
cliff and the sea far below is just the kind of description that an actor would
use on the non-scenic Jacobean stage to evoke a 'real' cliff. We are in the
theatre, and Gloucester is safe. Edgar, discarding the peasant role he has
used as he guided his blind father to Dover, now approaches the fallen
old man as if they were now at the bottom of the huge cliff, Gloucester
having fallen all that height. Edgar conjures up for his father a fantastic
story about a frightening monster standing at the crown of the cliff with
eyes like 'two full moons', 'a thousand noses' and 'Horns whelked and waved
like the enridgèd sea'. 'It was some fiend', Edgar declares, thus manufac-
turing a providential interpretation to account for what the father thinks
must have happened to him. 'Therefore, thou happy father, / Think that
the clearest gods, who make them honors / Of men's impossibilities,
have preserved thee' (4.6.11–74), Edgar concludes. This little drama that
Edgar has staged for his father works. 'I do remember now', says the old
man. 'Henceforth I'll bear / Affliction till it do cry out itself "Enough,
enough," and die' (75–6). Gloucester accepts the seeming truth that the
gods have saved him from his attempted suicide; he is to live until the gods
decree that the time has come for him to die.

These gods are, of course, Edgar's fiction; so too is the fiend looming at
the crown of the cliff. Edgar has practiced deception on his father to prevent a suicide. Why has he done so? In an aside to us, he suggests his motive:
'Why I do trifle thus with his despair / Is done to cure it' (4.6.33–4). Edgar
stages his fiction in this particular way because he knows his father well
enough to realize that the old man needs to believe in a cosmos presided
over by gods whose workings are mysterious but whose intents are ultimately just. Edgar invents a whole cosmology because his father cannot
live without one. Edgar is enough of a skeptic himself to see what fictions
we humans devise to shape the chaotic elements of our universe into some
semblance of a coherent pattern. This is not to say that Edgar is an athe-
ist, but rather to say that any gods in which he could believe must be understood to be immeasurably distant from the daily events of human life.

The Duke of Albany too seeks to understand what to make of humanity's seemingly limitless potential for savagery. Albany sees in this a test as
to whether the gods care about human injustice. When he learns of the
blinding of Gloucester, Albany immediately poses this as a challenge to
his understanding of divine intent. 'If that the heavens do not their visible spirits / Send quickly down to tame these vile offenses', he declares,
'It will come, / Humanity must perforce prey on itself, / Like monsters of

the deep' (4.2.47–51). His observation is close to that of the unnamed servants who have actually witnessed the blinding of Gloucester. In a postlude to the scene of blinding that is found only in the quarto version of the play, they posit a challenge to the very idea of divine purpose. 'I'll never care what wickedness I do, / If this man come to good', says one; if Regan and the others can perform such cruelty without divine punishment, then we all might just as well become criminals. A fellow servant agrees: 'If she [Regan] live long, / And in the end meet the old course of death, / Women will all turn monsters' (3.7.102–5). Yet these servants proceed at once to give aid to the blind old Gloucester, presumably at some risk to themselves for assisting a 'traitor'. Their own reasons for wanting to act charitably override their anxious suspicions that humans need not fear any corrective punishment from the gods.

Like these servants, Albany is aghast at the prospect of a godless universe. Accordingly, he seeks for reassurance by interpreting events to suit his philosophical view when he can. On learning that Cornwall has died in the aftermath of grinding out Gloucester's eyes, Albany sees purposefulness in the event. 'This shows you are above, / You justicers, that these our nether crimes / So speedily can venge!' he declares (4.2.79–80), laying stress on the rapidity of divine punishment he sees in this account. Yet what is Albany to make of the blinding of 'poor Gloucester'? Where is divine justice in that, or in Lear's sufferings? Later, in the play's final scene, Albany is quick to utter a similar pronouncement over the deaths of Goneril and Regan, whom he now knows to have been practiced villains. 'This judgment of the heavens, that makes us tremble, / Touches us not with pity' (5.3.235–6), he insists. Yet what is Albany to make of Kent's odyssey of suffering, and of the deaths of Cordelia and then Lear? As Kent asks, 'Is this the promised end?' (268). The ending of the story is so apocalyptic, so like the image of the Last Judgment when all life shall cease, that Albany is left without an answer. He tries one last time to see a pattern of reward for goodness by declaring that 'All friends shall taste / The wages of their virtue, and all foes / The cup of their deservings' (308–10), but when Lear then dies, Albany's vision of ultimate justice dissipates before his very eyes. To hope for justice at the hands of the gods is to set oneself up for inevitable disappointment. Perhaps it is better, like Edgar, to assume the worst and seek for strength in being true to one's interior moral sense without divine sanction or hope of reward.

Yet villainy in *King Lear* is punished and defeated at last. Goneril and Regan die what can perhaps be construed as edifyingly meaningful deaths:

Goneril confesses that she has poisoned her sister, presumably in jealous anger over their competition to have Edmund as a lover or husband, and then Goneril takes her own life. Their lifeless bodies are '*brought out*' (5.3.241.1) on stage as though to demonstrate that they have suffered just retribution for their crimes. We cannot be sure that the gods, if they exist, had anything to do with this, but at any rate the two sisters are dead, and no one mourns for them. Their own heartless self-assertions have led directly to their deaths. Giving themselves to unbridled lust and desire for power has resulted in their hating each other and themselves enough to commit murder and suicide. Their lives and deaths are thus instructive in a negative sense. Many readers and viewers of the play are apt to agree with Albany when he declares his wife to be a 'fiend' in 'woman's shape' (4.2.67–8).

Sexuality in *Lear* is presented, on the whole, as monstrous. Lear, in his madness, raves about what seems so monstrous to him in women's sexual appetites:

> To't, luxury, pell-mell, for I lack soldiers.
> Behold yond simpering dame,
> Whose face between her forks presages snow,
> That minces virtue and does shake the head
> To hear of pleasure's name;
> The fitchew nor the soilèd horse goes to't
> With a more riotous appetite.
> Down from the waist they're centaurs,
> Though women all above.
> But to the girdle do the gods inherit;
> Beneath is all the fiends'.
> There's hell, there's darkness, there is the sulfurous pit, burning, scalding,
> stench, consumption. Fie, fie, fie! Pah, pah! Give me an ounce of civet,
> good apothecary, sweeten my imagination.

> (4.6.117–31)

Sexuality is, in this apocalyptic vision, diabolical. The marriages and love affairs in the play, apart from the brief declaration of vows between Cordelia and the King of France in the opening scene, all tend to confirm this image of sexuality as corrupt and horrible. Wholesomely loving relationships in *King Lear* are for the most part non-sexual: Edgar's loving concern for his father, Cordelia's for her father, Kent's unending loyalty to Lear, and the Fool's constant companionship with the King (until the Fool unexplainedly vanishes from the text after 3.6, perhaps because Cordelia takes his place in ministering to Lear). Cordelia is aptly described as Lear's 'one daughter / Who redeems nature from the general curse / Which twain have brought her to' (4.6.205–7).

Edmund's death can similarly be interpreted in a meaningful way, albeit with uncertainties as to whether the gods have any part in this story. His final duel with Edgar raises many questions. Why, first of all, does Edmund consent to duel with an unnamed challenger? After Edmund has fallen in the combat, Goneril upbraids him for this choice. 'This is practice, Gloucester', she admonishes him (using the aristocratic title he has by now inherited from the old Earl of Gloucester who, as condemned traitor, no longer holds the title). 'By th' law of arms thou wast not bound to answer / An unknown opposite. Thou art not vanquished, / But cozened and beguiled' (5.3.154–7). Goneril knows whereof she speaks: according to the medieval law of arms, an aristocrat was under no obligation to answer the challenge of any unidentified person who might be of lower rank. Why then has Edmund chosen to fight?

One answer may be that Edmund sees here his chance to vindicate his name in the face of Albany's having made a move to arrest Edmund 'On capital treason' (85) for having conspired with Goneril to murder Albany and thus become Goneril's partner as Duke of Albany. That move would have given Edmund an unobstructed shot at absolute royal power as King of Great Britain, since Cornwall is now dead. The incriminating evidence written down in Goneril's letter (4.6.266–74) is now in the hands of Albany, having been found by Edgar on the dead body of Goneril's steward, Oswald, whom Edgar has killed in order to save the life of the old Earl of Gloucester. The handwriting in the letter is indisputably that of Goneril; she makes no attempt to deny her authorship, saying instead to Albany that 'the laws are mine, not thine', and taunting him by adding, 'Who can arraign me for't?' (5.3.161–2). Thus Edmund stands publicly accused of murder and conspiring to achieve the royal crown. How can Edmund best fend off such an accusation?

His solution seems to be at hand when he learns that he is challenged by an anonymous knight to a duel. This medieval ritual, a strange one from our modern perspective, is known as trial by combat. According to that ritual form of trial, the litigants are to swear the truth of what they allege and then fight to the death; the winner will be seen as having been vindicated by divine dispensation, since the very idea of such a trial is posited on the notion that the gods oversee the meting out of just rewards and punishments. This is the same sort of old-fashioned ideology about the gods that Edmund skeptically regards as mere superstition. Since he is confident that the gods will not intervene, why should he not accept the challenge, defeat the challenger, and thus 'prove' through the ritual of trial by combat that he is innocent? Those who credulously believe that such a trial will sort out justice according to the gods' decrees will accept Edmund's victory as demonstration that he has told the truth in asserting his innocence. Surely he ought to be able to defeat such a challenger; Edmund has sublime confidence in his own strength and agility.

What happens is that Edmund loses the fight and then his life. Is this simply because in any such encounter between two combatants, one of them must win, or is it a vindication of the sorely tested proposition that the gods will control the outcome of such important matters? Once more, the idea that Providence directs human affairs is being put to the test. Edmund, for his part, seems to interpret the outcome in providential terms. This is a surprising reversal of creed in such a hardened villain, and yet in this play it makes sense psychologically. Edmund has expected to win, and yet he has lost. What is more, he loses to the very brother whom he has so grievously wronged. Edgar, for his part, sees divine justice and reciprocity in this outcome. 'My name is Edgar, and thy father's son', he says to the dying Edmund. 'The gods are just, and of our pleasant vices / Make instruments to plague us. / The dark and vicious place where thee he got / Cost him his eyes' (5.3.172–6). If Gloucester had not sired the illegitimate Edmund in a moment of heated lust, Gloucester would not have lost his eyes. This is course literally true in that if Edmund had never been born he would not have been there to betray his father, but Edgar sees more to it than that. Surely there is a sense here that what goes around comes around, that the deeds we enact are never forgotten; they remain forever an integral part of who we are, and they can return to haunt us. To beget a child is an awesomely serious act; it creates life, and should be done reverently. A father must bear responsibility for the children he has sired.

Edmund comes at last to accept this proposition that there is a moral pattern of cause and effect in human action. 'Th' hast spoken right. 'Tis true', he replies to Edgar. 'The wheel is come full circle; I am here' (5.3.176–7). Edmund has not been able to evade at last the consequences of his villainous practices against Gloucester and Edgar. The sum of who he is and what he has done must be answered for. Perceiving that to be true in the last moments of his existence, Edmund attempts to undo his latest villainy. He has ordered the execution of Cordelia in the prison. Can she be saved? 'Some good I mean to do', he says, 'Despite of mine own nature' (248–9). He dispatches an attendant to hasten to the prison with his sword as evidence that he wishes now to reverse the order of death. But he is too late. Cordelia, hanged and lifeless, is brought on stage by her inconsolable father.

Why does Cordelia have to die? This is a question that we posed earlier, and that all readers down through the generations have agonized over. The death is manifestly so unfair, so unnecessary, so brutal. Even the villain who ordered her death now wishes her alive. All of Cordelia's selfless love and generosity, in leaving her new home in France and unwillingly invading England with a hostile army so that she might rescue Lear from the pitiless rejection practiced by her two sisters, apparently counts for nothing in the score card that the gods (if they exist) are presumably keeping. Why does Shakespeare do this, when his sources did not, and in view of the fact that Nahum Tate's 1681 revision reigned supreme in the theatre well into the nineteenth century with Cordelia happily restored at last to her father?

One possible answer is that Lear has simply asked too much of her. She has had to endure banishment at his hands because she has not been willing to say that he would be all in all to her. She has wanted to make clear that she has a new duty to her lord and husband, the King of France. She has wanted Lear to understand that. Yet when circumstances demand that she give her full loyalty and love to her father because of the inhumane way he suffers at her sisters' hands, she unhesitatingly and uncomplainingly does just what she had said she did not want to do: make him the center of her life. She leaves her home and marriage in France, comes to England, and ministers to him without a murmur of unwillingness. She understands the one thing that can bring Lear back to sanity and that she alone can provide: her unqualified love and presence as an assurance that he has not lost her love by banishing her. When Lear begins to regain his sanity under her patient care, his first thought is that he has so deeply wronged her as to be unforgivable. 'I know you do not love me', he tells her, 'for your sisters / Have, as I do remember, done me wrong. / You have some cause, they have not' (4.7.75–8). Her answer is utterly simple in its eloquence: 'No cause, no cause.' She assures Lear that he need not ask if she has forgiven him, because, she says, there is nothing to forgive. Hers is the incredibly generous act of forgiving the unforgivable, and in such a way that it does not even seem like an act of forgiveness at all. She simply is what she is. Her existence, her continual presence at Lear's side, is all that he need ask.

The cure is no less miraculous than the generosity of spirit that has enabled it to happen. Lear discovers what it is to be truly happy. He has Cordelia; let everything else go. He speaks with radiant contentedness of the prospect of being in prison with her. The two of them will sing 'like birds i'th'cage'. If Cordelia should offer to kneel to him in the usual token of filial duty, to ask the father's blessing, Lear will instead 'kneel down / And ask of thee forgiveness'. They will laugh at the world's follies as father and daughter feed on each other's precious company (5.3.8–19). Yet Cordelia does not speak with the same euphoric sense. She is concerned only with Lear's having been so fearfully abused; she is herself, like Edgar, prepared for her own part to 'outfrown false Fortune's frown' (5–6). She does not rhapsodize on what it means to find true happiness in the company of her father. Nor could she, honestly, for, however uncomplainingly she has done what she has done, this was not her choice as to how she had hoped to live. Her present circumstances provide no hope of her being able to enjoy her new marriage and children of her own.

King Lear, Act 5, scene 3. Lear and Cordelia captured. Valentina Shendrikova as Cordelia and Yuri Yarvet as King Lear in Grigori Kozintsev's 1971 film. (Lenfilm / The Kobal Collection)

Lear, then, is once again bargaining with the gods. Take away everything else, he seems to say, so long as I have Cordelia. But, as Edgar has learned the hard way, the gods do not accept bargains. If the gods are there at all, they seem not to be listening. The death of Cordelia underscores this hard truth, that justice in human affairs can claim no divine authority. And since Lear clings still to a sense of entitlement, to a selfish insistence that he be allowed to have his favorite daughter all to himself, that longing is an inappropriate one and must suffer the life-destroying consequence of its being denied. Case closed. As Edgar puts it, in counseling his father to find the patience to go on, 'Men must endure / Their going hence, even as their coming hither. / Ripeness is all' (5.2.9–11). Samuel Beckett says much the same thing, in a more modern idiom: 'I can't go on. I'll go on.'

7

The Tempest

The Tempest is such a superb summary and retrospective of Shakespeare's art as a dramatist that it affords an ideal model with which to consider how we can go about reading a Shakespeare play. One can read *The Tempest* in many different ways that are complementary to one another and at the same time illustrate the coherence and unity of this remarkable work. We might want to consider these possibilities:

- *The Tempest* is about a political struggle between the rulers of Milan and Naples that ends harmoniously, through marriage, in a settling of that long and bitter dispute.
- It is about the human propensity for brutal enmity on the one hand and loving grace on the other. It is a story of human frailty, of spiritual failure, of self-hatred, then of contrition and eventual forgiveness. To no less extent it is about the difficult search within oneself for the strength of spirit to be able to forgive one's enemies.
- Accordingly, it portrays a battle between the dark primitive inner self of libidinal instincts (Freud's Id) and the regulating superego that represents both individual self-control and the necessary constraints of civilization.
- *The Tempest* tells a story that is strikingly analogous in some ways to the colonizing by Europe of the New World across the Atlantic Ocean, with all the thorny ethical and political issues that come with colonization.
- The island of *The Tempest* is a utopia, in the literary tradition of Plato, Thomas More, and Montaigne. As such it invites us to dream about an ideal commonwealth that may never come into existence but that will continue to intrigue us with its unstable vision. Such a utopia seems

completely rational and yet is somehow unattainable in the fallen world of human imperfection.

- Act 4 of *The Tempest* features a courtly masque, a remarkable thing in that Shakespeare did not otherwise write any of the elaborate and very expensive entertainments staged at court for the king, the queen, and their select entourage.
- *The Tempest* is about dramatic art and about the inspiration that comes to the artist from some unseen and eternal power of creativity. In this reading, the island of the Tempest represents the theatre, where the theatre artist is in charge of his own play. He scripts the behavior of other characters and contrives a happy ending, at which point he acknowledges that his creative powers are coming to an end.
- The story is thus about the aging of the artist, his arranging family matters by marrying off his daughter, his acceptance of the necessity of retirement from the theatre, and his awareness that, as a mortal, he will eventually die. *The Tempest*, seemingly, celebrates Shakespeare's retirement as playwright. It is both a demonstration of, and a defense of, the kind of theatre he does best.

The political story line of *The Tempest* is about Prospero, Duke of Milan, who, having neglected the exercise of political power in favor of his magical studies, loses his dukedom to his ambitious younger brother, Antonio, aided by the King of Naples (Alonso), whereupon Prospero and his very young daughter Miranda are put to sea in a boat with the expectation that they will perish. Instead, they fetch up on an island, and manage to survive with no companion other than a native named Caliban, who had been born on this island to the witch Sycorax. Twelve years later, when Alonso and his son Ferdinand are returning with others to Italy from a marriage in Africa, Prospero and his airy spirit Ariel cause an extraordinary storm and shipwreck that casts the Italians ashore. The rest of the play follows their fortunes as Ferdinand meets Miranda, Alonso and his party of Italians are subjected to various tribulations and illusions of loss, and the clownish Trinculo and Stephano cook up with Caliban a conspiracy to take over the island from Prospero. The story is, unusually for Shakespeare, an invented plot in the main (though many details are borrowed from time to time from individual sources). Unusual also is the compactness of the plotting along neoclassical lines of unity of place and time: by telling how Prospero lost his dukedom as an event that took place some twelve years ago, Shakespeare neatly confines the dramatic action of the play to the island of the Tempest and to approximately two days. (In the second scene, Prospero promises to free Ariel 'after two days' (1.2.301), when they have completed all that they have to do.)

The political story of *The Tempest* is thus one of machiavellian chicanery committed long ago but not forgotten by its victim, Prospero. The realpolitik of mainland Italy is contrasted point by point with the idealized artistic landscape of the island, suggesting an adversarial and complementary relationship between life as it is ordinarily lived and life as it can be imagined by the creative artist. Prospero's account of the political takeover twelve years ago that toppled him from office is filled with bitter recriminations, mostly against his younger brother Antonio. Noting that Prospero had grown a 'stranger' to the affairs of state as a result of his being 'transported / And rapt in secret studies', Antonio moved quickly to take advantage of the situation. 'Being once perfected how to grant suits, / How to deny them, who t'advance and who / To trash for overtopping', Antonio 'new created / The creatures that were mine' (1.2.76–82): that is to say, Antonio practiced the art of doing political favors for the courtiers in the court of Milan, thus making those persons beholden to him rather than to Prospero. Antonio became in effect the Duke of Milan. His next ambitious move was to seek out the aid of the King of Naples by agreeing 'To give him annual tribute, do him homage, / Subject his coronet to his crown' (113–14) in return for Naples's military support in ousting Prospero from office.

> This King of Naples, being an enemy
> To me inveterate, hearkens my brother's suit,
> Which was that he, in lieu o'th' premises
> Of homage and I know not how much tribute,
> Should presently extirpate me and mine
> Out of the dukedom and confer fair Milan,
> With all the honors, on my brother.
>
> (121–7)

A 'treacherous army' did its dirty work at midnight, and soon Prospero found himself, with his crying infant daughter, consigned to a wretched vessel not fit to put to sea. Only the kindly intervention of a noble Neapolitan named Gonzalo made it possible for them to have food, water, a few other provisions, and, perhaps most importantly, the magical books that Prospero prized above his dukedom.

Such treachery invites reprisal, and Prospero, having had twelve years to brood on the ingratitude, now has Antonio and the others in his power.

What vengeance will he take? The play tantalizes us with the question, for Prospero deals harshly at first with his enemies. By separating young Ferdinand from his father Alonso in the shipwreck, Prospero creates for Alonso the illusion that his son has drowned, and Prospero is not quick to disabuse Alonso of that mistaken impression. He allows Alonso to wallow in grief and self-accusation. 'O thou mine heir / Of Naples and of Milan', Alonso meditates, 'what strange fish / Hath made his meal on thee?' (2.1.114–16). Following Prospero's instruction, Ariel appears before the Neapolitan party as a harpy, i.e., a fabulous and vengeful monster with a woman's face and breasts and a vulture's body, informing Alonso and the rest that their disastrous shipwreck is a sure sign of divine reprisal for sin: 'The powers, delaying, not forgetting, have / Incensed the seas and shores, yea, all the creatures, / Against your peace' (3.3.73–5). The harpy assures Alonso that his son is indeed dead, as a direct result of Alonso's terrible crimes: 'Thee of thy son, Alonso, / They have bereft' (75–6). Alonso's despairing response is suicidal: he vows that he will 'seek him [Ferdinand] deeper than e'er plummet sounded, / And with him there lie mudded' (101–2). Antonio and his companion in villainy, Sebastian (the younger brother of Alonso), are similarly denounced by the harpy as 'men of sin' (53), and are subjected to strange and frightening visions calculated to make them mad. Indeed, as Gonzalo observes, 'All three of them [Alonso, Antonio, and Sebastian] are desperate. Their great guilt, / Like poison given to work a great time after, / Now 'gins to bite the spirits' (105–7).

Gonzalo's observation may give us some clue as to why Prospero is inflicting such suffering on these three guilty men. In part the harrowing experience is meant to be punitive, like a working poison, but at the same time we can wonder if some spiritual health-giving benefit may arise from the workings of conscience. Alonso, most notably among the three, sees the punishment as just retribution for his sin, and so his sorrowing heart is open to the cleansing effect of contrition and remorse. When at last he is confronted by Prospero, Alonso's immediate response is to beg forgiveness: 'Thy dukedom I resign, and do entreat / Thou pardon me my wrongs' (5.1.118–19). Such genuine contrition makes forgiveness possible. Even at this late date, however, Prospero allows Alonso to remain in ignorance of his son's being alive. 'Irreparable is the loss, and Patience / Says it is past her cure', Alonso sadly concludes (140–1). The thought prompts him to wish not only that his son were alive, but that Ferdinand might have married Prospero's sole daughter: 'O heavens, that they were living both in Naples, / The king and queen there!' (150–1). Alonso's contrition takes the form of his wishing not only to restore Prospero's dukedom, which he fully intends to do, but also that he might resign his crown of Naples in favor of such a marriage.

We know, of course, that Ferdinand and Miranda are already engaged to be married, and that their betrothal has been celebrated in a masque devised for the purpose by Prospero. The betrothal that ends this play is more than a conventional way of ending a Shakespearean romantic comedy; it is also a political union of remarkable astuteness. The wedding of the heir to the throne of Naples with the daughter and sole heir of the Duke of Milan will unite those two contending principalities and thereby bring to a peaceful conclusion the strife that led twelve years ago to Prospero's banishment. The union is like those often used to form alliances in early modern Europe, as for example when Henry VII of England strengthened his own weak Lancastrian claim to the throne by marrying the female heir to the Yorkist line (Elizabeth, daughter of Edward IV) and then marrying his son Arthur to Catherine of Aragon and his daughter Margaret to James IV of Scotland. In the present instance, the alliance fulfills both Prospero's dream of recovering his dukedom of Milan and Alonso's dream of seeing his son married to Prospero's daughter and heir. Prospero and Alonso, having been mortal enemies for so long, now can look forward to being the grandfathers of a child that will be born to Ferdinand and Miranda as sole heir of the combined kingdoms.

Pardoning Antonio is another matter, as Prospero makes clear when he pronounces forgiveness: 'For you, most wicked sir, whom to call brother / Would even infect my mouth, I do forgive / Thy rankest fault – all of them; and require / My dukedom of thee, which perforce I know / Thou must restore' (5.1.130–4). What sort of pardon is this, coupled with such an expression of continuing hostility and even contempt? Antonio deserves no better; he remains a villain to the end, sarcastic, ruthless, deeply cynical about human nature. Prospero knows that Antonio will never willingly relinquish the dukedom of Milan unless forced to do so. Antonio has been found out and, for the time being at least, defanged, but he experiences not the slightest remorse. Can Prospero forgive such a brother? He repeatedly insists that he does do so: 'I do forgive thee, / Unnatural though thou art' (78–9). 'Unnatural' is a word advisedly chosen: Antonio has 'Expelled remorse and nature', and accordingly Prospero has devised 'inward pinches' that 'therefore are most strong' (76–7). This pardon is offered with no illusions that it will result in inner spiritual reform. Antonio is incorrigible and wholly guilty, yet he too must be pardoned. Why is this?

In part it shows us that such an act is all the more precious and meritorious because it requires such a generosity of spirit. 'The rarer action is / In virtue than in vengeance', Prospero discovers (27–8). He learns this from Ariel, who, though a spirit, is not without feelings and perceptions of right and wrong. Ariel hopes that Prospero's feelings will now turn pitiful toward his enemies, if only because the men have suffered so much in their instructive purgation. 'Dost thou think so, spirit?' asks Prospero, to which Ariel replies, 'Mine would, sir, were I human' (18–20). Prospero immediately sees the point: if a spirit can feel sorry for the villains, should not he, as a man, feel compassion also? 'Though with their high wrongs I am struck to th' quick', he says, 'Yet with my nobler reason 'gainst my fury / Do I take part' (25–7). Prospero struggles with his desire to avenge the injustices done to him, and concludes that forgiveness is of a higher moral order. He forgives the unforgivable.

Prospero must also come to terms with Caliban, whom he pardons by conceding that Caliban's darker nature is a part of Prospero himself. 'This thing of darkness I / Acknowledge mine', he declares (5.1.278–9). Even though Caliban is 'as disproportioned in his manners / As in his shape', and will always be remembered by Prospero as a 'demidevil' and 'a bastard one' who has plotted with Stephano and Trinculo to take Prospero's life (275–95), Prospero freely offers pardon, and arranges at the end of the play for Caliban to remain in sole possession of the island that he claims for his own as its first inhabitant. Caliban for his part seeks a reconciliation also: he promises to do as Prospero bids him, adding that 'I'll be wise hereafter / And seek for grace' (298–9). Such an accommodation promises a kind of harmony between the controlling superego of our human nature and our libidinal inner selves, even if the accommodation is in the nature of an uneasy truce.

To say that Caliban is a projection of our libidinal inner natures is not to condemn him as evil or deplorable, even if the play's ending does seem to opt for a resolution in which the primitive inner self submits more or less willingly to the control of human reason. Caliban is both dangerous and endearing, brutish and poetically sensitive. His early history is ambivalent in just this way. On the one hand, he is a 'freckled whelp, hag-born' of the 'damned witch' Sycorax, who, 'For mischiefs manifold and sorceries terrible', was banished from Argier and would have been executed had it not been 'For one thing she did' – presumably becoming pregnant with Caliban (1.2.265–85). According to Prospero, Caliban was 'got [i.e., begotten] by the devil himself / Upon thy wicked dam' (322–3), and, even though we might ascribe this allegation to inflated rhetoric, Caliban makes no attempt to deny this paternity. He is, to Prospero and Miranda, a 'poisonous slave', an 'Abhorrèd slave / Which any print of goodness wilt not take' (322, 354–5). On the other hand, Caliban is capable of great tenderness, and is more responsive to the natural beauty of the island than any other inhabitant on it. He alone is aware that

> The isle is full of noises,
> Sounds, and sweet airs, that give delight and hurt not.
> Sometimes a thousand twangling instruments
> Will hum about mine ears, and sometimes voices
> That, if I then had waked after long sleep,
> Will make me sleep again; and then, in dreaming,
> The clouds methought would open and show riches
> Ready to drop upon me, that when I waked
> I cried to dream again.
>
> (3.2.137–45)

No child of nature could express more poignantly what it is like to be in touch with the majesty of the universe.

If we search for clues as to Caliban's physical appearance and his eating habits (as theatre directors have done over the centuries), we come across the same ambivalence. On the one hand, he seems scarcely to be 'honored with / A human shape' (1.2.285–6). Miranda, upon seeing Ferdinand, reckons him to be 'the third man that e'er I saw' (449), evidently including Caliban in that number along with Prospero, but a little later we hear her confiding to Ferdinand that she has not seen 'More that I may call men than you, good friend, / And my dear father' (3.1.51–2). Perhaps she now forgets Caliban in her euphoria of being in love. At any rate, we find ourselves wondering what Caliban is like physically. The 'Names of the Actors' in the First Folio printing of this play describes him as a 'savage and deformed slave', though we cannot be sure that the description is by Shakespeare; it could be the work of his editors. Other than that, we gather that Caliban has 'long nails' that he uses to dig pignuts (tuberous roots) or to pry 'Young scamels from the rock' (whatever they may be, perhaps shellfish), or to pick the flesh out of crabs (unless Caliban is referring simply to crab apples; 2.2.165–70). He likes 'Water with berries in't' (1.2.337). He knows how to fish (2.2.159) and to find jay's nests, from which he presumably eats the eggs, and how 'To snare the nimble marmoset' or small monkey. According to Trinculo, 'a very ancient and fishlike smell' emanates from Caliban as he lies cowering under his cloak, but Trinculo's further diagnosis that the strange creature he has found has 'fins like arms' does not mean that Caliban actually has fins, or gills; it means that Trinculo finds arms where he expected, from the fishlike odor, to find fins (2.2.26–34). Generations of stage directors have fitted Caliban out with amphibian qualities suggesting that he is some strange monster slowly making his way up the evolutionary chain of being, but the text of the play is more lightly suggestive. His name, Caliban, is transparently an anagram for 'canibal' or 'cannibal', and yet his diet is chiefly that of berries, roots, eggs, and an occasional bit of fish or meat. He has shown Prospero and Miranda where to find precious resources on the island, such as 'fresh springs', along with 'brine pits, barren place and fertile' (1.2.341; see also 2.2.158–9), none of them remotely suggestive of cannibalism.

Caliban's language similarly places him ambivalently between the natural world and the presumably civilized order of Western Europe. He recalls how Prospero and Miranda, when they first arrived and found him an orphan, made much of him, teaching him 'how / To name the bigger light, and how the less, / That burn by day and night', namely, the sun and the moon (1.2.337–9). At first he loved them for this, but by now he has bitterly concluded that the only benefit that has accrued to him from learning their language is that he knows 'how to curse' (367). What was his language like before? Miranda charges that he did not 'Know thine own meaning, but wouldst gabble like / A thing most brutish'; only when Miranda and her father have 'endowed' Caliban's 'purposes / With words' was he enabled in any way to make those purposes 'known' (358–61). The implication is that Caliban did not in fact have any language at all; nor does he deny that implication. Language, then, is a crucial marker of civilization for Miranda and her father, the lack of which is simply 'brutish'. Yet an aura of genuine debate hovers over this conversation. Is Caliban better off for having learned a Western European language? The question forcefully underscores the matter of evaluating what Freud will later identify as the 'discontents' of civilization, the imposing of discipline without which social order is impossible and yet which is undeniably a kind of repression.

Certain it is that Caliban has attempted to force himself on Miranda as a sexual partner. Indeed, he is still unrepentant: 'Oho, oho! Would it had been done! / Thou didst prevent me; I had peopled else / This isle with Calibans' (1.2.352–4). Evidently he lived in harmony with Prospero and Miranda when they first arrived; 'with humane care' (349) they lodged him in their cell, taught him language, and treated him as a member of their family, so that he and Miranda must have been playmates. Perhaps then Caliban came of age sexually at about the same time Miranda reached the age of early womanhood, at which point a genetic craving for procreation asserted itself. Caliban's ebullient lack of repentance for the attempted assault is of course offensive to Prospero and Miranda, since from their point of view what he tried to do was a rape. Still, this is not the same sort of impenitence we see in Antonio and Sebastian. Caliban sees no reason why sexual desire should not have fulfilled itself in an act designed by nature to further the propagation of the species. To him, the attraction is as simple as 'You girl, me boy.' His forthright ethics of desire as natural is thus pitted in debate against the self-restraining ethics of Miranda and Ferdinand. In them, desire is no less great, especially in Ferdinand, who, as an eager male, is explicitly the counterpart of Caliban as potential sexual partner for Miranda. She gets to choose between Caliban and Ferdinand, and of course the choice is entirely clear to her.

Ferdinand is explicit about the urgency of his sexual desire: on the day of his wedding to Miranda, he will think 'or Phoebus' steeds are foundered / Or Night kept chained below' (4.1.30–1). That is, he will be frantically impatient for the day to pass so that he can possess his dear Miranda as his wife. At the same time, he makes a deep vow to her and to her father that no opportunity for sex, however inviting, could induce him to 'melt / [His] honor into lust, to take away / The edge of that day's celebration' when they are to be married (23–9). They are, to be sure, on an island, with no church or priest and with manifold chances to be alone together. Why should they not enjoy sex since they have promised themselves to each other for all eternity? The question answers itself, for both Miranda and Ferdinand. Their desire will be infinitely more honorable and proper if they wait until they are married. They do not need Prospero's repeated insistences that Ferdinand not 'break her virgin-knot before / All sanctimonious ceremonies may / With full and holy rite be ministered' (15–17).

Does this mean that they are right and that Caliban is wrong to defend the natural idea of sex as a healthy instinct to be obeyed without restraint? The play does seem to privilege the Western Christian tradition of sex only after marriage, since the betrothal of Ferdinand and Miranda is the appropriate highpoint and conclusion of this romantic comedy, and is attended by the celebration of the gods (albeit gods that Ariel and Prospero have manufactured for the occasion). Still, the play accentuates a debate between European and non-European mores as a way of inviting us to consider all possibilities. Caliban's attractively poetic sensibility, and his readiness to challenge all European customs from a refreshingly skeptical vantage point, are the very stuff of entertaining drama. Shakespeare revels in the entertaining and the dramatic.

Perhaps the most compelling of Caliban's challenges to European tradition and authority is that of protesting against his enslavement. He is indeed a slave, and is called so repeatedly in the language of the play ('Thou most lying slave', 'Abhorrèd slave', etc., at 1.2.346–54, also 311, 316). To be sure, Ariel is called 'slave' also, and is so in that he has little choice but to obey; Prospero refers to him as 'Thou, my slave', and Ariel responds by addressing Prospero as 'master' (272, 302). 'Slave' can mean a number of things, including 'servant' and 'wretch'. Even so, Caliban is a slave in the more oppressive sense of one who performs involuntary servitude and without hope of eventual release. Ever since his attempted assault on Miranda he has been confined in a 'hard rock' (346, 364), and is obliged to 'make our fire, / Fetch in our wood', and serve in other offices that profit Prospero and Miranda (314–15). (When Ferdinand too is obliged to carry firewood in 3.1, the stage image underscores the parallelism between him and Caliban.) Caliban of course hates his enslavement, and is given opportunity to protest against it in ways that seem strikingly modern. Whose island is this, after all? 'This island's mine', he insists, 'by Sycorax my mother.' To Prospero he justifiably complains, 'I am all the subjects that you have, / Which first was mine own king' (1.2.334–44). When Trinculo and Stephano show up and seem to offer Caliban assistance in a revolt against slavery, he accepts with alacrity. Why should he not?

Still, Prospero is not a slavemaster and colonialist in the style of the Spanish *conquistadores* in Central and South America, for example, or the white operators of the slave trade (some of them British) in the eighteenth century. Prospero never asked to come to the island of the Tempest, and at the end he leaves Caliban in full possession. He never reaps any economic reward by maintaining an exploitative trade relationship with an underdeveloped country able to supply free or cheap labor and raw materials. Prospero enslaves Caliban chiefly as a means of protecting the chastity of Miranda, though he does then force Caliban to perform the disagreeable tasks that Prospero doesn't want to do for himself. A truer model of colonialism is to be found in Stephano and Trinculo, the drunken butler and jester who wash ashore from the shipwreck, with Stephano having managed to escape on a 'butt of sack' (i.e., barrel of Canary wine) that the sailors heaved overboard (2.2.121–2). Their manipulation of Caliban is strikingly anticipatory of the French and Indian wars in North America in the eighteenth century, for example: they ply Caliban with drink, enslave him with a new-found appetite for alcohol, represent themselves to him as gods to be worshiped, and stir up rebellion. Trinculo's first thought, when he comes upon a strange 'monster' hiding under a gaberdine cloak, is that such a savage would surely be marketable. 'A strange fish!' he exclaims. 'Were I in England now, as once I was, and had but this fish painted, not a holiday fool there but would give a piece of silver. There would this monster make a man.' Trinculo goes on to describe such a circus freak-show event in terms that any Londoner would instantly recognize, since the parading of exotic dark-skinned foreigners brought back by opportunistic adventurers to the New World, Asia, or Africa was not an uncommon event. 'Any strange beast there makes a man', Trinculo explains. 'When they will not give a doit to relieve a lame beggar, they will lay out ten to see a dead Indian' (2.2.27–33).

'Indian' can presumably mean any native brought back from beyond the seas, but the name has a special resonance for us in terms of the Americas, and elsewhere we do find hints in *The Tempest* of that New World across the Atlantic. Ariel recalls having been ordered by Prospero to fetch dew at midnight 'From the still-vexed Bermudas' (spelled 'Bermoothes' in the First Folio, 1.2.229–30), probably echoing one or more recent accounts of shipwreck in the Bermudas, by Sylvester Jordain (1610) and by William Strachey (written but not published in 1610–11), with which Shakespeare seems to have been familiar. Sycorax's god, Setebos, mentioned by Caliban at 1.2.376 and 5.1.263, was worshiped by the natives of Chile in South America, according to the account of Magellan's circumnavigation of the globe in Richard Eden's *History of Travel* (1577). In narrative terms, the island would appear to be somewhere in the western Mediterranean, since Prospero and Miranda were able to get there by boat when put out to sea from the Italian mainland, and since Alonso and the rest are shipwrecked on the island as they make their journey back to Naples from the marriage of Alonso's daughter Claribel to the King of Tunis in north Africa. Yet the island's New World resonances are undeniable, too, as when Miranda exclaims, 'Oh, brave new world / That has such people in't!' (5.1.185–6). The island, then, is at least two places at once, belonging both to the familiar old landscape of Mediterranean Europe and to a fascinating unknown terrain lying somewhere far off to the west. It is some place and no place, a world of the imagination, like Plato's floating island in *The Republic*.

As such, the island is a utopia. It is a place of dreams, of fantastic imaginings. When the Neapolitan party washes ashore, most of them are fearful, cynical, even despairing, except for old Gonzalo, the gentle-hearted courtier who, some twelve years ago, thought to provide Prospero and his daughter with enough provisions for their unseaworthy boat to enable them to live. And now, Gonzalo alone urges that the Neapolitans rejoice in having survived the shipwreck instead of gloomily deploring their precarious state. He alone notices that their garments, having been drenched in the sea, 'hold notwithstanding their freshness and glosses, being rather new-dyed than stained with salt water' (2.1.64–7). The phenomenon is indeed remarkable, but only a dreamer can be attuned to such a hopeful sign. He chides Sebastian and Antonio for oppressing Alonso with their certainty that his son Ferdinand is truly lost forever (115–34). Gonzalo speaks very much in character, then, when he proceeds to imagine what an ideal commonwealth might be like in such new surroundings, so far away from Western Europe:

> I'th'commonwealth I would by contraries
> Execute all things; for no kind of traffic
> Would I admit; no name of magistrate;
> Letters should not be known; riches, poverty,
> And use of service, none; contract, succession,
> Bourn, bound of land, tilth, vineyard, none;
> No use of metal, corn, or wine, or oil;
> No occupation; all men idle, all,
> And women too, but innocent and pure;
> No sovereignty. . . .
> All things in common nature should produce
> Without sweat or endeavor. Treason, felony,
> Sword, pike, knife, gun, or need of any engine
> Would I not have; but nature should bring forth,
> Of its own kind, all foison, all abundance,
> To feed my innocent people. . . .
> I would with such perfection govern, sir,
> T'excel the Golden Age.
>
> (2.1.151–72)

This reverie is taken, almost word for word, from Montaigne's essay 'Of the Cannibals' (in his *Essays*, first translated into English by John Florio in 1603). It nicely captures the skeptical spirit of Montaigne's inquiry into the mores of Western Europe. Seen from the vantage point of an imagined native culture overseas, can Europe really claim to be superior to the rest of the world? Might not some as-yet-undiscovered society find a better way for humans to live, with no selfish accumulation of wealth and hence no poverty, no oppressive laws, no competition for survival, no war, no violence? Would not such a world of innocent sufficiency for everyone be indeed a Golden Age? Thomas More's *Utopia* (1516) similarly imagines a classless society free from any dependence on wealth, set in some imagined island in the Caribbean. More contrasts this Utopia to early sixteenth-century Europe, in which princes gather around them a parasitic class of courtiers bent on oppressing the poor and fighting endlessly among themselves out of vainglory and covetousness. Shakespeare's Gonzalo is indeed a dreamer to fantasize about an ideal communal society, and so he is mocked at by his cynical companions, but truly the island invites such dreaming.

The 'realists', Antonio and Sebastian, are the ones who are truly out of place in this magical landscape. Their plot to assassinate Alonso and the other Neapolitans while they sleep is patently absurd. What good will it do them? They are on an island, with no hope of rescue, since they believe their ship to have been totally wrecked. They might better turn cooperatively to the business of survival. How will they eat and drink and find shelter? Their assassination attempt is the *reductio ad absurdum* of the rootless homicidal ambition they have practiced so long that it has become habitual, like some narcotic-driven compulsion. This plot is parodied in turn by the fruitless attempt of Stephano and Trinculo, aided by Caliban, to carry out a similar assassination plot against Prospero: Stephano is to be king of the island, with Miranda as his queen and Trinculo and Caliban as their viceroys (3.2.107–8). Sixteenth-century Europe is seen at its worst in its insane desire to desecrate and colonize every unspoiled land it can territorialize, imprinting its own decadent power structures and competitive mores on foreign lands that have everything to lose and nothing to gain from being taught the ways of European culture.

Both of these plots are foiled from the start by Ariel, who, in fulfillment of Prospero's bidding, invisibly overhears the conspiracies and makes sure that the plots will not succeed. It is Ariel who causes Alonso, Gonzalo, and their companions to sleep, so that Antonio and Sebastian will have a seeming opportunity to kill them all; it is Ariel who then awakens the sleepers '*with music and song*' (2.1.300.1) just in time to prevent the massacre. 'While you here do snoring lie, / Open-eyed conspiracy / His time doth take', sings Ariel '*in Gonzalo's ear*' (304–6). The seeming opportunity for murder is only an illusion, then, designed to test the villains and reveal them to be wholly lacking in decency or loyalty. The same thing happens when the buffoonish Stephano and Trinculo, together with Caliban, cook up their mischievous plot against Prospero. Ariel, entering '*invisible*' (3.2.40.1), mimics Trinculo's voice with such skill that the jester receives a thrashing from Stephano. Thereafter, Ariel keeps track of everything the clowns intend to do. 'This will I tell my master', vows Ariel, when Caliban has explained to his co-conspirators how they are to seize Prospero's books and fall upon him as he lies asleep in the afternoon (87–117). Ariel continues to play his beneficial role of deceiver at Prospero's cell by hanging out '*glistering apparel*' on a lime or linden tree to distract the clowns from their homicidal purpose. And finally Ariel and his fellow 'goblins' (4.1.260) become the agents of a satirically comic retribution. First, Ariel leads the conspirators 'through / Toothed briers, sharp furzes, pricking gorse, and thorns' to a 'filthy-mantled pool' near Prospero's cell where they are left 'dancing up to th' chins' and smelling 'all horse piss' (4.1.179–99). Then Ariel's goblins become '*divers spirits, in shape of dogs and hounds, hunting them* [*Stephano, Trinculo, and Caliban*] *about, Prospero and Ariel setting them on*' (256.2–4). The spirits are further instructed to 'grind their [the conspirators'] joints / With dry convulsions, shorten up their sinews / With agèd cramps, and more pinch-spotted make them / Than pard or cat o' mountain' (260–3). In both plots, events proceed as though some invisible power hovers over humankind, testing intentions, exposing conspiracy in all its evil, and protecting the innocent.

Ariel and his spirits are the instruments of many awesome shows and illusions in *The Tempest*. In the guise of '*several strange shapes*', they bring in '*a banquet*' to the awed Neapolitans '*and dance about it with gentle actions of salutations*', inviting Alonso and the rest to eat (3.3.19.1–4). The banquet is sumptuous but tantalizing: as the Neapolitans approach the table, Ariel enters amid thunder and lightning '*like a harpy, claps his wings upon the table, and with a quaint device the banquet vanishes*' (52.1–3). Once Ariel has lectured Alonso, Antonio, and Sebastian on their heinous sins and has promised them 'Ling'ring perdition, worse than any death' as their punishment lying in store, Ariel '*vanishes in thunder*' while, '*to soft music*', the spirits enter again '*and dance, with mocks and mows, and carrying out the table*' (77–82.1–3). Small wonder that the villains are 'desperate' (105). The banquet is to vanish suddenly by '*a quaint device*', i.e., by a *trompe l'oeil* contrivance that will be as visually astonishing to the spectators in the theatre as it is to Alonso and his companions. Like other late plays in part or wholly by Shakespeare (*Cymbeline, The Winter's Tale, Henry VIII, The Two Noble Kinsmen*), *The Tempest* is unusually full of such theatrical special effects.

The masque in Act 4 is thus one magical show among many in the play; it is certainly the most impressive and ornate. Again, it is the work of Ariel and his goblins. The three goddesses that celebrate the betrothal of Ferdinand and Miranda, together with the nymphs and reapers who dance gracefully in a kind of antimasque, are all stage illusions: as Prospero explains afterwards to Ferdinand, 'These our actors, / As I foretold you, were all spirits and / Are melted into air, into thin air' (4.1.148–50). Prospero's wish, put into practice by Ariel and his 'meaner' (i.e., lesser) fellows, is to 'Bestow upon the eyes of this young couple / Some vanity of mine art' (35–41), The word 'vanity' suggests a trifle, an illusion. Repeatedly, Prospero stresses the theatrical nature of his contrivance, underscoring his own role as author and director. Ariel and his assistants are instructed not to appear until Prospero calls them. He dismisses them no less imperiously: 'Avoid; no more!' (142). What the young couple have seen, he assures them, are 'Spirits, which by mine art / I have from their confines called to enact / My present fancies' (120–2). Prospero is both stage manager and magician. He enjoins the spectators to silence, 'Or else our spell is marred' (59, 127).

As a piece of dramatic fiction, the masque itself is in a markedly different style from the various styles found elsewhere in *The Tempest*. It is ceremonious, formal, declamatory, elevated in diction, ornate, and rich in invocations, as befits the diction of classical gods and goddesses. The three deities who preside are carefully chosen for the celebration of a nuptial. Iris is Juno's messenger and goddess of the rainbow, signifying hope and promise for the future; Ceres (played by Ariel, 4.1.167) represents the generative force of nature as embodied in foison and bountiful harvests; and Juno is the presiding deity of marriage. 'Honor, riches, marriage blessing, / Long continuance, and increasing, / Hourly joys be still upon you!' she greets the betrothed couple. 'Juno sings her blessings on you' (106–9). The masque has no plot; it is instead an allegorical declamation in which the chaste virtues of these three goddesses are pointedly contrasted with their opposite numbers in the pantheon of the gods. Juno and her companion goddesses are here to defeat the insinuating tactics of 'dusky Dis' or Pluto, god of the underworld who carried off Ceres's daughter Proserpina to be his bride in Hades and thereby set in motion the seasonal death of the year. Juno, Ceres, and Iris are no less hostile to Venus and her wanton son Cupid, who have intended to have done 'Some wanton charm upon this man and maid [i.e., Ferdinand and Miranda], / Whose vows are that no bed-right shall be paid / Till Hymen's torch be lighted' (88–97).

These goddesses stoutly defend the sexual code that Prospero has sought to impress on the young couple: no sex before marriage. (Hymen is the god of marriage.) As dramatist, Prospero stages an elaborate pageant in which the heavens themselves appear to sanction the moral code of Western Christian tradition. Venus (called 'Mars's hot minion' in recollection of her celebrated tryst with the god of war) and her 'waspish-headed son', blind Cupid, are completely disempowered: Cupid 'has broke his arrows', and 'Swears he will shoot no more, but play with sparrows' (98–100). Sparrows are traditionally lustful and sacred to Venus.

Shakespeare never wrote a masque for performance at court. This is surprising in view of his eminence as poet and dramatist in an age when most of his contemporaries did write such masques: Ben Jonson, George Chapman, Francis Beaumont, Samuel Daniel, John Webster, John Marston, Thomas Middleton, Thomas Campion, John Ford, James Shirley, and still others. Perhaps Shakespeare preferred to write for the public theatre, and to stage for his London audiences a distilled version of the court masque in a form they could appreciate and afford. Court masques were exclusively presented to the very rich and powerful, and were elaborate exercises in the conspicuous consumption of wealth. They were performed on a single occasion only, with costly and impressive scenic effects designed by Inigo Jones and others on the model of Italian extravaganzas. The courtly persons who witnessed these masques and then danced as part of the evening's entertainment spent fortunes on the clothes needed for such a display of wealth and social position. *The Tempest*, on the other hand, was written to be acted on repeated occasions in a public theatre to which any person might come who was willing and able to pay a relatively modest price of admission (a penny throughout most of Shakespeare's career, if one wanted to stand in the yard around the platform stage). To be sure, *The Tempest* was taken to court in 1611, and then in 1613 as part of the elaborate festivities celebrating the marriage of King James I and VI's daughter Elizabeth to Frederick, the Protestant Elector Palatine. Still, *The Tempest*'s masque is essentially written for a commercial theatre catering for the most part to those who would never be invited to court. Shakespeare knows that his patrons are his paying customers. Prospero says as much in the play's epilogue, when he unabashedly asks for the audience's applause.

Considerations such as these invite us to think about the island as a place of theatre, with Prospero as playwright-magician. From the very start, he orchestrates the action of the play as its presiding genius and master. Nothing happens without his knowledge and supervision. He causes the storm with which the play begins. In many modern productions he hovers over this action in his magic cloak and with his magic wand. The text itself does not mandate such an effect, but in the scene that follows Prospero makes it clear to Miranda that the storm was his illusion and that 'There's no harm done' (1.2.15). Throughout the play, in fact, the human agony and sense of loss, the conspiratorial plotting, the frustrating of those schemes, and the joys of falling in love are all presented in the benignly ironic light of Prospero's omniscience and his powerful control of circumstances. Aided by Ariel, he arranges the landing on the island of the Italian visitors in such a way that Alonso thinks his son is dead, Antonio and Sebastian think they see an opportunity for a coup d'etat, Ferdinand meets Miranda, and Stephano and Trinculo encounter Caliban. Prospero scripts these individual actions with a view to testing and scourging his various characters by means of dramatic illusion. He freely acknowledges that 'Providence divine' is somehow important in the overall scheme of things, and that 'accident most strange' and 'bountiful Fortune, / Now my dear lady' are crucial factors that have made possible this present opportunity which he must seize upon lest his fortunes 'ever after droop' (160, 179–85), but within the precinct of the island and its shores Prospero is in charge. He is indeed godlike, able to make himself invisible, all-powerful. Yet he is also mortal, and subject to strong emotions of hatred and irritability which he controls only with considerable difficulty, so that he is godlike only in the limited environment of the island, his theatre. He is a magician, but he knows that he must die.

Prospero's relationship to Ariel is thus temporal and limited. Prospero has freed Ariel from a terrible imprisonment in a 'cloven pine', where Ariel has remained for a dozen years rather than carry out the 'earthy and abhorred commands' of the witch Sycorax (1.1.274–81). Prospero has freed Ariel in return for Ariel's becoming Prospero's 'slave' (272), but it is an enslavement now limited to two more days (301). More importantly, perhaps, it is a servitude of performing tasks that Ariel approves of; Ariel would rather suffer unimaginable torture than obey Sycorax, but he has no such compunctions about obeying Prospero. Never does Ariel question his master's judgment or motives, though he does finally urge forgiveness of Prospero's enemies. Ariel clearly makes moral distinctions. He seems to represent some supernal power, something like the Muses that can inspire the writing of great poetry; he is eternal, and lends his gift of creativity to certain mortals who are somehow worthy to be thus chosen. He will not assist wicked men, and indeed seems to rejoice in performing tasks that foil villainy. Ariel seems to represent a creative power of art that insists on the triumph of goodness.

Prospero is fully aware that he is mortal, enabled for a limited time only to create his own artistic universe. He senses that the inspiration has come to him from some eternal source, and that without that inspiration he himself is nothing. The burden of creativity is thus for him a heavy one indeed, one that he is glad, in a way, to set aside once his work has been done. When he sums up what he has accomplished with his magical powers, he describes for us what is awesome, daunting, and even transgressive in its daring to attempt things that are usually reserved for the gods alone:

> Ye elves of hills, brooks, standing lakes, and groves,
> And ye that on the sands with printless foot
> Do chase the ebbing Neptune, and do fly him
> When he comes back; you demi-puppets that
> By moonshine do the green sour ringlets make,
> Whereof the ewe not bites; and you whose pastime
> Is to make midnight mushrooms, that rejoice
> To hear the solemn curfew; by whose aid,
> Weak masters though ye be, I have bedimmed
> The noontide sun, called forth the mutinous winds,
> And twixt the green sea and the azured vault
> Set roaring war; to the dread rattling thunder
> Have I given fire, and rifted Jove's stout oak
> With his own bolt; the strong-based promontory
> Have I made shake, and by the spurs plucked up
> The pine and cedar; graves at my command
> Have waked their sleepers, oped, and let 'em forth
> By my so potent art. But this rough magic
> I here abjure, and when I have required
> Some heavenly music – which even now I do –
> To work mine end upon their senses that
> This airy charm is for, I'll break my staff,
> Bury it certain fathoms in the earth,
> And deeper than did ever plummet sound
> I'll drown my book.

$$(5.1.33–57)$$

That these lines are borrowed from Arthur Golding's English translation of Ovid's *Metamorphoses* (7.197–219) adds to their Promethean audacity, for in Ovid the speech is by Medea, that fearsome if heroic practitioner of black magic. Like Medea, then, Prospero has been able to command spirits and thereby create storms. He has wielded Jove's own thunderbolt, and has dared to bring the dead back to life. This seems like a fearsome blasphemy, especially in a Christian society for whom Christ's raising of Lazarus from the dead is a miracle vouchsafed only to the Godhead and practiced only on rare occasions even by Him. Yet dramatists create illusions of a similar kind in their theatres. Marlowe's Doctor Faustus prevails on the devil Mephistopheles to conjure up Helen of Troy, along with Alexander and his paramour. The deed is blasphemous, and yet it is what any poet intoxicated with the beauty of classical languages and civilizations longs to do. Prospero revels in the power of language that has enabled him to do things like this, and yet he also abjures this 'rough magic', vowing to break his magic staff and drown his book – the book or books that in former days he prized above his dukedom (1.2.168–9). And whereas Doctor Faustus is damned eternally, Prospero renounces his artistic power. He renounces something he has loved perhaps too much, and does so in the same spirit with which he acknowledges that as a mortal he cannot practice such hubristic endeavors forever. He cannot aspire to be a god. At the play's end, his last act is to release Ariel: 'Then to the elements / Be free, and fare thou well!' (5.1.321–2). Ariel departs without a word.

We are often reminded in this play that theatre is an emblem of life itself, in its fragile beauty, its evanescence, its poignant brevity. Theatre is also like a dream, just as life is like a dream. The point is nowhere more eloquently expressed than in these famous lines:

> Our revels now are ended. These our actors,
> As I foretold you, were all spirits and
> Are melted into air, into thin air;
> And, like the baseless fabric of this vision,
> The cloud-capped towers, the gorgeous palaces,
> The solemn temples, the great globe itself,
> Yea, all which it inherit, shall dissolve,
> And, like this insubstantial pageant faded,
> Leave not a rack behind. We are such stuff
> As dreams are made on, and our little life
> Is rounded with a sleep.
>
> (4.1.148–58)

Prospero's immediate subject is the masque he has just presented to Ferdinand and Miranda, but his larger topic has to do with the fascinating resemblance between dream, sleep, theatrical illusion, and life itself. As in the passage taken from Ovid about opening graves by means of Prospero's potent art, this passage seems at once proud of artistic creativity and keenly aware of its insubstantiality. The artist exults in his achievement even while he discounts it as a 'baseless fabric', a mere 'vision'.

When Prospero announces that 'Our revels now are ended' (4.1.148), he is surely thinking about his own retirement. As he later says, his plan for the future is to 'retire me to my Milan, where / Every third thought shall be my grave' (5.1.314–15). Not every thought, but perhaps a third of them. Is Shakespeare also thinking about his own retirement from the theatre, his moving back to his family home in Stratford-upon-Avon, and, eventually, his death? Many are the reasons for supposing so, even though the play never says it explicitly. *The Tempest* occupies first place in the First Folio of 1616, as though to proclaim it, in the opinion of Shakespeare's editors and fellow actors, as his culminating work. The printed text is carefully prepared on the basis of a scribal copy by the scrivener Ralph Crane. Lacking a single narrative source of the sort Shakespeare used in most of his plays, *The Tempest* reads like a summation and display of the kinds of comedy Shakespeare had learned to do so well, with its imagined landscapes, its delightful character types, and its festive ending in marriage. The very idea of theatre as a kind of fantastic dream, as insubstantial and evanescent as life itself, echoes what Theseus says about the lunatic, the lover, and the poet in Act 5 of *A Midsummer Night's Dream*. The play-within-the-play masque in *The Tempest* calls to mind Shakespeare's fascination with similar plot devices in *Love's Labor's Lost*, *The Taming of the Shrew*, *A Midsummer Night's Dream*, *Hamlet*, and still others. Shakespeare did continue writing after *The Tempest*, but only in collaboration with his successor, John Fletcher, on what appears to have been a part-time basis; the result was *Henry VIII* and *The Two Noble Kinsmen*, both in 1613. Shakespeare may not have been in the best of health by this time; he died in 1616. *The Tempest* reads plausibly as his farewell to the stage.

Another reason for thinking of *The Tempest* as a last play is that it brings to completion a family saga of father and daughter, together with some reflections on a lost son and a sometimes disappearing wife, that seem to have fascinated Shakespeare in his late years. He himself had married Anne Hathaway when he was eighteen and she nearly eight years his senior, in a hastily arranged ceremony necessitated by the fact that Anne was already three months or so pregnant when the ceremony took place. The birth of their daughter Susannah in 1583 was followed some twenty months later by the birth of twins, Hamnet and Judith. Some time after that, Shakespeare made his way to London, where he took up a career in the theatre but never moved his family from Stratford-upon-Avon. He bought handsome real estate there, and eventually was laid to rest in the chancel of Holy Trinity church as a wealthy 'gentleman' and first citizen of the town. He must have gotten home from time to time in the two decades or so of his career as a London actor and dramatist, but he and Anne had no more children after 1585. In 1596 his only son Hamnet died suddenly. In that same year Shakespeare instituted proceedings to enable his father, John Shakespeare, to bear a coat of arms and thus be styled a gentleman. Shakespeare seems to have gotten on well with his elder daughter Susannah and her husband, the physician John Hall, for he bought a splendid house for them (known today as Hall's Croft) at the time of their marriage in 1607. In 1616 Judith married a man, Thomas Quiney, with whom Shakespeare quarreled. Later in that same year, Susannah and her husband moved into Shakespeare's own fine house, New Place (no longer standing today), where they provided a home for Anne as well. Anne is mentioned only briefly in Shakespeare's rather detailed last will and testament (1616) as the recipient of their 'second best bed'. Whether or not this is a churlish slight is still in dispute, but may indicate a certain distancing of affection.

Can one find traces of this family saga in Shakespeare's plays, and especially in *The Tempest*? Shakespeare is notably reticent about himself, and he generally dramatizes plots that are taken from literary sources; he does not write autobiographically. At the same time, his choice of stories to dramatize does provide him an opportunity to choose ones that have some personal meaning for him, and in any event *The Tempest* is not based extensively on any known sources and may therefore have a special relevance to the dramatist himself.

The loss by a father of his only son and heir is one place to look, since Shakespeare's own loss of Hamnet in 1596 at the age of eleven was presumably traumatic to him, and especially so in view of Shakespeare's vivid interest in the importance of having such a son; this is a repeated theme of the Sonnets, in which a young man is urged to marry and procreate as one means of achieving a kind of immortality. Yet, oddly enough, although Shakespeare dramatizes the subject with poignant intensity in an early play like *1 Henry VI* in the deaths of Lord Talbot and his son John, and in *King John*, which may precede the death of Hamnet, he is laconic about such personal tragedies in the years following 1596. Not until *Twelfth Night*, in 1600 or 1601, do we find an intriguingly relevant situation: when

Viola's twin brother, Sebastian, is presumed drowned, she adopts a male disguise, in effect replacing the loss by her playing a male role until finally, in the happy finale, the lost twin turns out not to be dead after all. Hamnet was Judith's twin brother. One can perhaps speculate about this as a kind of dreamwork, not uncommon in such losses. At about the same time, Shakespeare writes *Hamlet* about a son called upon to avenge his father's dishonor and death, as though in memory of Shakespeare's own efforts at obtaining a coat of arms for his father and himself, and by way of mourning his loss of a son who might do likewise for him in the future. Subsequent plays like *Othello* and the main plot of *King Lear* are notably lacking in sons. Macbeth, haunted by his own lack of male heirs, attempts unsuccessfully to destroy the male line of his chief rival, Banquo, who has been promised that he will be the father of kings. Sons are absent from *Pericles* and *The Winter's Tale*. *Cymbeline* (c. 1608–10) does provide a happy ending for the King in which his two sons, long thought dead, are restored to him and thus provide a line of royal succession. In *The Tempest*, Ferdinand is restored to his father after having been thought drowned, like Sebastian in *Twelfth Night*, but the play's protagonist, Prospero, has no son. Instead he finds a son-in-law in Ferdinand, and he seems content with that. Ferdinand thus serves to replace the missing son.

In the frequent absence of sons in the late plays, a single daughter is often the chief hope and consolation of the aging male, with a corresponding capacity to render him miserable when that consolation fails. Ophelia, the sole daughter of Polonius in *Hamlet*, is a source of anxiety for her father; she becomes distracted and dies when he is killed by her one-time wooer, Hamlet. Desdemona, in *Othello*, is her widower father's constant companion and housekeeper; when she deserts him (as he views the matter) for Othello, the father eventually dies of a broken heart. Cordelia, in *King Lear*, keenly disappoints her father when she tells him exactly what Desdemona has told her father Brabantio, that a marriageable young woman must transfer her first loyalty to a husband, even though she will continue to honor the father to whom she owes so much. Lear sees this as a desertion, just as Brabantio did when Desdemona eloped with Othello. Cordelia does return to Lear as a ministering angel in his madness and forlorn condition, bringing a brief euphoric happiness the likes of which he has never known, but this happiness proves to be his undoing: having lost so much, he now accepts those losses gladly so long as he can have Cordelia for his own. He has not learned to let go of her, to let her have her own life, as she so urgently begged in the play's opening scene. In these terms,

King Lear is the tragedy of a father who cannot learn how to loosen the bond of a father–daughter love to which he feels he is entitled.

Shakespeare's so-called late Romances pursue the saga of father and daughter with an intensity that suggests a preoccupation on the part of the aging dramatist. The wife and mother moves in and out of the story as though representing a deep uncertainty as to her place in the family constellation. In *Pericles*, the titular hero escapes from a prospective marriage to a princess when he discovers that she is in fact sleeping with her father, Antiochus. Fleeing in alarm, Pericles has the good fortune to fall in love with another princess, Thaisa, whose father, the King of Pentapolis, puts on an initial show of hostility to the young man but gladly bestows his blessing on the couple. Thaisa and her father are thus the instructive and virtuous opposite of the incestuous father Antiochus and his daughter. When Thaisa seemingly dies in childbirth aboard a vessel at sea, Pericles sorrowfully accedes to the demands of the mariners that he pacify the gods of the storm by committing Thaisa's body to the deep. She washes ashore in her coffin and is revived by a magician-figure who places her as a priestess in the temple of Diana. The infant girl, Marina, comes to marriageable age in the course of time, having gone through a series of hair-breadth escapes until she is eventually reunited with her father. He, having languished in despair, is restored to happiness by her, and together they find her mother at the temple of Diana. This story is one of eventual restoration of the family, though without a son. It is also the story, if you like, of a husband who has thrown away his wife and has been restored to her by the beneficence of the gods far in excess of his own deserving. Even though Pericles had no choice other than to let her be buried at sea, the narrative has the dimensions of a husband's abandoning his wife, and that fact may explain why he is so inconsolable when Marina finds him and restores him to happiness. As a fantasy, it bears an intriguing resemblance to the circumstance of Shakespeare's own marriage and eventual reunion in Stratford with his family. Again, we must suppose that Shakespeare chose this story for personal reasons, since the narrative is in the play's source (a prose version by Laurence Twine of the ancient story of Apollonius of Tyre). Shakespeare seems not to have written the play unassisted, but the outline of the narrative, and especially the ending, do seem to be his.

Cymbeline (c. 1608–10) is about a father who, like King Lear, angrily banishes his only daughter, Imogen, when she marries against his wishes. He has also lost his two sons; they were stolen from his court long ago by a disappointed courtier named Belarius, and, unbeknownst to him, have been raised in the mountains of Wales far from the corruptions of court life. The King, thus deprived of his own family and widowed by the death of his queen, marries a woman who turns out to be a thoroughly despicable step-mother to Imogen. Her own son, the King's new step-son, Cloten, is the parodic opposite of what a true courtier ought to be. In the course of her wanderings and in the protective disguise of a young man, Imogen encounters her brave young brothers in their wilderness cave, and is instinctively drawn to them as they to her. Eventually, all are reconciled with the King, who also learns that Cloten has been killed (by one of the King's sons) and that the wicked Queen has died confessing that she intended to poison her husband. Thus the family is restored to happiness, albeit under remarkable circumstances if we view this as a kind of fantasy reenactment of Shakespeare's own family history: the sons are restored to life, like Sebastian in *Twelfth Night*, and the father regains the precious love of his sole daughter, while the mother figure is grotesquely transformed into that of an evil step-mother. Folklorists no doubt would regard this part of the story as a transference onto the hated step-mother of qualities that no child would want to attribute to the true mother. The mother is thus an especially unstable figure in this working out of the family saga.

The Winter's Tale (c. 1609–11) makes ample amends to the mother, with the result that this play seems especially interesting as a fantasy about the dramatist's own family. King Leontes of Sicilia, the father, is the most guilty of all such fathers in late Shakespeare. When he becomes insanely and unjustifiably jealous of his wife Hermione chiefly because her nine-months' pregnancy began at the same time as the arrival in Leontes's court of his dearest friend, King Polixenes of Bohemia, Leontes insists on putting Hermione on trial for adultery. Everyone but the King knows that she is innocent. The trial proves too much for her, and she dies of shock and grief. So does the young son Mamillius. And in fact he really is dead; later we learn that Hermione is alive, but not the son. Is this a pattern of dreamwork on the part of the dramatist, through which he comes at last to acknowledge that the lost son will not come back? In any event, Hermione does come back. Leontes goes about furiously to destroy his own happiness: he instructs that the newborn daughter, Perdita, be abandoned on a distant shore. Perdita, found on the coast of Bohemia, is raised by shepherds as a young shepherdess. When her grace and beauty attract the attention of King Polixenes's son, Florizel, the King is furious at the mismatch, so much so that the young couple are obliged to flee by ship. They end up in Sicilia, where Perdita is restored to her father. Leontes, still endlessly remorseful for his terrible crimes of killing Hermione (as he thinks) and being responsible for his only son's death, is given back a happiness he knows that he does not deserve. Part of his happiness too is in having a son-in-law to take the place of the lost Mamillius. A still greater joy awaits Leontes: a seeming statue of Hermione, guarded carefully by a lady of the court named Paulina, turns out to be Hermione herself. Paulina has kept her safe all these years until Perdita has come of age and has been found: as the oracle has predicted, that which was lost has been found. Leontes is fascinated by the skill of the sculptor who has created this 'statue', since it uncannily resembles Hermione not as she was some sixteen years ago but as she would have aged. She is older, like Leontes, and she is beautiful to him; his love for the woman he attempted to destroy is renewed. As a story (one that Shakespeare found in Robert Greene's prose novel *Pandosto*), this one seems especially close to that of a man like Shakespeare who might plausibly accuse himself of having abandoned his family and who, at the time he wrote *The Winter's Tale*, must have been wondering what it would be like to retire from his profession and his life in London to the quieter company of Anne in Stratford. The fantasy is a hopeful one, in which the aging wife is lovable and forgiving and true as ever to their marriage contract.

If we regard *The Tempest* as the culmination of this continuing saga, then we can perhaps see it as a resolution of what has for so long fascinated the dramatist. Prospero is, like Brabantio, Lear, and Cymbeline, a widower. (Earlier instances are to be found in the Duke in *The Two Gentlemen of Verona*, Baptista Minola in *The Taming of the Shrew*, and Shylock in *The Merchant of Venice*.) Unlike his predecessors, however, Prospero works hard at discovering how to let go of the potentially incestuous hold on his single daughter. He playacts at being the angry parent, much as the King of Pentapolis did in *Pericles*, partly because he is acting out his own fantasies, partly because he knows that a story of young lovers needs a series of hurdles to make it interesting, and partly because he wants the young people to consider seriously what it is that they are about to embark upon. Like Brabantio and Lear with their sole daughters, Prospero has meant everything to Miranda and she to him. They have lived together, virtually as a couple. Indeed, *The Tempest* intensifies this aspect of the story to its purest form by casting Prospero and Miranda on a remote island where they literally see no one for twelve years other than Caliban and the spirit Ariel. How can Prospero bear the prospect of losing his companion, his student, his housekeeper? Yet he knows that he must give her away in marriage, and he actively embraces the task by arranging matters so that Ferdinand and Miranda will meet. He overhears their conversations, or at least some of them, in his invisible presence. To them he poses as the stern and forbidding parent of the literary tradition, playing his role with gusto, but to us as audience he confesses his delight. 'Fair encounter / Of two most rare affections!' he exults, in an aside. 'Heavens rain grace / On that which breeds between 'em!' (3.1.74–6). And, when the two young people have left the stage at one point, after exchanging vows of eternal love, Prospero is no less happy: 'So glad of this as they I cannot be, / Who are surprised with all; but my rejoicing / At nothing can be more' (93–5).

Prospero is not a deeply flawed protagonist, like Leontes in *The Winter's Tale* or King Cymbeline. Still, he has had to struggle with his anger at his enemies and with his emotional dependency on Miranda as his sole child, his daughter. He succeeds in that struggle because he sees, rationally, the deep necessity of such a life-change as he grows older. He rectifies the errors his predecessors have made, and does so as part of the difficult process of coming to terms with aging and the approach of death. Prospero gives up his daughter to further her happiness, and sees that he has gained a son in Ferdinand. Indeed, Shakespeare idealizes the son-in-law as one who sees his new father-in-law as quite wonderful. 'Let me live here ever!' Ferdinand exclaims, when he has witnessed the amazing masque put on for his benefit by Ariel and the spirits at Prospero's behest. 'So rare a wondered father and a wise / Makes this place paradise' (4.1.122–4). The First Folio text, with its tall 's' resembling an 'f', could read 'wife' in place of 'wise', but the preferred reading of 'wise' makes the tribute to Prospero especially intense (and rhymes with 'paradise'). In either case the young man seems deliriously happy not only with his new mate but with her father as well. Is this a self-congratulatory fantasy on Shakespeare's part in which his new son-in-law thinks of the father as wonderful beyond description? Does it reflect at all how Shakespeare and his son-in-law John Hall, Susannah's husband, got along with each other? We do not know, other than knowing that Shakespeare certainly bought a handsome house for John and Susannah when they married. At any rate, *The Tempest* is in this regard a happy meditation about an aging playwright who learns how to release his hold on his daughter at the same time that he releases his hold on Ariel, the source of his artistic creativity.

The story of *The Tempest* is one in which human intents, so often misguided and poorly understood, somehow become part of a complex narrative in which everything works out better than the participants could have hoped or planned. 'This falls out better than I could devise!' exults Puck in *A Midsummer Night's Dream* (3.2.35). Through a similar sort of providential shaping, *The Tempest* is steered toward its happy conclusion in a way that most of the persons involved could not possibly have foretold. Old Gonzalo sees this pattern in the story, and he sees in it a series of benignly ironic reversals. 'Was Milan thrust from Milan, that his issue / Should become kings of Naples?' he says, wonderingly. 'Oh, rejoice / Beyond a common joy, and set it down / With gold on lasting pillars: In one voyage / Did Claribel her husband find at Tunis, / And Ferdinand, her brother, found a wife / Where he himself was lost; Prospero his dukedom / In a poor isle; and all of us ourselves / When no man was his own' (5.1.207–15). As in *The Winter's Tale*, what was lost has been found. Everything that has happened can now be seen to have contributed by integral steps to the happy ending. What appeared tragic before now emerges as a necessary part of a providential design. What Gonzalo does not say, however, is that on the island of the Tempest Prospero guides that providential force. He alone understands where everything is ultimately leading; he creates unhappiness as a necessary prelude to forgiveness and rejoicing. The gods of the island are at his beck and call, or are of his creating. And, since Prospero is above all the master dramatist of the theatrical world of the island, his providential guiding of events is the work of the playwright. All is under his control, including his own self-awareness and emotional ripening as he prepares to confront the inevitability of death.

One plaintive note mars this great synthesis of art and life in *The Tempest*. Prospero has no wife; he is a widower. He does not recover a seemingly dead wife he had abandoned, as in *Pericles* and *The Winter's Tale*. Prospero's wife is mentioned only once. While Prospero is telling Miranda the story of their past, and describes how 'Thy father was the Duke of Milan and / A prince of power', Miranda is understandably puzzled. 'Sir, are not you my father?' she asks, and Prospero chooses to take the question in a jesting spirit. 'Thy mother was a piece of virtue, and / She said thou wast my daughter', he tells Miranda (1.2.45–7). This is an old joke, reflecting the male's perennial anxiety that a woman can know for certain whose child she brings forth from her body, whereas the male can only hope that his wife has been true to their marriage bed. The joke turns up repeatedly in Shakespeare (e.g., *1 Henry IV*, 2.4.399–402, and *King Lear*, 2.4.130–1), as it does in other writers of the period. It is the misogynistic jest of a patriarchal culture, bespeaking a fear of cuckoldry. In the present instance, it offers only a poor remembrance of the woman who was once Prospero's companion and the mother of his child. The wife is written out of this final version of the family history as told in the late plays. What it suggests about Shakespeare's retirement years in Stratford with Anne can only be guessed at, but it may put us in mind of that odd provision in Shakespeare's will about the second best bed.

8

Epilogue

Shakespeare mentions epilogues rarely, and does so only with a characteristic self-effacing modesty. When Bottom the Weaver asks Duke Theseus, at the conclusion of 'Pyramus and Thisbe' in *A Midsummer Night's Dream*, 'Will it please you to see the epilogue, or to hear a Bergomask dance between two of our company?', Theseus does not hesitate in his choice: 'No epilogue, I pray you; for your play needs no excuse. Never excuse; for when the players are all dead, there need none to be blamed' (5.1.348–53). Rosalind is no less self-deprecating at the end of *As You Like It*, when the boy actor playing her part is left alone on stage to address the audience: 'If it be true that good wine needs no bush, 'tis true that a good play needs no epilogue. Yet to good wine they do use good bushes, and good plays prove the better by the help of good epilogues. What a case am I in then, that am neither a good epilogue nor cannot insinuate with you in the behalf of a good play!'

Despite the apologetic tone, the epilogues to *A Midsummer Night's Dream* and *As You Like It* are masterful in their defense of the art of theatrical illusion. So too are the epilogues to *Troilus and Cressida* and *The Tempest*. Other plays like *Romeo and Juliet* and *Twelfth Night* end with speeches or songs that provide a suitably choric ending to the action. *Much Ado about Nothing* ends with a dance. As in so many other ways, Shakespeare knew when and how to make a graceful and effective exit.

I hope that the argument of this present book is clear enough that it needs no elaborate recapitulation. We have explored the idea that Shakespeare's plays cannot be reduced to simple moral equations, so that the art of reading him is an art of being open-minded and attuned to multiplicities of meaning. Reading is an act of involvement. We need to commit ourselves to the proposition that reading a Shakespeare play is a two-way process to which we both respond and contribute. Richness of meaning is continually enhanced by the active use of our imagination in reading this most imaginative of dramatists. We must stage his plays in our minds, clothing the actors, finding the right nuance for their utterances, setting them in space and time in such a way as to flesh out Shakespeare's script with our thoughts. Whenever Shakespeare seems to be talking about his dramatic art, in the opening chorus of *Henry V*, or in Theseus's ruminations about the lover, the madman, and the poet in Act 5 of *A Midsummer Night's Dream*, or in Mercutio's speech about Queen Mab in *Romeo and Juliet*, or in Prospero's farewell to his art in *The Tempest*, he asks us to engage ourselves in this creative act of bringing to life the stories he has dramatized.

How does one start reading Shakespeare? We might end this book with a paradoxical answer: namely, to start not with reading, in fact, but with Shakespeare in performance. Many young people have learned to delight in Shakespeare by being involved in a school or community production, such as *A Midsummer Night's Dream*. Even if one doesn't have the opportunity or desire to be in such a show, one can often be in the audience when a play is put on locally. Professional productions are increasingly available to large numbers of potential viewers, and for extended seasons, at Stratford-upon-Avon, London, Bristol, New York, Chicago, Washington, DC, and at Shakespeare festivals in Ontario (Stratford), Oregon (Ashland), Utah, Alabama, Connecticut, and many others. Again and again, the experience of seeing a live Shakespeare production convinces spectators that the language is not really a problem after all. When capable and well-trained actors deliver Shakespeare's lines with interpretive skill, they can engage us in intellectual and emotional ways even while entertaining us with what is supposed, after all, to be a play. One can have a wonderful experience seeing a Shakespeare play for the first time and even before one has read it, watching and listening as it unfolds. One can resonate to the brilliance of Shakespeare's language even when some words and phrases are a bit puzzling.

Good sound recordings can be surprisingly effective as a way of enjoying and understanding Shakespeare in performance. That is because gifted actors can convey meaning and interpretation in their voices, by the way they react to what another character has said, by their showing surprise or dismay or amusement or scorn. Listening to a good recording is in fact a liberating experience: one is free to imagine what the characters look like, how they are dressed, what gestures they make, and where they are located. As one listens to the play's conversations, monologues, crowd scenes, and battle sequences, images come into one's mind as a pictorial projection of what the actors are saying. One particularly successful recording, for example, is that of Richard Burton in the role of *Coriolanus*. Burton, surely one of the most gifted actors of the twentieth century, never appeared in a film version of this seldom-seen play, but he did record the script with a group of professional actors. Burton's steely, acerbic, rapid-fire delivery is magnificently suited to the role of the patrician, elitist, yet honorable Roman general who comes to despise his city for giving in to the will of the plebeians. My own visual and aural memory of the play is derived chiefly from listening again and again to this recording. Another personal favorite, one indeed that got me started on the road to becoming a serious Shakespearean, is a 1952 recording on RCA of *Romeo and Juliet*, with Claire Bloom as a very young Juliet and Alan Badel as Romeo, Athene Aylmer as the Nurse, and a generally stellar cast. This was my wife's and my first Shakespeare recording, given to us as a wedding present. We played it over and over, much as one might put on music in the evening on one's record player. During a car trip some time later, we discovered that between us we could recite the play more or less word for word down through the first three acts. That was so much fun that I got serious about tape-recording BBC productions of plays (by Shakespeare and others) when they were broadcast over the radio. That way I collected a perfectly marvelous *As You Like It* and *The Merry Wives of Windsor*, among others. Another professional recording that I have cherished is of *A Midsummer Night's Dream* with Robert Helpmann as Oberon, Moira Shearer as Titania, and Stanley Holloway as Bottom the Weaver. The productions I have staged in my head from listening to these recordings are very personally my own.

Shakespeare plays on screen are widely available. Some of these versions are so bad that they should never be watched at all, even if no alternatives are to be found. Many of the productions in the BBC series called The Shakespeare Plays manage to do the unforgivable and, one would have hoped, the impossible: they make Shakespeare boring. Such is a frequently voiced critical verdict of their *The Winter's Tale, Cymbeline, The Tempest, A Midsummer Night's Dream* (not funny), *Love's Labor's Lost, Antony and Cleopatra, Romeo and Juliet, Troilus and Cressida, Coriolanus, Pericles, Timon of Athens,* and *As You Like It*; I found all these disappointing, though it has been a long time since I have looked at them. Not all viewers have been as dismayed as I, but the press coverage has often been unfavorable. One should say at once that the series offers important exceptions to this generally dreary scenario. Derek Jacobi is excellent in *Hamlet* and *Richard II*. *Twelfth Night*, with Alec McCowen as Malvolio, is better than most; so is *Henry VIII*. *Measure for Measure* and *All's Well That Ends Well* are well worth watching; small-scale, intimate dramas of psychological conflict seem well suited to the BBC idiom. *Henry IV, Part I* is straightforward, not exciting but well spoken. *The Comedy of Errors* is passable, especially since there are few alternatives. Some of the BBC series are not really bad but are easily outshone by other available productions, as is the case with *Julius Caesar, King Lear, Much Ado about Nothing, The Merchant of Venice, Othello* (quirky and boring), *Macbeth* (murky), *The Taming of the Shrew* (bizarre), *Titus Andronicus, Richard III*, and *Henry V*. As a rule, please be wary of the BBC plays. Consult your doctor before using.

Fortunately, many of the plays one might like to get to know visually are well served on screen. Among the most serviceable film Shakespeares during the last seventy or so years are the following, listed by title, director, date, and notable leading players.

Love's Labor's Lost

Kenneth Branagh, 2000, with Branagh, Matthew Lillard, Alessandro Nivola, Adrian Lester, Natasha McElhone, and Alicia Silverstone.

The Taming of the Shrew

Franco Zeffirelli, 1967, with Richard Burton and Elizabeth Taylor.
A *commedia dell'arte* production by the American Conservatory Theatre, 1976, with Marc Singer and Fredi Ostler.
John Allison, 1983, with Franklyn Seals and Karen Austin.

A Midsummer Night's Dream

Max Reinhardt, 1935, with James Cagney, Mickey Rooney, and Olivia de Havilland.
Peter Hall, 1969, with Ian Richardson, Judi Dench, Diana Rigg, Helen Mirren, David Warner, Ian Holm, Derek Godfrey, Barbara Jefford, and Paul Rogers.

Epilogue

Michael Hoffman, 1999, with Kevin Kline and Michelle Pfeiffer.

(All three versions are seriously flawed but have their rewarding moments.)

The Merchant of Venice

Jonathan Miller, 1969, with Laurence Olivier and Joan Plowright.
Trevor Nunn and Chris Hunt, 2001, with Harry Goodman and David Bamber.
Michael Radford, 2005, with Al Pacino, Joseph Fiennes, and Lynn Collins.

Much Ado about Nothing

Kenneth Branagh, 1993, with Branagh and Emma Thompson.

Twelfth Night

Trevor Nunn, 1996, with Imogen Stubbs, Toby Stephens, Helena Bonham Carter, Nigel Hawthorne, and Ben Kingsley.

Richard III

Laurence Olivier, 1955, with Olivier, John Gielgud, and Ian Richardson.
Richard Longraine, 1995, with Ian McKellen, Nigel Hawthorne, Maggie Smith, and Jim Broadbent.

Henry IV, Parts I and II

Orson Welles (*The Chimes at Midnight*), 1966.

Henry V

Laurence Olivier, 1944, with Olivier, Harcourt Williams, Max Adrian, Leo Genn, Renée Asherson, and Robert Newton.
Kenneth Branagh, 1989, with Branagh, Emma Thompson, Richard Briers, Paul Scofield, Michael Maloney, and Robert Stephens.

Titus Andronicus

Julie Taymor, 1999, with Anthony Hopkins, Laura Fraser, Alan Cumming, and Jessica Lange.

Romeo and Juliet

Franco Zeffirelli, 1968, with Leonard Whiting and Olivia Hussey.
Baz Luhrmann (*Romeo + Juliet*), 1996, with Leonardo DiCaprio and Claire Danes.

Julius Caesar

Joseph L. Mankiewicz, 1953, with Marlon Brando, James Mason, and John Gielgud.

Hamlet

Laurence Olivier, 1948, with Olivier, Eileen Herlie, Basil Sydney, Jean Simmons, Felix Aylmer, and Stanley Holloway.
Grigori Kozintsev, 1964, with Innokenti Smoktunovsky and Elsa Radzina. In Russian, with subtitles.
Tony Richardson, 1969, with Nicol Williamson.
Rodney Bennett, BBC Shakespeare, 1980, with Derek Jacobi, Claire Bloom, Patrick Stewart, and Eric Porter.
Franco Zeffirelli, 1990, with Mel Gibson, Glenn Close, Alan Bates, and Helena Bonham Carter.
Kevin Kline and Kirk Browning, 1990, with Kline, Dana Ivey, Diane Venora, Brian Murray, and Michael Cumpsty.
Kenneth Branagh, 1996, with Branagh, Derek Jacobi, Julie Christie, and Kate Winslet.
Michael Almereyda, 2000, with Ethan Hawke, Kyle MacLachlan, Diane Venora, Bill Murray, and Julia Stiles.

King Lear

Peter Brook, 1970–1, with Paul Scofield, Irene Worth, Jack MacGowran, and Anne-Lise Gabold.

Epilogue

Grigori Kozintsev, 1970, with Yuri Yarvet, Valentina Shendrikova, Oleg Dal, Elsa Radzina, and Galina Volchek. In Russian, with subtitles.

Michael Elliott, 1983, with Laurence Olivier, Anna Calder-Marshall, Dorothy Tutin, Diana Rigg, Leo McKern, and Robert Lindsay.

Akira Kurosawa's *Ran*, 1985, is in Japanese and contains none of Shakespeare's text, but as an adaptation it is remarkably insightful.

Othello

Orson Welles, 1952, with Welles and Micheál MacLiammóir.

Stuart Burge, 1965, with Laurence Olivier, Derek Jacobi, Maggie Smith, and Joyce Redman.

Janet Suzman, 1988, with John Kani and Joanna Weinberg.

Trevor Nunn, 1990, with Willard White, Ian McKellen, and Imogen Stubbs.

Oliver Parker, 1995, with Kenneth Branagh and Laurence Fishburn.

Macbeth

Orson Welles, 1948, with Welles, Jeanette Nolan, and Dan O'Herlihy.

Roman Polanski, 1971, with Jon Finch and Francesca Annis.

Trevor Nunn, 1979, with Ian McKellen and Judi Dench.

Akira Kurosawa's *Throne of Blood*, 1957, is an adaptation with none of Shakespeare's text, but it is an extraordinary film.

Antony and Cleopatra

Trevor Nunn and Jon Scoffield, 1974–5, with Janet Suzman, Richard Johnson, Corin Redgrave, Patrick Stewart, Ben Kingsley, Tim Piggott-Smith, and Mary Rutherford.

Charlton Heston tried hard in 1972, but even he admitted that his version was a failure.

The Tempest

Derek Jarman, 1979, with Heathcote Williams, Toyah Wilcox, Karl Johnson, and The Incredible Orlando, a.k.a. Jack Birkett.

Peter Greenaway (*Prospero's Books*), 1991, with John Gielgud.

(Both are interesting but bizarre.)

You will notice some obvious omissions from this list. For our purposes, there just are not any very satisfactory film versions of the following:

The Comedy of Errors
The Two Gentlemen of Verona
The Merry Wives of Windsor
As You Like It (Paul Czinner's 1936 film is painful)
All's Well That Ends Well
Measure for Measure
Troilus and Cressida
The *Henry VI* plays
King John
Richard II
Henry VIII
Coriolanus
Timon of Athens
Pericles
Cymbeline
The Winter's Tale

Some of these can be filled in with adequate presentations in the BBC television series, notably *Richard II, Henry VIII, Measure for Measure, All's Well That Ends Well*, and *The Comedy of Errors*, so that overall the coverage on film or video is not bad.

Spinoffs or adaptations usually give us none of Shakespeare's language, and thus are not really pertinent to a discussion of how to read Shakespeare. At the same time, a number of them are important films in their own right and can indeed be instrumental in helping us to see the greatness of ideas and dramatic conflict in Shakespeare's plays. Some notable ones are listed here by director, name of the film, and date:

The Taming of the Shrew: George Sidney, *Kiss Me Kate*, 1953; Gil Junger, *10 Things I Hate About You*, 1999
Henry IV, Part I: Gus Van Sant, *My Own Private Idaho*, 1991
Romeo and Juliet: Robert Wise and Jerome Robbins, *West Side Story*, 1961
Othello: Tim Blake Nelson, *O*, 2000
King Lear: Akira Kurosawa, *Ran*, 1985 (as mentioned above)
Macbeth: Akira Kurosawa, *Throne of Blood*, 1957 (as mentioned above)

Epilogue

All of these suggestions about stage productions, films, televised renditions, and sound recordings are meant to address three points: first, that Shakespeare is a dramatist whom we need to experience in the theatrical medium for which he wrote; second, that good actors can give rich insights into interpretation that might easily escape us without their help; and third, that Shakespeare in performance will then redirect us back to the written words in which he lives eternally. Shakespeare is a great writer and poet whose unequalled mastery of the English language needs to be studied and admired on the printed page. Only when we have the script in front of us can we look closely and repeatedly at the astonishing poetic and dramatic achievement that is his gift to humanity. As Hamlet says, with his unfailing skill in finding just the right phrase: 'The play's the thing.'

Further Reading

The following list is meant to accomplish two purposes: first, to offer suggestions for reading in case you would like to follow up on questions that have been raised by the chapters of this book, and second, to acknowledge my indebtedness. Although this book lacks detailed citations, I do need to give credit for many of the ideas in what I have written. I have read and taught Shakespeare for so long (going back to 1957, in fact) that I am sure I no longer remember all my indebtednesses, but the list here is at least a significant effort in that direction.

Throughout this book, act-scene-and-line references to the plays of Shakespeare are to David Bevington, ed., *The Complete Works of Shakespeare*, 5th edn., New York: Pearson Longman, 2003. The line numberings may differ from those of other editions owing chiefly to different column widths in the printing of prose and to differing editorial views of where line breaks occur in verse, but generally one ought to be able to find a particular passage close to where it is cited in this book.

Chapter 1 How to Read a Shakespeare Play

Bullough, Geoffrey, ed. *Narrative and Dramatic Sources of Shakespeare*. 8 vols. London, 1957–75.
Dessen, Alan C. *Recovering Shakespeare's Theatrical Vocabulary*. Cambridge, 1995.
Empson, William. *The Structure of Complex Words*. London, 1951; 3rd ed., 1977.
Hulme, Hilda M. *Explorations in Shakespeare's Language*. London, 1962.
Kermode, Frank. *Shakespeare's Language*. New York, 2000.
Mahood, M. M. *Shakespeare's Wordplay*. London, 1967.
Partridge, Eric. *Shakespeare's Bawdy*. London, 1947, 1955.
Spurgeon, Caroline. *Shakespeare's Imagery and What It Tells Us*. Cambridge, 1935.

Further Reading

Vickers, Brian. *The Artistry of Shakespeare's Prose*. London, 1968.
Wheeler, Richard P. *Shakespeare's Development and the Problem Comedies*. Berkeley, 1981.

Chapter 2 A Midsummer Night's Dream

Barber, C. L. *Shakespeare's Festive Comedy*. Princeton, 1959.
Bevington, David. ' "But We Are Spirits of Another Sort": The Dark Side of Love and Magic in *A Midsummer Night's Dream*', *Medieval and Renaissance Studies*, ed. Siegfried Wenzel. Chapel Hill, NC, 1978, pp. 80–92.
Frye, Northrop. 'The Argument of Comedy', *English Institute Essays 1948*. New York, 1949.
———. *A Natural Perspective: The Development of Shakespearean Comedy and Romance*. New York, 1965.
Kirsch, Arthur. *Shakespeare and the Experience of Love*. Cambridge, 1981.
Leggatt, Alexander. *Shakespeare's Comedies of Love*. London and New York, 1974.
Montrose, Louis Adrian. ' "Shaping Fantasies": Figurations of Gender and Power in Elizabethan Culture', *Representations* 2 (1.2, Spring 1983), 61–94.
Nuttall, A. D. '*A Midsummer Night's Dream*: Comedy as *Apotrope* of Myth', *Shakespeare Survey* 53 (2000), 49–59.
Rose, Mary Beth. *The Expense of Spirit: Love and Sexuality in English Renaissance Drama*. Ithaca, NY, 1988.
Salingar, Leo. *Shakespeare and the Traditions of Comedy*. Cambridge, 1974.
Wall, Wendy. 'Why Does Puck Sweep?: Fairylore, Merry Wives, and Social Struggle', *Shakespeare Quarterly* 52 (2001), 67–106.
Warren, Roger. '*A Midsummer Night's Dream*': Text and Performance. London, 1983.
Young, David. *Something of Great Constancy: The Art of 'A Midsummer Night's Dream'*. New Haven, 1966.

Chapter 3 Romeo and Juliet

Dickey, Franklin. *Not Wisely But Too Well: Shakespeare's Love Tragedies*. San Marino, CA, 1957.
Evans, Robert O. *The Osier Cage: Rhetorical Devices in 'Romeo and Juliet'*. Lexington, KY, 1966.
Halio, Jay. '*Romeo and Juliet*': Texts, Contexts, and Interpretation. Newark, DE, 1995.
Levenson, Jill L. *Shakespeare in Performance: 'Romeo and Juliet'*. Manchester, 1987.
Novy, Marianne. *Love's Argument: Gender Relations in Shakespeare*. Chapel Hill, NC, 1984.

Chapter 4 Henry IV, Part I

Barber, C. L. *Shakespeare's Festive Comedy*. Princeton, 1959.

Blanpied, John W. *Time and the Artist in Shakespeare's English Histories*. Newark, DE, 1983.

Calderwood, James L. *Metadrama in Shakespeare's Henriad: 'Richard II' to 'Henry V'*. Berkeley, 1979.

Hodgdon, Barbara. *The End Crowns All: Closure and Contradiction in Shakespeare's History*. Princeton, 1991.

Howard, Jean E., and Phyllis Rackin. *Engendering a Nation: A Feminist Account of Shakespeare's English Histories*. London and New York, 1997.

Kastan, David Scott. *Shakespeare and the Shapes of Time*. Hanover, NH, 1982.

McMillin, Scott. *Shakespeare in Performance: 'Henry IV, Part One'*. Manchester, 1991.

Norwich, John Julius. *Shakespeare's Kings: The Great Plays and the History of England in the Middle Ages: 1337–1485*. London, 1999; New York, 2000.

Porter, Joseph. *The Drama of Speech Acts: Shakespeare's Lancastrian Tetralogy*. Berkeley, 1979.

Rackin, Phyllis. *Stages of History: Shakespeare's English Chronicles*. Ithaca, NY, 1990.

Saccio, Peter. *Shakespeare's English Kings: History, Chronicle, and Drama*. New York, 1977.

Watson, Robert N. *Shakespeare and the Hazards of Ambition*. Cambridge, MA, 1984.

Chapter 5 Hamlet

Bednarz, James P. *Shakespeare and the Poets' War*. New York, 2001.

Bowers, Fredson T. 'Hamlet as Minister and Scourge', *PMLA* 70 (1955), 740–9.

Bradley, A. C. *Shakespearean Tragedy*. London, 1904.

Charney, Maurice. *Style in 'Hamlet'*. New York, 1983.

Danson, Lawrence. *Tragic Alphabet: Shakespeare's Drama of Language*. New Haven, 1974.

Ferguson, Francis. *The Idea of a Theater*. Princeton, 1949.

Goldman, Michael. *Acting and Action in Shakespearean Tragedy*. Princeton, 1985.

Greenblatt, Stephen. *Hamlet in Purgatory*. Princeton, 2001.

Jenkins, Harold, ed. *Hamlet*. The Arden Shakespeare, 2nd series. London and New York, 1982.

Jones, Ernest. *Hamlet and Oedipus*. London, 1949.

Kirsch, Arthur. *The Passions of Shakespeare's Tragic Heroes*. Charlottesville, VA, 1990.

Mack, Maynard. *Everybody's Shakespeare: Reflections Chiefly on the Tragedies*. Lincoln, NE, 1993.

——. 'The World of *Hamlet*', *Yale Review* 41 (1952), 502–23.

Rose, Mark. 'Hamlet and the Shape of Revenge', *English Literary Renaissance* 1 (1971), 132–43.

Rosenberg, Marvin. *The Masks of 'Hamlet'*. Newark, DE, 1992.

Wilson, J. Dover. *What Happens in 'Hamlet'*. London and New York, 1935, 1951.

Chapter 6 King Lear

Bradley, A. C. *Shakespearean Tragedy*. London, 1904.

Cavell, Stanley. *Must We Mean What We Say?* New York, 1969. (The chapter on *King Lear* is reprinted in Cavell, *Disowning Knowledge in Six Plays of Shakespeare*, Cambridge, 1987.)

Colie, Rosalie L., and F. T. Flahiff, eds. *Some Facets of 'King Lear'*. Toronto, 1974.

Elton, William R. *King Lear and the Gods*. San Marino, CA, 1966.

Foakes, R. A. *'Hamlet' Versus 'Lear': Cultural Politics and Shakespeare's Art*. Cambridge, 1993.

——, ed. *King Lear*. The Arden Shakespeare, 3rd series. Walton-on-Thames, 1997.

Kirsch, Arthur. *The Passions of Shakespeare's Tragic Heroes*. Charlottesville, VA, 1990.

Kubler-Ross, Elisabeth. *On Death and Dying*. New York, 1969.

Leggatt, Alexander. *Shakespeare in Performance: 'King Lear'*. Manchester, 1991.

Mack, Maynard. *King Lear in Our Time*. Berkeley, 1965.

Rosenberg, Marvin. *The Masks of 'King Lear'*. Berkeley, 1972.

Snyder, Susan. *'King Lear* and the Psychology of Dying', *Shakespeare Quarterly* 33 (1982), 449–60.

Spivack, Bernard. *Shakespeare and the Allegory of Evil*. New York, 1958.

Taylor, Gary, and Michael Warren, eds. *The Division of the Kingdoms: Shakespeare's Two Versions of 'King Lear'*. Oxford, 1983.

Chapter 7 The Tempest

Bishop, T. G. *Shakespeare and the Theatre of Wonder*. Cambridge, 1996.

Kernan, Alvin B., *The Playwright as Magician: Shakespeare's Image of the Poet in the English Theater*. New Haven, 1979.

Mowat, Barbara. *The Dramaturgy of Shakespeare's Romances*. Athens, GA, 1976.

Vaughan, Virginia Mason, and Alden T. Vaughan, eds., *The Tempest*. The Arden Shakespeare, 3rd series. Walton-on-Thames, 1999.

William, David. *'The Tempest* on the Stage', *Jacobean Theatre*, eds. John Russell Brown and Bernard Harris. Stratford-upon-Avon Studies 1. London, 1960, pp. 133–57.

Index

Index

Index

Index